THE AMERICAN HERITAGE
BOOK OF

FISH COOKERY

by Alice Watson Houston

drawings by James Houston

Published by
AMERICAN HERITAGE PUBLISHING CO., INC., New York

Book Trade Distribution by
Charles Scribner's Sons, New York

The American Heritage Book of Fish Cookery

EDITOR/DESIGNER
Kate Slate

ART DIRECTOR
Murray Belsky

ASSISTANT EDITOR
Donna Whiteman

AMERICAN HERITAGE PUBLISHING CO., INC.

CHAIRMAN AND PRESIDENT
Samuel P. Reed

PUBLISHER
Beverley Hilowitz

CORPORATE ART DIRECTOR
Murray Belsky

PRODUCTION DIRECTOR
Elbert Burr

Library of Congress Cataloging in Publication
Data

Houston, Alice Watson, 1938-

The American heritage book of fish cookery

Includes index.
1. Cookery (Fish) 2. Cookery (Shellfish) I.
American heritage. II. Title.
TX747.H68   641.6'92   80-12469
ISBN 0-8281-0401-8, regular
ISBN 0-8281-0405-0, deluxe (with The Ameri-
can heritage cookbook, in two-volume boxed
set: ISBN 0-8281-0402-6)

Table of Contents

1: Fish Cookery

The art of fishing must certainly be as old as man himself. Living on a planet whose surface is over 70 percent water, and whose waters support an abundance of edible life, man early on developed tools and techniques for harvesting food from both fresh and salt water. In North America (in whose waters swim over 300 varieties of edible fish and shellfish), prehistoric man left ample evidence of his craft: bone, ivory, and shellfish hooks; ingenious fish spears; elaborate stone weirs; and clever nets woven of plant fibers or human hair.

Fish Poacher

Somewhere along the line, of course, the craft became a sport as well as a survival skill. The challenge was no lónger simply to catch fish, but to do it at the right time of day, in the right spot, with the right touch, and the right gear. Discussing the fine points of fishing technique and equipment became second only to the sport itself. But the rewards stayed the same. After a successful day on the river, lake, bay, or open sea, the fisherman not only feels the thrill of having outsmarted a wily and elusive prey, but also gets to turn that catch into a nourishing meal. Fishing is one of the few sports in which the prizes are edible.

Nutrition

Not only are fish edible, they are also one of the world's most efficient and healthy sources of food. Calorie for calorie, fish has more digestible protein than any other food, and several species—cod and haddock, for example—are up to 20 percent protein. Fish are also high in vitamins A, B, D, and K, as well as calcium, iodine, magnesium, phosphorus, potassium, and iron. Shellfish are particularly high in iron, and all saltwater fish have high levels of iodine. All fish (including saltwater varieties) are low in sodium, and their fats are polyunsaturated, making them low in cholesterol.

The level of polyunsaturated fats in fish varies from species to species. Those with less than five percent oil are considered lean fish, such as cod, halibut, catfish, and all shellfish; those with six to ten percent oil are considered medium fish, such as herring, salmon, and pompano; and those with over ten percent oil are considered fat fish, such as mackerel, trout, and shad. However, the actual oil content in any fish can vary considerably with diet, time of year, and age. As a general rule, fatter fish tend to have darker, more distinctively flavored flesh and do not keep as well as leaner fish. Lean fish have whiter meat, will keep longer, but have a greater tendency to dry out when cooked, and are therefore best prepared with sauces, additional oils, or moist heat (poaching or steaming). Of course, recipes for

◀*In 1908, a wealth of Pacific salmon and Dungeness crab crowded the counters of this Washington fish market.*

lean and fat fish are basically interchangeable, as long as care is taken to keep lean fish from drying out.

Buying Fish

When buying whole fish, look for those that have clear, bulging (not collapsed) eyes. The gills should be bright pink to red, not muddy brown. The skin should have tight, shiny scales and be covered with a natural slime. The flesh should be firm and elastic and spring back if pressed. Saltwater fish and shellfish should have the clean smell of the sea, and fish taken from fresh water should have almost no smell at all. The flesh in fillets and steaks should glisten and be translucent (old fish will look dried and dull), with no yellowing around the edges—or in the case of flounder, the flesh should not have a blue tinge.

MARKET FORMS: **Whole** or **round** fish are those that have not been cleaned at all. **Dressed** fish are scaled, gutted, and have had the gills removed. And some species, such as eels and catfish, have also been skinned. **Pan-dressed** fish are cleaned as for dressed fish, but have had head and fins removed. **Steaks** are 1″ to 1½″ cross-sections of dressed round fish. **Fillets** are nearly or completely boneless sides of the fish that have been cut away from backbone and rib cage and are most often skinned. When having the fish market pan-dress or fillet a whole fish, be sure to ask for the head and trimmings to make fish stock.

HOW MUCH TO BUY: The average serving per person is ⅓ to ½ pound of edible fish (i.e., no bones, head, tail, skin, etc.). About 50 percent of an undressed fish is edible, while fillets and steaks are nearly 100 percent edible. Therefore, figure on ⅔ to 1 pound of whole, undressed fish per serving; ½ to ¾ pound of pan-dressed fish per serving; and ⅓ to ½ pound of steaks and fillets per serving.

Keeping Fish Fresh

As a general rule, fresh fish should be cooked within two or three days of purchase, or else frozen for future use (see HOW TO FREEZE FISH, page 199). Most fish, refrigerated and properly covered with foil or plastic wrap, will keep only two or three days; while fatter species, such as mackerel, will last only a day or two. However, some fishermen believe that freshly caught salmon will not only keep for up to 7 days (refrigerated), but will actually improve with age. (Although the Fisheries Research Board of Canada has proven that fresh fish can be kept up to 12 days at 31.5° F. without spoiling, few home refrigerators are this cool.)

"Every species generally of Salt water Fish are best fresh from the water . . . but as generally, live ones are bought first, deceits are used to give them a freshness of appearance. . . . Experience and attention will dictate the choice of the best. Fresh gills, full bright eyes, moist fins and tails, are denotements of their being fresh caught; if they are soft, its certain they are stale, but if deceits are used, your smell must approve or denounce them, and be your safest guide."
—American Cookery, Amelia Simmons, 1796

Homemade pole in hand, this fisherman shows off the 14½-pound Dolly Varden he took from Alberta's Smoky River.

Cooks who get fish fresh from the river or sea will have a little more leeway than with fish from the market. However, care should be taken to keep the fish fresh on the journey from sea or river to kitchen. If the angler has the time, one of the best ways to retard spoilage in fish is to bleed and clean them right after catching. In any case, the fish should be kept cool and out of the sun, and should be well ventilated. Keeping fish cool, once it is dead, by submerging it in water is *not* a good idea, and shouldn't be done unless there's no alternative. A cooler filled with ice is ideal; or, for old-fashioned fishermen, a creel lined with ferns. Most important, fish should never be put in a stuffy plastic bag or a hot automobile trunk.

Frozen Fish

With modern flash-freezing techniques, the packaged catch in supermarket freezers can taste fresh and flavorful—although never as varied or delicately flavored as fresh fish. Frozen fish should be thawed slowly in the refrigerator, never at room temperature, to reduce moisture loss. Thawed, or even partially thawed, fish should not be refrozen or it will be rubbery and dull tasting. Thawed fish should be cooked within a day of thawing, as frozen fish are much more susceptible to spoilage. Fish can be cooked still frozen by doubling the cooking time, and pre-stuffed frozen fish *must* be cooked unthawed.

Sheltered from the wind by a snow wall, an Eskimo woman jigs for lake trout or Arctic char through a hole in one of the vast frozen lakes west of Hudson Bay.

Basic Cooking Methods

To prepare freshly caught fish for cooking, see Chapter 7. To keep hands relatively free of fish odor, chill hands in cold water before handling raw fish. After handling fish, rub hands with salt and a little cold water, vinegar, or lemon juice, then rinse under hot water and wash with soap. Rinse cooking pans in warm salt water and then wash with soap.

Unlike meat, which has a fair amount of tough connective tissue, fish has delicate flesh that will cook in a short amount of time (see the Canadian Fish Cooking Rule, page 14). Overcooking will make it dry and flavorless. In all methods of fish cookery, fish will be done when the flesh has turned from translucent to opaque and it flakes easily when tested with a fork. Fish can be broiled, baked, steamed, poached, boiled, sautéed, pan-fried, deep-fried, or barbecued. General guidelines for cooking shellfish are included in Chapter 5.

BAKING: Baking is excellent for whole stuffed fish, stuffed fillets, and thick steaks; but since it's a dry-heat method, the fish should be kept moist with butter, oil, strips of bacon, wine, or sauce. Fish should be placed in a buttered baking dish and baked in a preheated 350° F. to 450° F. oven. Covered baking dishes, stuffed fish, and fish in a great deal of sauce will take slightly longer to cook.

BROILING: Broiling works well for butterfly-style fillets, regular fillets, steaks, and some whole fish. Broiled fish must be basted, and leaner fish basted frequently, to keep them from drying out. Fillets should be cooked on only one side 2" to 4" from the heat. Steaks should be cooked 2" to 4" from the heat, and turned halfway through the cooking time. Whole fish must also be turned and should be cooked 5" from the heat. Guidelines for broiling also apply to grilling over an open fire (see HOW TO GRILL, page 209).

STEAMING: This method is excellent for keeping leaner fish moist and preserving a fish's delicate flavor. To steam fish, place it on a rack above 2" of boiling water and cover the pan; or use an Oriental bamboo steamer tray. Seasonings can be added to the boiling water. Wrapping the fish in cheesecloth will make it easier to lift out when it's done.

STEAM-BAKING: Fish can be steamed by wrapping it closely in aluminum foil or parchment paper and baking it in the oven (see HOW TO PREPARE FISH EN PAPILLOTE, page 208). The foil traps the fish's natural moisture and uses it to steam-bake. If a liquid or sauce is added, the effect will be more like braising or poaching. Steam-baked fish should be cooked about 5

Isaak Walton, in the first edition of his famous book The Compleat Angler (1653), wrote, "There we sit on cowslip banks, hear the birds sing and possess ourselves in as much quietness as these silent silver streams which we now see glide so quietly by us. Indeed, we may say of angling as Doctor Boteler said of strawberries, 'God doubtless could have made a better berry, but doubtless God never did.'"

minutes longer than the time it would take for straight baking. In an unusual variation, which is said to be Alaskan-Chinese in origin, fish stuffed with several pats of butter is very tightly wrapped in aluminum foil and run through two cyles of a dishwasher (without soap, of course).

POACHING: In another moist-heat method, excellent for whole fish, steaks, and large fillets, fish are poached (see HOW TO POACH, page 208) in a simmering liquid: a wine-water mixture, a court bouillon (Chapter 6), or milk. Milk is best when poaching smoked fish. Fish can also be boiled, but, except in large-scale fish boils (see WISCONSIN FISH BOIL, page 92), this method tends to extract too much flavor from the fish.

SAUTÉING AND PAN-FRYING: Good for small whole fish, fillets, and steaks, fish are sautéed, very simply, in butter (or oil) for a little over half the cooking time on one side, the rest of the cooking time on the second side. Thicker pieces of fish should be cooked over medium heat, thinner pieces over high heat. To pan-fry, fish is dredged in seasoned flour, cornmeal, or bread crumbs, and beaten egg, and then sautéed in butter (or oil).

STIR-FRYING: Best for cubes or strips of fish (often marinated), fish are moved around very quickly over very high heat in a small amount of oil—usually in a wok. Seasonings and coating sauces as well as vegetables can also be added. Watch the fish carefully as it will cook in a matter of minutes.

DEEP-FRYING: Deep-frying works well for small whole fish— such as whitebait or smelt—small chunks of fillet, and fish cakes or croquettes. The fish is dried, dipped in batter or seasoned flour and dropped into hot oil (or fat) at 375° F. and cooked until golden brown, which should take about 3 to 5 minutes per batch. Never add a lot of fish at once or the temperature of the oil will drop too far. The temperature of the oil should remain steady in order to cook the fish evenly: if the oil is too hot it will burn the fish on the outside before cooking the inside; if it's not hot enough, the fish will be soggy with oil before it browns. After cooking, the fish should be drained on paper toweling.

◄*An Idaho camper fries up a handsome feast of small, crisp, pan-sized fish.*

Fish peddlers such as this one once sold fresh seafood door to door, a custom whose passing must surely have disappointed its share of cats.

OTHER METHODS: Fish can also be plank cooked (see page 210), cooked Indian style (see page 209), and smoked (see page 199-201).

Canadian Fish Cooking Rule

Cooking time for fish will vary according to fish type and size. However, the Canadian Department of Fisheries and Marine Service, in a scientific study of fish cookery, has developed a simple but excellent rule of thumb. The Canadian method recommends cooking fish for 10 minutes per inch of thickness, measuring the fish at its thickest point. This rule applies to all cuts of fish: whole, fillets, steaks, stuffed fish, and rolled or stuffed fillets. For example, a fillet ½″ thick should be cooked about 5 minutes. A whole fish (which should be measured by laying it on its side and measuring the highest part) that measures 3″ should be cooked for 30 minutes. For stuffed whole fish or fillets, or rolled fillets, measure the fish *after* it's stuffed or rolled. When cooking frozen fish or fish blanketed in heavy sauce, double the cooking time.

This rule also applies to all methods of cooking, but assumes that the fish will be cooked over high heat: at 450° F. for baking and steam-baking; 2″ to 4″ from the heat for broiling; over boiling water for steaming; in simmering liquid for poaching; over high heat for sautéing, pan-frying, and stir-frying; in 375° F. oil for deep-frying. The Canadian Fish Cooking Rule does not apply to shellfish, nor, of course, to microwave cooking.

Other Ingredients

Very flavorful fish, such as dolphin, trout, salmon, swordfish, and tuna, are best prepared with the simplest of ingredients: butter, lemon juice, a sprinkling of dill or parsley, a splash of wine. Less distinctively flavored fish, on the other hand, are perfect foils for sauces and herbs.

Sauces (Chapter 6) should not fight with the fish for attention, but should enhance its flavor. The simplest sauces are those made with the pan juices, dry white wine (or dry vermouth), and lemon juice. White wine slightly darkens fish flesh, but lemon juice counteracts this. Simple white sauce, or the slightly more complicated velouté, can be flavored with any number of vegetables, herbs, or cheese. Pickled green peppercorns, horseradish, and capers are delicious as condiments and as additions to sauces. Cheeses used should have a mellow flavor, such as Swiss, mild Cheddar, or Muenster. Avoid such overpowering cheeses as blue cheese. White pepper, although less conspicuous in sauces or against the whiteness of fish, tastes the same as black pepper. All pepper should be freshly ground.

In general, herbs used to flavor fish and fish sauces should not be too strong (see FISH HERBS, page 185). Use fresh herbs when possible, and when using dried herbs use only half the amount of fresh called for. Some regional fish recipes do, of course, call for some fairly strong and unusual herbs or spices. Creole cooks, for example, use such spices as filé (ground sassafras leaves), cloves, allspice, and hot pepper sauces.

All recipes in the book list butter in the ingredients, but margarine is certainly recommended as a substitute for the cholesterol conscious. Unless otherwise specified, vegetable oil can be olive oil, corn oil, safflower oil, or peanut oil. Oil for deep-frying should be a vegetable oil with a high smoke point. When sautéing at high heat in butter or margarine, the addition of a little vegetable oil will reduce the chance of the butter or margarine burning.

"Flower Salad. Arrange a fringe of parsley on the outer rim of each plate. Then a ring of very dark slices of beet, moistened with plain mayonnaise dressing. The next ring should be of pink beets with a bit of whipped cream in the dressing. Fill the center with lighter beets and cream. In the very center rice a bit of cooked yolk of egg."
—Good Housekeeping Family Cookbook, 1909

Side Dishes

Vegetables and salads served with fish should not be so strongly flavored that they overwhelm the fish. In fact, they are often best served *after* the fish in order not to compete with the fish's delicate flavor. Boiled new potatoes and steamed rice are perfect complements to fish and shellfish. Barely cooked, fresh, green vegetables are excellent accompaniments; but vegetables should also be used to make the fish look attractive. Steamed green beans, buttered orange carrots, broiled red tomatoes all add color to a serving dish, along with a garnish of yellow lemon wedges and bright green parsley sprigs.

2: Trout & Salmon

Trout and salmon are among the most popular game and table fish in North America, offering the cook or angler 25 separate species. They belong to the same extended family (*Salmonidae*) and all species of trout and salmon spawn in fresh water and run in lakes or rivers. Yet many of them spend an important part of their lives in the sea (some for a few months, others for a number of years). Hence, trout and salmon have been given their own chapter. However, although these two fish are closely related, they do not overlap, despite the tendency of some markets and restaurants to use the misnomer "salmon trout" in describing what is actually a young salmon or a sea-run char.

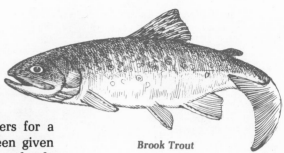

Brook Trout

Trout

There are 19 species of trout found in North American waters. Many of them range throughout Canada and may be found everywhere in the United States, except those few southern states where the waters are too warm to support them. Trout require cold, fast-flowing water, with abundant oxygen.

Although all trout are accessible to sportsfishermen, only lake trout are permitted to be caught wild and sold commercially. All other trout are restricted from commercial sale unless spawned and raised in hatcheries—from which they may be purchased (in large quantities) by restaurants, by markets, for commercial smoking, or for stocking purposes. Most trout sold on the U.S. market are rainbow trout from Idaho hatcheries.

The flesh of trout is finely textured, with subtle hues ranging from white to yellow to red, depending on the type of trout, its diet, the season of the year and whether it is in salt or fresh water. These flesh colors, however, make little if any difference in flavor. It is generally believed that trout taste their best in spring and autumn, when the waters are cold. A female trout just after spawning is likely to be lean and somewhat less flavorful. In the fall, the more northern trout accumulate a layer of belly fat, off which they live during lean winter months, sometimes spent beneath the ice. Although this belly fat was prized by most native peoples, some cooks today prefer to remove it. Because of their controlled diet, the flesh of hatchery trout can be slightly softer and perhaps less flavorful than that of trout living in the wild state.

Another factor affecting the taste of a trout's flesh is the age of the fish. Just as lamb is more delicate than mutton, a younger trout is likely to be more subtle in taste than an older one. Adult trout range in size from a half pound to a record 120 pounds. Most trout, however, are caught or sold in smaller sizes, from a half pound to four pounds, depending on the species.

Trout are relatively easy to prepare for cooking. Their skeletal

◀Perched on a fishing platform on the banks of Oregon's Rogue River, this fisherman seems to have lost the attention of his two primly dressed companions.

Clearly a family of avid anglers, these campers at Lake San Cristobal, Colorado, display their remarkable catch.

structure is simple to remove, and their scales so small that they should be considered a part of their skin, making scaling unnecessary. (The skin of a properly-cooked trout is every bit as tasty as the skin of a well-baked Idaho potato.) A 14-inch fish will cut nicely into two 10-inch fillets. If serving fillets, allow approximately one-third pound per person.

BROOK TROUT: When colonists first came to New England and New France, they discovered the brook trout (*Salvelinus fontinalis*—fish of the fountains) in vast numbers. This spectacularly beautiful game fish, with its distinctive square tail, its glorious back design, its glowing spots of blue, and brilliant scarlet sides, must have been one of the most delicious mainstays in the early colonists' diet. Brook trout (called **speckled trout** in Canada) is still widely fished throughout much of America. Taken on the very lightest tackle, a brook trout of 10 to 14 inches (under a pound) is a wily prize, and three-pound brooks today are treasures. (The record is a mammoth 15 pounds 2 ounces—taken in 1969 from a river on the Labrador.) The average size available in the markets is 8 to 10 inches and is usually gilled and gutted and then cooked whole, including head and tail. Brook trout has a firm delicate flesh that ranges in color from pink to snow white.

RAINBOW TROUT: The rainbow trout (*Salmo gairdneri*), a table fish of world renown, is also a spectacular game fish. Originally native to western North America, it has been widely stocked in lakes and streams throughout this continent and the world. The color of the rainbow trout is highly variable; most

often it has a dark back and is spotted, with an iridescent pink along its sides. However, this pink almost completely disappears in sea-run rainbows. The rainbow has several close relatives, such as the **Western Kamloops trout,** and the famous **West Coast steelhead,** which is actually a sea-run rainbow. The average weight of a rainbow taken by an angler is one to five pounds, but in the famous fishing rivers of northwest Canada and Alaska, the steelhead variety occasionally weigh up to 40 pounds. Hatchery rainbows, however, rarely exceed one pound.

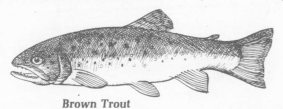

Brown Trout

BROWN TROUT: Brown trout (*Salmo trutta*) are brown-backed with notably large spots on the body and often on the fins and upper tail, which is distinctly square in shape. As the brown trout gains size, its under jaw protrudes. The teeth in the upper jaw are sharp and well developed. (Similar in appearance to the brown trout is the much rarer **Gila trout** of the southwestern United States.) The brown trout, which will readily take a dry fly, is a hardy species, quick and aggressive, and can thrive in lakes and streams that have become too polluted for the brook or rainbow trout. Perhaps this is one of the reasons why the brown trout in American waters is more respected as a fighter than as a table fish. Brown trout taste better taken from cool waters during colder weather, and are usually caught weighing from a half pound to five pounds, although some have been taken weighing more than 30 pounds.

CUTTHROAT TROUT: The cutthroat trout (*Salmo clarki*) is a sporting fish that usually occupies the same habitat as the rainbow trout and shares some similarities in appearance. The cutthroat is most easily identified by two red slashes on either side of its lower jaw. Cutthroats become densely spotted when they live in fresh water, but the spots fade when they run to the sea. Unlike the rainbow, the cutthroat trout has teeth on the back of its tongue. (The rare **golden trout**—*Salmo aguabonita*—somewhat resembles the cutthroat.) The cutthroat commonly returns from the sea weighing one to three pounds. A 10-pound cutthroat is remarkable, and the world's record on a rod is 41 pounds, taken in 1925 at Pyramid Lake, Nevada.

DOLLY VARDEN TROUT: This colorfully spotted trout was named for a dress—with a flowered skirt draped over a brightly colored petticoat—worn by Dolly Varden, a character in Charles Dickens's *Barnaby Rudge*. The strong-fighting Dolly Varden (*Salvelinus malma*) usually lives in fast, cold rivers from Alaska to northern California, and runs, when it has access, to the sea. The Dolly Varden usually averages from a half to two pounds; its record weight is 32 pounds. The Dolly Varden is a splendid table fish, so similar to the Arctic char (*see below*) that some experts say there is scarcely any difference. It may also be a close relative of the **Aurora trout** (*Salvelinus aureolus*), a rare fish today found mostly in Ontario.

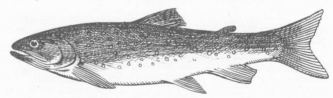

Arctic Char

ARCTIC CHAR: The Arctic char (*Salvelinus alpinus*) is North America's most northern game fish. This fish is very similar to the Dolly Varden, which is also a true char species. Chars (genus *Salvelinus*) have smaller scales and rounder bodies than trout of the genus *Salmo*. The Arctic char is silver in the sea, but turns dark with a spectacular scarlet side banding when it returns to the rushing rivers in the autumn. These char then spend the long Arctic winter locked beneath lake ice. The char's lean Arctic diet not only improves its flavor, but also slows its rate of growth: Arctic char can live as long as 35 years. The **Quebec red**

On their trip west, *Lewis and Clark discovered what was probably a cutthroat trout (whose Latin name is* Salmo clarki *in honor of the discovery). It resembled, Lewis wrote, "our mountain or speckled trout in form and in the position of their fins, but the specks on these are of a deep black instead of the red or goald colour of those common to the U'. States. these are furnished long sharp teeth on the pallet and tongue and have generally a small dash of red on each side behind the front ventral fins."*

trout and **blueback trout** are also char species found in Canada and parts of the northern United States; and the **Sunapee trout** is a char species that survives in the cold, deep lakes of New Hampshire and Maine. Three-pound char are common, 20-pounders very rare. Char has a delicate pink flesh, considered by members of the Cordon Bleu society of Paris to be the most delicious of any fish in the world. Today Arctic char are netted or speared by some Eskimo communities and are commercially available in southern Canada in restaurants and a few marketing outlets.

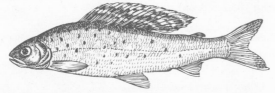

Arctic Grayling

ARCTIC GRAYLING: The Arctic grayling (*Thymallus arcticus*) is a species that is half way between trout and whitefish (another member of the salmonid family). Noted for its quick fighting qualities, the Arctic grayling has a dramatically high, winglike dorsal fin, a small mouth, large eyes and a forked tail. They seldom weigh more than five pounds. This fish will take both wet and dry flies and presents a real challenge to the sportsman. Unlike most trout, the Arctic grayling has fairly large scales, which should be removed. It is also bonier than most trout, but has a fine, delicate yellowish flesh that when lightly cooked remains one of the rare fish treats on earth. The grayling takes its Latin name, *thymallus*, from the faint odor of the herb thyme, which rises pleasantly from its flesh. It has an extraordinarily fine flavor when smoked or grilled, and is considered at its best when caught during the brief northern summer. The **Montana grayling** is indistinguishable from its Arctic cousin. However, its range has been so seriously decreased that only through careful restocking does this fish now survive in the United States.

LAKE TROUT: The lake trout (*Salvelinus namaycush*) prefers cold, deep water and inhabits the northern part of the continent as far north as Alaska. It has a deeply forked tail, a gray-green back and is lightly spotted. It has prominent teeth on the roof of its mouth. Lake trout will take a surface lure in spring and fall, and may be taken by deep trolling in cold waters during summer. The lake trout is commonly caught at weights of 10 pounds, but giants have been taken that weigh well over 100 pounds and are 35 to 40 years old. Unfortunately, great weight and age are more impressive to anglers than to cooks. The best,

" 'What a delightful thing is fishing!' have I more than once heard some knowing angler exclaim, who, with "the patience of Job," stands or slowly moves along some rivulet twenty feet wide, and three or four feet deep, with a sham fly to allure a trout, which, when at length caught, weight half a pound. Reader, I never had such patience."

—John James Audubon

most delicate flesh is found in the younger, smaller fish from two to 10 pounds. These fish are taken commercially from the Great Lakes in considerable numbers.

SPLAKE: Not actually a species, the splake is a newly-recognized hybrid. The "sp" stands for speckled trout (Canadian name for brook trout), and the "lake" for lake trout. The cross between these two species has produced a fish of increased size but undiminished food and fighting qualities. The pale-colored, fine-grained flesh is similar to the lake trout. The splake is sometimes called a **tiger trout**, because the cross occasionally produces a tigerlike banding (instead of the usual spots) on the fish's sides.

On his way to Florida in 1774, William Bartram described this trailside trout dinner: "I now, with difficulty and industry, collected a sufficiency of dry wood to keep up a light during the night and to roast some trout which I had caught when descending the river. Their heads I stewed in the juice of oranges, which, with boiled rice, afforded by a wholesome and delicious supper."

TROUT À LA MEUNIÈRE

**2 pan-sized trout, 9″ to 14″,
  with or without heads**
**Flour seasoned with salt and
  freshly ground pepper, for
  dredging**
Butter, for sautéing

1. Dredge the trout in seasoned flour.
2. In a frying pan, melt about 2 tablespoons of butter and when hot add fish. Cook 5 to 8 minutes on one side, then turn and cook 5 minutes on second side. Add more butter, if needed, to keep fish from sticking.

Note: Be sure to cook over moderate heat, since too great a heat will brown the skin and cause it to break when turning; and if cooked too slowly, the fish will get soft.

3. Serve with lemon wedges and a few capers, or melt more butter and pour foaming over fish.

Yield: 2 servings

TROUT AMANDINE

**All of ingredients for TROUT À
  LA MEUNIÈRE**
2 tablespoons sliced almonds
Lemon juice

1. Prepare as for TROUT À LA MEUNIÈRE, through Step 2.
2. Remove trout from pan and place on a warm serving plate. Add almonds to the frying pan and cook over high heat for 1 minute. Spoon almonds and drippings over the trout and flavor with a few drops of lemon juice.

Yield: 2 servings

A day of trout fishing on the *Rio Brazos* seems to have been a profitable one for this slightly scruffy *New Mexican* fisherman and his sidekick.

TROUT POACHED IN WHITE WINE

5 quarts water
4 cups dry white wine
¾ cup white wine vinegar
2 large carrots, roughly sliced
1 large onion, roughly sliced
4 sprigs fresh parsley

1 sprig fresh thyme, or 1
    teaspoon dried
1 small bay leaf
2 tablespoons salt
1 trout, 4 to 6 pounds*

1. Make a court bouillon: combine water, wine, vinegar, vegetables, herbs, and salt in a large pot and bring to a boil. Reduce heat and simmer gently for 5 minutes. Strain and cool slightly.
2. Clean the trout, but leave the head and tail on.
3. Place fish on the rack of a poacher (see Chapter 7), or wrap in cheesecloth to prevent sticking to bottom and place in pan large enough to hold fish. Pour warm court bouillon over the fish to cover.
4. Place over low heat and poach gently, allowing 10 minutes for every inch of the trout's thickness (see Canadian fish cooking rule, Chapter 1).
5. When done, lift the rack carefully out of the poacher and slide the trout gently onto a hot platter.
6. Serve hot with Hollandaise sauce (Chapter 6).

*Allow ½ pound per person.

Mayfly

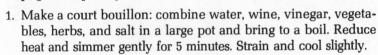

BAKED STUFFED TROUT

2 1½-pound trout
6 soda crackers, crushed, or 1
    cup dried bread crumbs
1 teaspoon salt
1 teaspoon freshly ground
    pepper
2 tablespoons chopped fresh
    parsley, or 1 tablespoon dried

2 tablespoons chopped fresh
    tarragon, or 1 tablespoon
    dried
1 tablespoon butter
Salt and freshly ground pepper,
    for seasoning
Corn meal, for dredging
4 slices bacon

1. Clean trout, cutting off heads and tails. Place heads and tails in a saucepan with water to cover and simmer about 20 minutes. Discard heads and tails and reserve the broth.
2. In a bowl, combine crackers (or bread crumbs), salt, pepper, herbs and butter. Moisten with 5 tablespoons of the reserved fish broth.
3. Preheat oven to 350°F.
4. Wipe body cavities of trout and sprinkle lightly with salt and pepper, inside and out. Stuff fish beginning at tail end and sew up with heavy thread and large darning needle, or use skewers (see Chapter 7).

5. Butter a baking dish, place trout in it and cut a couple of shallow slashes across fish. Sprinkle with salt, pepper and corn meal, and lay the bacon slices on top.
6. Bake in a 350°F. oven until done, about 30 minutes. The fish is done when it flakes easily when tested with a fork.

Yield: 4 servings

Variation: Add heated stewed tomatoes to baking dish before serving.

CLAY BAKER STUFFED TROUT

**All of ingredients for BAKED
    STUFFED TROUT**
½ cup dry white wine

1. Prepare a clay baker according to manufacturer's instructions for pre-soaking (or soak it for 10 minutes in water to cover).
2. Prepare the trout as for BAKED STUFFED TROUT, through Step 5, placing the fish in the clay baker instead of a buttered baking dish.
3. Moisten the fish with wine and bake in a 400°F. oven for 30 minutes.

Yield: 4 servings

TROUT STUFFED WITH CRAB

**2 trout, 9″ to 12″, with or
    without heads**
**Salt and freshly ground pepper,
    to taste**
1 tablespoon butter
**1 cup cooked, shredded
    crabmeat**
2 tablespoons heavy cream
**2 teaspoons chopped fresh
    parsley**
2 tablespoons lemon juice

1. Preheat oven to 350° F.
2. Season cleaned trout inside and out with salt and pepper.
3. In a frying pan, melt butter and add crabmeat, stirring till covered. Add cream and parsley.
4. Stuff trout beginning at tail end and sew up with heavy thread and large darning needle, or use skewers (Chapter 7). Lay stuffed trout in buttered baking dish and sprinkle with lemon juice.
5. Bake in a 350° F. oven for 15 minutes. Fish is done when it flakes easily when tested with a fork.
6. Serve with walnut sauce (Chapter 6).

Yield: 2 servings

"I, like other boys, fished with worms until a generous fisherman . . . gave four of us three artificial flies each. They proved powerfully productive. It never occurred to me that they were perishable. In any event, I nursed those three flies and used them until all the feathers were worn off— and still the trout rose to them. . . . A brand-new fly of any variety, even when carefully treated with cosmetics and attached to gut leaders and expensive rods, has nothing like the potency of that bamboo pole and the fly tied directly upon the end of a string."

—Herbert Hoover

TROUT STUFFED WITH HERBED RICE

2 tablespoons butter
1 cup long-grain rice
2 cups chicken stock
1 teaspoon dried marjoram
1 teaspoon dried dill
1 teaspoon dried parsley
1 tablespoon minced onion

1 teaspoon salt
¼ teaspoon freshly ground pepper
2 1½-pound trout, heads and tails left on
Salt, freshly ground pepper and dried dill, for seasoning

1. In a heavy saucepan, heat butter. Add rice and sauté gently for 1 minute. Do not let it brown.
2. Add chicken stock, herbs, onion, salt, and pepper. Bring to a boil and allow to boil for 2 minutes only. Reduce heat and simmer, tightly covered, until tender and fluffy, or about 20 minutes. Do not stir rice or uncover pot before rice has cooked.
3. Allow rice to rest for 5 minutes before stuffing fish.

Nineteenth-century New England fly fishermen still dressed for the sport in the British manner, and belonged to angling clubs that only permitted fishing from after tea until sundown.

4. While rice is resting, prepare fish. Wipe body cavities of trout and sprinkle lightly with salt and pepper, inside and out.
5. Preheat oven to 350°F.
6. Stuff fish with the herbed rice, beginning at the tail end. Sew up with heavy thread and large darning needle, or use skewers (see Chapter 7).
7. Butter a baking dish and place the trout sewn side down, so the fish is resting on its belly, not lying on its side. Cut a couple of shallow slashes across fish. Sprinkle with salt, pepper and dill.
8. Bake in a 350°F. oven until done, about 30 minutes. The fish is done when it flakes easily when tested with a fork.
9. Serve the fish in swimming position (the same way it was baked) surrounded by greens. Garnish with lemon wedges and dill sauce (Chapter 6).

Yield: 4 servings

Bound by no streamside etiquette, Western fishermen developed their own methods of plucking big Dolly Vardens from the snowfed streams.

BAKED DILL TROUT

2 trout, 10″ to 17″, with or without heads
Salt and freshly ground pepper, to taste

3 tablespoons butter
Juice of 1 lemon
2 teaspoons chopped fresh dill, or 4 teaspoons dried

1. Preheat oven to 350°F.
2. Dry the cleaned trout thoroughly inside and out. Season inside and out with salt and pepper.
3. Butter an ovenproof dish and lay trout in it. Top with pats of butter, lemon juice, salt, pepper and dill.
4. Bake in a 350°F. oven for 10 minutes. Fish is done when it flakes easily when tested with a fork.
5. Serve with lemon wedges and dill sauce (Chapter 6).

Yield: 2 servings

Variation: After baking, cover with 1 cup warmed heavy cream, a sprinkle of bread crumbs seasoned with dill, and brown under the broiler.

At the Dalles in Oregon, Lewis and Clark came across a fish they called "salmon trout," but which was probably a steelhead trout. Lewis described it as a fish of "silvery white colour on the belly and sides, and a bluish light brown on the back and head . . . narrow in proportion to their length."

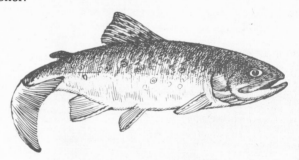

TROUT FILLETS MIREPOIX

4 trout fillets, 8″ to 10″
Flour seasoned with salt and freshly ground pepper, for dredging
Butter, for sautéing
½ cup chopped onion
½ cup chopped carrots

⅓ cup chopped celery
½ teaspoon thyme
Salt and freshly ground pepper, to taste
¼ cup medium cream

1. Dredge fillets in seasoned flour.
2. In a large frying pan, heat 2 tablespoons butter. Add vegetables and sauté until vegetables begin to soften. Add thyme, salt and pepper and move all to one side of the pan.
3. Add 1 more tablespoon of butter. Add trout fillets and sauté 2 to 3 minutes on each side, using more butter if necessary to keep fish from sticking.
4. Place fillets on hot platter. Add cream to pan, warm with vegetables, and serve over fish.

Yield: 4 servings

FILLETS WITH SHRIMP AND MUSHROOMS

4 trout fillets, 8" to 10"
Flour seasoned with salt and
   freshly ground pepper, for
   dredging
Butter, for sautéing

½ pound whole shrimp,
   cleaned and deveined
¼ pound mushrooms, sliced
½ teaspoon thyme
¼ cup medium cream

1. Dredge the trout fillets in seasoned flour.
2. In a large frying pan, heat about 2 tablespoons of butter. Add shrimp and mushrooms and sauté 3 to 5 minutes until shrimp are cooked and mushrooms begin to soften. Add thyme, salt and pepper to taste and move all to one side of pan.
3. Add 1 more tablespoon of butter. Add trout fillets and sauté 2 to 3 minutes on each side, using more butter if necessary to keep fish from sticking.
4. Place fillets on hot platter. Add cream to pan and warm with shrimp and mushrooms, serve over fish.

Yield: 4 servings

Variation: A splash of dry white wine can be substituted for cream and added to the pan juices just before serving.

New York State hatcheries were the first to introduce brown trout to North American waters, importing eggs from Germany and Scotland in the late 1800s. This Seneca Ray Stoddard photograph shows men at work in a New York hatchery at Glen Falls.

GRILLED ARCTIC CHAR STEAKS

This recipe can be used with other large fish—such as lake trout—that can be cut into steaks.

4 1″-thick char steaks (about 2 pounds)
3 tablespoons lemon juice
1 teaspoon grated lemon rind
¼ cup salad oil

⅛ teaspoon freshly ground pepper
¼ teaspoon marjoram
1 tablespoon finely chopped onion

1. In an outdoor grill or fireplace, start a wood or charcoal fire and burn until you have hot coals.
2. Meanwhile, place char steaks in a single layer in a shallow pan. Combine remaining ingredients and pour over char. Marinate 30 minutes, turning once.
3. Place fish in a well-greased, hinged, wire grill (see Chapter 7) and barbecue about 4″ from hot coals. Cook 10 minutes on each side, or until fish flakes easily when tested with a fork.

Yield: 4 servings

Eskimos camped on the beach at Port Clarence, Alaska, wind dry Arctic char on strings hung from an upturned umiak.

TROUT SOUFFLÉ

3 tablespoons butter
3 tablespoons flour
1 cup milk
1 cup (or less) cooked, flaked
  trout
¼ cup shredded carrot
2 tablespoons chopped fresh
  dill, or 1 tablespoon dried

3 eggs, separated
¼ teaspoon salt
⅛ teaspoon paprika
½ teaspoon lemon juice
  (optional)

1. Preheat oven to 325°F.
2. Make a white sauce: in a saucepan, melt butter, add flour, mixing with a wire whisk, and cook over low heat for 1 minute. Stirring constantly, gradually add milk and cook over medium heat until slightly thickened and smooth.
3. Add trout, carrot and dill.
4. When hot, remove from heat and stir in beaten egg yolks. Add salt, paprika, and lemon juice (if desired).
5. Whip egg whites until stiff, but not dry, and fold into fish mixture.
6. Pour into a buttered 1½-quart soufflé dish. Bake in a 325°F. oven for 35 minutes, or until firm.
7. Serve with mushroom sauce (Chapter 6) or tomato sauce (Chapter 6).
Yield: 4 servings

TROUT À LA NEWBURG

3 tablespoons butter
3 tablespoons flour
1½ cups milk
1 cup cooked, flaked trout
2 egg yolks

Salt and freshly ground pepper,
  to taste
4 slices white or whole wheat
  bread
3 tablespoons sherry

1. Make a white sauce: in a saucepan, melt butter, add flour, mixing with a wire whisk, and cook over low heat for 1 minute. Stirring constantly, gradually add milk and cook over medium heat until slightly thickened and smooth.
2. Add flaked trout and remove from heat.
3. Beat egg yolks lightly, then, stirring constantly, gradually add them to the fish mixture. Add salt and pepper.
4. Stirring constantly, cook barely at simmering point for 2 to 3 minutes. If it thickens too much, add a bit more milk.
5. Toast bread and slice diagonally in half.
6. Add sherry to the creamed trout and serve surrounded with toast points. Garnish with a sprinkling of capers.
Yield: 4 servings.

Fly fishing is only one of many ways to catch a trout, but for two thousand years it has been thought to be the most sporting. The Roman, Aelian, who died in 170 B.C., may have written the earliest description of fly fishing. "They fasten red wool around a hook and fix onto the wool two feathers which grow under a cock's wattles and which in color are like wax. Their rod is six feet long and their line is the same in length. Then they throw their snare, and the fish attracted and maddened by the color comes straight at it thinking from the pretty sight to get a dainty mouthful."

TROUT-STUFFED CUCUMBERS

4 medium cucumbers (about 2 pounds)	1 3-ounce package cream cheese, softened
2 cups water	2 teaspoons lemon juice
2 tablespoons salt	1 tablespoon chopped fresh dill
1 cup cooked, flaked trout	Salt, to taste
⅓ cup cottage cheese	Paprika

1. Peel cucumbers and cut in half lengthwise. With a spoon, scoop out seeds and discard. In a large bowl, combine water and salt and submerge cucumbers in mixture. Cover and refrigerate 1 hour, turning cucumbers occasionally.
2. In blender or food processor, blend the trout, cottage cheese, cream cheese, lemon juice, dill and salt.

Note: For a chunkier stuffing, mix with a fork.

3. Preheat oven to 350° F.
4. Drain cucumber halves and pat dry. Divide trout mixture evenly and spread into hollow of cucumbers. Sprinkle with a dash of paprika.
5. Place in buttered baking dish and bake in a 350° F. oven for 20 minutes.
6. Serve with dill sauce (Chapter 6).

Yield: 4 to 8 servings

PICKLED TROUT

1 cup sliced onions	1 quart distilled vinegar
½ cup olive oil	1 quart water
1 tablespoon mustard seed	10 pounds trout, without heads
½ teaspoon bay leaves	and tails
½ teaspoon whole cloves	⅓ cup salt
1 tablespoon peppercorns	

1. In a large saucepan, cook onions in olive oil until they are soft. Add spices, vinegar and water, and simmer gently for 45 minutes. Remove from heat and allow to cool.
2. While pickling solution is simmering, prepare the trout. Cut trout into individual serving portions, rinse in cold water and drain. Place in a glass, enamel, plastic, or stainless-steel bowl (*not* aluminum) and cover with salt. Toss to coat the trout thoroughly.

"As the shadow of the king-fisher moved up the stream, a big trout shot upstream in a long angle, only his shadow marking the angle, then lost his shadow as he came through the surface of the water, caught the sun, and then, as he went back into the stream under the surface, his shadow seemed to float down the stream with the current, unresisting, to his post under the bridge, where he tightened, facing up into the current."

—Big Two-Hearted River, Ernest Hemingway

3. Let trout sit for about 30 minutes, then rinse salt off. Place trout in a saucepan with water to cover and simmer gently until done. Trout is done when flesh is opaque and flakes easily when tested with a fork.

4. Drain the cooked trout and place, while still warm, in a crock (or glass or enamel container) and cover with pickling solution. Make sure all pieces are completely covered.

5. Allow to stand in the pickling solution for 24 hours before serving.

6. Serve as an hors d'oeuvre, plain or with a dab of sour cream.

Yield: 24 to 30 servings

TROUT SOUP

6 cups fish stock (Chapter 6)	½ cup heavy cream
1 cup cooked, flaked trout	Salt and freshly ground pepper,
1 cup cooked, chopped spinach	to taste

1. Bring fish stock to a boil. Lower to a simmer and add trout and spinach. Cook for 5 minutes, or until trout and spinach are heated through.

2. Remove from heat and add cream and salt and pepper.

3. Serve in bowls ungarnished or with croutons or sea biscuit crackers, a spoonful of sour cream and chopped chives.

Yield: 8 servings

COLD SMOKED TROUT IN MAYONNAISE

Smoked trout can be prepared in one of several ways (see Chapter 7) and then stored in the refrigerator for up to two weeks, or frozen. Serve smoked trout as an hors d'oeuvre, as below, or in any recipe that calls for cooked trout.

1 or more smoked trout	Chopped parsley
Mayonnaise	Lemon wedges
Capers	

1. Skin the trout from the tail to gills and place it on a serving dish. Lightly frost with mayonnaise. Sprinkle with garnish of capers and parsley, and edge with lemon wedges.

2. Serve on lettuce or sandwich bread, with a squeeze of lemon.

Variation: Add garnish of sliced hard-boiled eggs and tomatoes.

Salmon

There are six species of salmon that inhabit North American waters. Only one of these salmon species (*Salmo salar*) lives in the Atlantic; the other five varieties of salmon (genus *Oncorhynchus*) range along the Pacific coast. Although the most common names for the five Pacific salmon types are Chinook, coho, sockeye, chum, and pink, they are also known by myriad local names, such as tyee, king, blueback, spring, dog, or humpback. In addition to these main anadromous varieties of salmon (ie., those that return from the sea to spawn in rivers), there are also two species of landlocked salmon: **ouananiche**—a *Salmo salar* found in northeastern lakes—and **kokanee**—a variation of the sockeye, found in northwestern lakes.

The principal difference between the Atlantic salmon and the five Pacific salmon species is that the adult Atlantic salmon runs up river from the sea, enters smaller streams to spawn, then returns to the ocean, repeating this cycle several times. All five of the Pacific salmon species, when they are adults, run from the ocean into the rivers where they were born, spawn only once, then continue up river to die. Very young salmon are called fingerlings, which grow to become parr. They then run to the sea where they become silver-sided smolts, growing to lengths of three to seven inches. In their next phase before adulthood they are called grilse, and some grow to weigh as much as four pounds. In this stage many will gain almost half their adult weight. Most salmon are caught as adults.

All types of salmon prefer cold, clear, fast-moving water to supply them with the large amount of oxygen they require. Their sleek, streamlined bodies allow them to leap up 12-foot waterfalls. Both male and female salmon (often referred to by fishermen as cocks and hens, or bucks and does) usually turn a darker color during the autumn spawning season. At that time, the male develops a large undershot lower jaw that it uses to scoop out shallow trenches on the river bottom where the female salmon lays thousands of eggs. The male then deposits a thick white milt, which fertilizes and gives a protective covering to the eggs until the young are hatched, usually in the following spring. The orange roe taken from a freshly caught female salmon makes delicious caviar and should be no more overlooked than the nutritious and flavorful white milt from a male.

The quality of salmon flesh varies with species, age, season and location. Some salmon is oily and particularly well suited to salads or smoking; some salmon is lean and is at its very best when poached or baked. Flesh colors range from white to red and, according to most experts, have little to do with taste; but market prices are always higher for the red-fleshed salmon and

▶ *This dignified looking gentleman has just won a battle with a huge tyee salmon.*

Isaak Walton wrote of salmon: "He has, like some other persons of honor and riches which have both their winter and summer houses, the fresh water for summer and the salt water for winter . . ."

canneries make a distinction between red and white. There is, however, a difference in the flavor of salmon depending on whether it is ocean-run or has spent considerable time in the river. The best salmon are those caught just after they've run in from the sea and are bright silver. A salmon whose skin is turning dark has been in the river a while and should not be considered a prime food fish. Small or medium-sized salmon generally have finer texture and flavor than very large fish.

Many experienced fishermen/cooks feel that salmon is best taken directly from the water and cooked immediately. However, salmon stored in a cold place, with guts and gills removed, will keep nicely for four or five days; and some connoisseurs believe that this holding period actually improves the flavor of a salmon's flesh. In any case, salmon are relatively easy to prepare for cooking. Depending on variety and age, and the recipe to be used, large salmon sometimes need a quick scaling, but most salmon do not. When cooking salmon, allow a half pound of cleaned fish per person or one-third pound of fillets. Commercially, salmon is sold whole, cut in steaks, as smoked fillets, or in cans.

Salmon stands up admirably to being canned. It is tasty and convenient, and although the flavor varies with the species and brand, price is a fairly reliable indication of quality. Most salmon used in canning comes from the Pacific, usually pinks, sockeye, and Chinook. There are several recipes in this chapter that call for canned salmon, but naturally leftover fresh salmon will serve as well.

Atlantic Salmon

ATLANTIC SALMON: The Atlantic salmon (*Salmo salar*) is the best known of all the *Salmonidae*. Once, together with cod, it was considered America's most important table fish. It was certainly one of the greatest of all game fish. Atlantic salmon ran so plentifully in the New England rivers in the 18th and 19th centuries that the fish was considered a poor man's staple; servants actually complained when fresh salmon appeared on their table more than twice a week. Unfortunately, the Atlantic salmon has been driven from many of its spawning rivers by industrial pollution, relentless netting and half-hearted international controls. On this side of the Atlantic, the salmon may still be found in the cold waters of eastern Canada from which it will soon disappear if conservation measures are not taken. Today the Atlantic salmon that reaches U.S. markets is shipped in from European or Canadian sources. Atlantic salmon has rich pink flesh and an average weight of 10 to 14 pounds, three to six pounds for a grilse. For sports fishing in the rivers of eastern Canada, early summer is the best season.

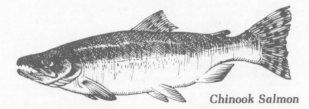

Chinook Salmon

CHINOOK SALMON: Chinook or **king salmon** (*Oncorhynchus tshawytscha*) is the largest of the five Pacific species, with a wide range and a record weight of 126 pounds. There are occasionally two runs of chinook during their spawning season. Chinook salmon, also called **spring** and **tyee**, are rich in oil and have a slightly higher fat content than other salmon. Its cooked flesh has a medium-firm, flaky texture. The average Chinook runs eight to 20 pounds and is best taken in the ocean in spring and autumn when it has bright silver sides.

COHO SALMON: The coho or **silver salmon** (*Oncorhynchus kisutch*) is an excellent sporting fish that ranges from Alaska to the coast of California, usually weighing from eight to 15 pounds, with a record weight of over 30 pounds. Coho spawn from late summer into midwinter, depending on their location, and the eggs hatch correspondingly in late spring or early summer. This silver salmon is a delicious table fish with fine-textured flesh that is usually pink, although some are white-fleshed. It is best for eating when caught in the sea just before it enters a river to spawn, or when newly in the river and still in its silver phase. This fish has recently been successfully transplanted to the Great Lakes and the Connecticut River system.

SOCKEYE SALMON: Sockeye salmon (*Oncorhynchus nerka*) is not much regarded as a game fish since it rarely takes lures or bait, but it is a splendid commercial fish taken by seiners and trawlers. When canned, it is labelled **blueback** or **red** salmon, and it is slightly oily, deep-colored and truly delectable. Its range is from Alaska south to Oregon. The sockeye when returning to the river for spawning has an average weight of six to seven pounds. During spawning the sockeye develops a large hump on its back and its outer skin takes on a vivid red coloration, at which time it is good eating.

CHUM SALMON: The chum or **dog salmon** (*Oncorhynchus keta*) is usually thought of as a netted fish, but it is also a sporting

Thank you, good selectman,
For your salmon.
A finer fish or fatter
Never swam a river
Nor smoked on any platter.
—A New England traveller

one to be taken with a line and various types of lure. They range from northern California to Alaska and usually return to their spawning river after four years at sea, weighing six to 10 pounds. During spawning the males turn dark-backed with brilliant red and green side splashes. When they are too red, they are not good to eat. The native peoples of the Northwest Coast prefer this fish above all other salmon because it is so delicious when smoked or dry-cured.

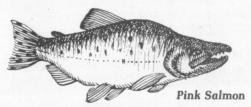

Pink Salmon

PINK SALMON: Pink salmon (*Oncorhynchus gorbuscha*) is both a sporting and commercial fish with a delicious, savory flesh, and it represents nearly half of all salmon tinned in America. The pink is in larger numbers off California than other salmon species, and it ranges as far north as Alaska, providing excellent fishing in late summer and autumn. It reaches maturity in its second year when it commonly weighs about four pounds. The pink develops a considerable hump during spawning and so has earned the nickname **humpback.**

POACHED NOVA SCOTIA SALMON

1 whole salmon, 6 to 12 pounds*
3 to 4 tablespoons butter, depending on fish size
Salt and freshly ground pepper, to taste

1 onion, quartered
½ cup coarsely chopped celery
2 bay leaves
2 teaspoons rosemary

1. Preheat oven to 300° F.
2. Using your hands, rub entire salmon with softened butter, closing all the fish's pores. Season with salt and pepper, and wrap in cheesecloth.
3. Place in baking dish and add boiling water to above salmon's backbone. Add remaining ingredients to water.
4. Place in 300° F. oven for approximately 45 minutes. Allow 10 minutes for every inch of the salmon's thickness (see Canadian fish cooking rule, Chapter 1). Test for doneness with a knife point in flesh around backbone. Salmon is done when flesh is opaque, no longer translucent.
5. Remove fish from oven, drain, and allow it to cool. Do not refrigerate. Skin just before serving and garnish.

*Allow ½ pound per person.

◄An angler kills an Atlantic salmon on the famous Miramichi River in New Brunswick. Eastern Canadian rivers such as this one have traditionally provided world sportsmen with the best in fishing, but poor laws and river management now sadly threaten the destruction of these great salmon runs.

SALMON IN ASPIC

One of the simplest ways to dress up a fish is to serve it in a clear gelatin coating called aspic. Salmon, with its beautiful pink flesh, is particularly well suited to this method. It can be done with a whole salmon (as here), one long fillet, or a number of steaks. Also, pieces of cooked salmon may be flaked into small dishes or shells and covered with aspic. If time permits, the presentation can be made even fancier as in DECORATED COLD SALMON.

1 whole salmon*, poached in court bouillon (Chapter 6)	2 envelopes unflavored gelatin
½ cup water	3 cups court bouillon

1. Let the salmon cool in its court bouillon. Then remove it to a large serving platter (or a wooden plank). Remove the skin from both sides of the fish, leaving it on head and tail. Remove any brown meat to leave the fish all pink.
2. Put water in a large saucepan, sprinkle gelatin into water and let stand several minutes.
3. Meanwhile, in another saucepan, reheat 3 cups of the court bouillon. Then strain hot court bouillon through a fine sieve, carefully removing any bits of vegetables. Add to gelatin and simmer briefly to dissolve gelatin thoroughly.
4. Cool the aspic by setting the saucepan in a bowl of ice cubes and water. Slowly stir the aspic; it will thicken as it cools. When properly set, it will have the consistency of heavy cream. Do not allow it to cool too much or it will form lumps.
5. Quickly coat the fish by ladling the aspic along its length. This must be done in 4 or 5 seconds while the aspic remains the correct consistency. If it hardens, reheat it briefly and finish the job.
6. Surround the fish with parsley or watercress and serve with green sauce (Chapter 6) or mayonnaise (Chapter 6), and toast spread with parsley butter.

*Allow ½ pound per person.

DECORATED HOT SALMON

1 whole salmon*, poached or baked	Sauce (Chapter 6): Hollandaise, dill or green sauce

1. Lay the fish on a large serving platter (or a wooden plank). Remove skin from both sides of fish, leaving it on head and tail. Remove any brown meat to leave the fish all pink.

Traditional salmon recipes often included egg sauce, as in this recipe from a turn-of-the-century cookbook:
"BOILED SALMON: Sew up the fish in a piece of thin muslin, or mosquito-netting, fitted well to it, and boil in salted boiling water to which two tablespoonfuls of vinegar have been added. Take off the cloth carefully when the fish has boiled twelve minutes to the pound, and lay upon a hot platter. Pour over it a few spoonfuls of egg sauce into which has been stirred a tablespoonful of capers, and serve the rest in a gravy-boat. Garnish with nasturtiums, or parsley, or cresses."

2. Spread a line of mounded sauce head to tail down the middle of the fish. Choose the sauce to be used according to which color will best complement the side dishes: yellow (Hollandaise), very pale green (dill sauce) or dark green (green sauce).

3. Surround the fish with cooked vegetables (to be served as side dishes) or in any of the ways suggested in Step 4 of DECORATED COLD SALMON.

4. Serve any leftover sauce in a sauce boat.

*Allow ½ pound per person.

DECORATED COLD SALMON

To give salmon, king of fish, the royal treatment it deserves, serve it whole and adorned in one of the ways suggested below.

1 whole salmon*, poached or   Various garnishes
   baked, and cooled
Aspic glaze (see SALMON IN
   ASPIC)

1. Lay the cooled fish on a large serving platter (or a wooden plank). Remove the skin from both sides of the fish, leaving it on head and tail. Remove any brown meat to leave the fish all pink.

2. Replace the fish's eye, if you wish, with a stuffed olive or a slice of hard-boiled egg.

3. To dress the salmon, any of several vegetables or herbs are arranged on the fish in a decorative pattern, and the whole is coated with aspic (see SALMON IN ASPIC for instructions). The decorations must be dipped in hot aspic before placing on the salmon so that they will stick in place when the aspic glaze is applied. Some suggested decorations follow: 1) a row of thin lemon slices running head to tail down the salmon's middle, 2) thin lemon, egg or cucumber slices arranged in an overlapping fish-scale pattern, 3) small bits of diced pimiento or sliced olives to accent any of the preceding, 4) fresh tarragon or chervil sprigs arranged in stripes or a branch pattern.

4. To finish off the fish, surround it with fresh parsley studded with cherry tomatoes, uncooked carrot sticks or cooked carrot rounds. Other ingredients well suited to dressing the platter are: black olives, anchovies, sliced red or green peppers, cooked shrimp, sliced mushrooms, lemon wedges or a sprinkling of capers.

*Allow ½ pound per person.

Once, in June and early July, Atlantic salmon appeared in such great numbers that there were celebration menus of poached salmon with white potatoes and green peas. Although their numbers have decreased, salmon is still a Fourth-of-July food tradition in New England.

By the turn of the century, gill netting for salmon was a way of life in Washington State, one man to a boat and no coming home until the fish were sliding over the gunwales.

GRILLED STUFFED SALMON

This recipe is a variation on one used by fishermen who, camped alongside a salmon river, put quartered onions inside their newly caught and cleaned salmon, wrap it in aluminum foil and grill it over an open fire.

1 whole salmon, 4 to 5 pounds
1 potato, unpeeled, sliced
1 onion, sliced
¼ pound mushrooms, thickly sliced

1 lemon, sliced
2 cups white wine

1. In an outdoor grill or fireplace, start a wood or charcoal fire and burn until you have hot coals.
2. In the meantime, clean the salmon, removing head and tail, and stuff with the vegetables and lemon slices. Place the stuffed fish on two layers of heavy aluminum foil large enough to enclose fish.
3. Turn up the sides of the foil and pour wine over all. Seal the aluminum pouch around the salmon.

4. Place on a grill and cook for about 1½ hours, or until the salmon flakes easily when tested with a fork. Since temperatures of live coals vary greatly, fish should be carefully watched.
5. Serve with tartar sauce (Chapter 6) and lemon wedges.

Yield: 8 to 10 servings

SALMON STEAKS IN RED WINE

2 shallots, finely chopped
1 tablespoon lemon juice
¾ cup dry red wine
1 teaspoon cornstarch
1 tablespoon water

2 salmon steaks (about ½ pound each)
Salt and freshly ground pepper, to taste
1 tablespoon butter

Isaak Walton speaks of the cock and hen salmon as the "melter and spawner." He wrote in The Compleat Angler, published in 1653, "The salmon is accounted the King of fresh-water fish, and is ever bred in rivers relating to the sea . . ."

1. Preheat oven to 400° F.
2. In a saucepan, combine shallots, lemon juice and red wine. Bring to a boil and cook over medium heat for 5 minutes.
3. Dissolve cornstarch in 1 tablespoon water. Stir into wine mixture and return to boil. Allow sauce to thicken slightly. Set aside.
4. Place salmon steaks in buttered baking dish, sprinkle with salt and pepper and dot with butter. Place under broiler for 5 minutes.
5. Turn steaks, and cover with red wine sauce, and bake in a 400° F. oven for 5 minutes.
6. Serve on heated plates with sauce poured over the steaks.

Yield: 2 servings

SALMON CROWN ROYAL

6 salmon steaks (about ½ pound each)
2 tablespoons chopped fresh chives

Salt, to taste
½ cup (1 stick) butter
3 ounces (6 tablespoons) Crown Royal, Canadian rye whiskey

1. Place salmon steaks in a buttered baking dish. Sprinkle with chives and salt.
2. Melt the butter and pour half of it over the fish.
3. Broil steaks until they start to brown, about 5 minutes. Remove fish from broiler and flip steaks over. Add the Crown Royal to the remaining melted butter and pour over fish.
4. Place under the broiler again and cook until the fish is done, about 5 minutes. Fish is done when it flakes easily when tested with a fork.

Yield: 6 servings

SALMON MEDALLIONS FLORENTINE

4 salmon steaks (about ½ pound each)
1 pound spinach
Butter, for sautéing
2 medium onions, coarsely chopped

¼ cup dry vermouth
Salt and freshly ground pepper, to taste
½ cup heavy cream
Dash of nutmeg

1. Prepare the salmon. To shape salmon steaks into boneless medallions, remove outer skin, then cut out the central bone and the three sets of long, thin bones attached to it. This will give you two comma-shaped pieces per steak. Invert one of the commas so that it will fit snugly into the rightside-up comma. Press the two commas together to form a compact circle and pin the comma tails in place with toothpicks (see Chapter 7 for an illustration). Repeat for each steak.
2. Steam spinach briefly and chop coarsely. Set aside.
3. In a frying pan, heat about 2 tablespoons butter and sauté onions until soft. Add spinach and vermouth and keep mixture warm.
4. In a large frying pan, heat about 1 tablespoon butter, or enough to keep salmon from sticking. Sauté medallions on one side for approximately 3 minutes. Turn and sprinkle the cooked sides with salt and pepper. Add about 1 more tablespoon butter and cook reverse sides about 5 minutes, until steaks look opaque and are firm in the center but not dry. Season with salt and pepper, remove from heat and keep warm.
5. While salmon medallions are cooking on the reverse sides, add cream and nutmeg to spinach mixture. Heat, stirring constantly, to allow to reduce slightly.
6. Pour spinach mixture onto a warmed deep serving platter and place salmon medallions in the center.

Yield: 4 servings

Highlander

SALMON OMELET

½ cup cooked or canned salmon
4 to 6 eggs
3 tablespoons milk

Salt and freshly ground pepper, to taste
2 tablespoons butter

1. Flake the salmon, removing any skin and bones.
2. Beat the eggs with milk, salt and pepper until well mixed but not frothy. Mix in the salmon.
3. In an omelet or frying pan, melt butter, rotating pan so butter

coats bottom and lower sides. The pan will be ready for cooking when a drop of water sizzles, or the faintest bit of steam rises. Do not allow the butter to brown.

4. Turn heat to low and quickly pour in the salmon and egg mixture. Cook until the eggs thicken on the bottom. Then slide a spatula or fork under the edge of the omelet, lift up the edge of the cooked eggs, tilt the pan, and allow the uncooked eggs to flow underneath the cooked part.

5. When the entire mixture has just barely thickened, use a spatula to lift one half of the omelet and fold it over the other half, forming a half-moon shape. Slide out of pan onto a warmed platter.

Yield: 2 to 4 servings

Variation: For a special occasion, top each portion with a spoonful of black caviar and sour cream. Black caviar should never be cooked inside an omelet because it turns the eggs a spotted gray-green.

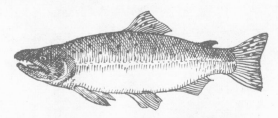

SALMON POTATO CASSEROLE

1 egg
¾ cup milk
3 large potatoes, peeled and thinly sliced
½ pound smoked salmon (fresh* or canned), or 1 7-ounce can regular salmon

1 large onion, thinly sliced
2 tablespoons flour
4 slices bacon
½ teaspoon salt
8 black peppercorns

1. Preheat oven to 400° F.
2. Whip egg into milk.
3. Grease a 2-quart casserole and fill it in layers as follows: half of the potato slices, all of the salmon, all of the onion slices, sprinkle lightly with 1 tablespoon of the flour. Then, the rest of the potato slices, all of the bacon, sprinkle lightly with the remaining tablespoon of flour, the salt and peppercorns.
4. Pour milk and egg mixture over the whole casserole.
5. Bake in a 400° F. oven for about 1 hour, or until potatoes are done.

Yield: 4 servings

*See Chapter 7 for smoking techniques.

"The fly to be used is any of the large Salmon flies, the larger and gaudier the better. None is more taking than an orange body with peacock and bluejay wings and black hackle legs; but any of the well-known Salmon flies will secure him, as will the scarlet bodied fly with scarlet ibis and silver pheasant wings. . . ."
—Frank Forester's Fish and Fishing of the United States and British Provinces of North America, 1849

A stylish young woman, with her split Tonkin bamboo rod in hand, holds up her hard-won prize: a Pacific salmon over half her size.

SALMON CRÊPES

Crêpes:
1 cup flour, white or buckwheat
½ teaspoon salt
3 eggs
¾ cup milk
¼ cup water
Butter, for frying

Creamed Salmon:
4 tablespoons butter
4 tablespoons flour

2 cups milk
1½ cups cooked, flaked salmon
2 tablespoons chopped fresh dill
1 tablespoon sherry (optional)
Salt and freshly ground pepper,
  to taste

1. In a large bowl, sift together the flour and salt.
2. In a small bowl, beat eggs. Add milk and water.
3. Pour the egg mixture into the flour and stir together with as few strokes as possible. Small lumps may be ignored.
4. Refrigerate the batter for 3 to 12 hours to allow the flour to absorb the liquid ingredients.
5. When you're just about ready to make the crêpes, make the creamed salmon: in a saucepan, melt butter, add flour, mixing with a wire whisk, and cook over low heat for 1 minute. Stirring constantly, gradually add milk and cook over medium heat until slightly thickened and smooth. Add the salmon and dill, and sherry (if desired) to the cream sauce and heat until warmed through. Season with salt and pepper.
6. Grease a crêpe pan (or a small frying pan with curving sides) and heat until a drop of water flicked into it bounces and sizzles. Gently ladle a small amount of batter into pan and quickly tip and rotate pan to spread batter around bottom. Cook over medium heat for a minute or two. When it browns, turn crêpe and brown other side for about a minute.
7. Repeat this procedure until all batter is used, regreasing pan for each crêpe. Fill crêpes with salmon mixture right away, or stack crêpes with pieces of waxed paper between them to keep from turning soggy. Keep warm in a 150° F. oven until ready to be filled.

Note: Crêpes can also be frozen for future use.

8. To fill crêpes, place a large spoonful of the salmon mixture in the center of each crêpe and roll it into a tube. As each crêpe is filled, place in a serving dish kept warm in a 150° F. oven.
9. Serve crêpes as is, or cover with remaining filling (if any) or dill sauce (Chapter 6).

Yield: 6 servings

Variation: Minced, sautéed onions may be added to the crêpe batter.

After a successful day on the river, try skinning and slicing fresh salmon and eating it on crackers or brown bread. It is delicious and has not the slightest fishy taste; but for the not so sure beginners, add a few drops of lemon juice, or Worcestershire sauce, or a touch of mustard. Follow this with a short shot of chilled aquavit or vodka, or a dram of whiskey, and you're set.

SALMON MOUSSE NANTUA

2 tablespoons butter	1 envelope unflavored gelatin
2 tablespoons flour	¼ cup heavy cream
1¼ cups milk	½ cup coarsely chopped shrimp
1½ cups cooked, flaked salmon	or crayfish
1½ cups mayonnaise	1 egg white
Salt and freshly ground pepper,	Watercress
to taste	1 teaspoon tomato juice
3 tablespoons fish stock	3 drops Tabasco sauce
(Chapter 6) or water	

1. Make a white sauce: in a saucepan, melt butter, add flour, mixing with a wire whisk, and cook over low heat for 1 minute. Stirring constantly, gradually add milk and cook over medium heat until slightly thickened and smooth.
2. In blender or food processor, blend salmon, white sauce, and 1 cup of the mayonnaise. Add salt and pepper.
3. Put the fish stock (or water) in a small saucepan and sprinkle gelatin into the liquid. Cook over low heat, stirring, until gelatin dissolves. Fold gelatin into salmon mixture.
4. Whip heavy cream until it is partially whipped and fold into salmon mixture along with shrimp (or crayfish).
5. Whip egg white until stiff. Fold into salmon mixture.
6. Turn into a lightly oiled 1½-quart mold and chill until firm.
7. To serve, turn out onto a bed of watercress. Mix remaining ½ cup mayonnaise with tomato juice and Tabasco sauce, and use this to frost the mousse. Garnish with extra shrimp if desired.

Yield: 6 servings

In his journals, William Clark described an Indian method of preparing salmon. "I was furnished with a mat to set on and one man set about pre-pareing me something to eate . . . he lay'd [pine chips] open on the fire on which he put round Stones, a woman handed him a basket of water and a large Salmon about half dried, when the Stones were hot he put them into the bas-ket of water with the fish which was soon sufficiently boiled for use, it was then taken out put on a platter of rushes neatly made, and set before me . . . after eateing the boiled fish which was deli-cious, I set out."

SALMON MOUSSE

4 cups cooked salmon, or 2	2 tablespoons grated onion
15½-ounce cans red salmon	1 tablespoon horseradish
¾ cup fish stock *, or liquid	1 teaspoon salt
from canned salmon	¼ teaspoon freshly ground
1 cup mayonnaise	pepper
4 tablespoons chopped fresh	2 envelopes unflavored gelatin
parsley	1 cup heavy cream
2 tablespoons lemon juice	

1. If using canned salmon, drain the salmon and reserve the liquid. Add enough water to salmon liquid to make ¾ cup. Set aside.
2. In a large bowl, flake fish and add mayonnaise, parsley, lemon juice, onion, horseradish, salt and pepper. If preferred, this step can be done, in two batches, in a blender or food processor.

3. Put the fish stock (or reserved liquid from the can) in a small saucepan, sprinkle the gelatin into liquid. Cook over low heat, stirring, until gelatin dissolves. Add to the salmon mixture. In two batches, blend thoroughly in a blender or food processor.
4. Whip heavy cream. Fold into the salmon mixture. Pour into a lightly oiled 2½-quart mold and chill until firm.
5. Unmold on lettuce and garnish with egg and cucumber slices.

Yield: 12 main-course servings, 20 first-course servings, or multiple hors-d'oeuvre servings.

Note: Cans labelled "red" salmon will produce a more deeply colored mousse.

*Water may be substituted for fish stock.

SALMON QUICHE

1 9″ pie shell	3 eggs
1 small onion, finely chopped	1 egg yolk
2 tablespoons butter	1 cup light cream
2 cups cooked, flaked salmon, or 1 15½-ounce can	Salt and freshly ground pepper, to taste
2 tablespoons chopped fresh dill	⅛ teaspoon nutmeg

1. Preheat oven to 325° F.
2. Roll out pastry, fit in pie or quiche pan and make a high edge with fork patterns. Prick air holes in crust and bake in a 325° F. oven for 10 minutes till light brown. Remove quiche shell from oven and set aside.
3. Turn oven up to 350° F.
4. In a frying pan, sauté onion in butter until soft. Set aside to cool.
5. If using canned salmon, drain, and pick out bones, if any. Flake salmon with a fork. Combine cooled onions with salmon and spread mixture on bottom of pie shell. Sprinkle with dill.
6. Combine eggs and egg yolk with cream, salt, pepper and nutmeg, and lightly mix with a whisk. Pour over salmon.
7. Bake in a 350° F. oven for 30 to 40 minutes, until the custard is set. The quiche may be removed from the oven without the center being fully done. Let stand at room temperature for at least 5 minutes before cutting.

Yield: 6 to 8 servings

Variation: For a colorful variation, place two rings (one inside the other) of thinly-sliced tomatoes on top of the custard for the last 10 minutes of baking.

A solid man of Boston
A comfortable man with dividends,
And the first salmon and the first green peas.
—Henry Wadsworth Longfellow

SALMON PIE

Crust:
1½ cups flour
½ teaspoon salt
½ teaspoon freshly ground pepper
½ cup shredded cheese (Muenster or young cheddar)
½ cup (1 stick) butter

Filling:
2 cups cooked, flaked salmon, or 1 15½-ounce can

3 eggs
¼ cup fish stock*, or liquid from canned salmon
1 cup sour cream
½ cup shredded cheese (Muenster or young cheddar)
¼ cup mayonnaise
1 tablespoon grated onion
3 drops Tabasco sauce

1. Preheat oven to 400° F.
2. Make the crust: Combine flour, seasonings, and shredded cheese. Cut in butter and mix until mixture forms crumbs.
3. Reserve 1 cup of crust mixture to use as topping. Pat remaining crumbs into deep pie dish to form a bottom crust.
4. Make the filling: if using canned salmon, drain and reserve liquid. Flake salmon, removing all bones and skin.
5. In a separate bowl, beat eggs lightly. Add fish stock (or ¼ cup reserved liquid from can), sour cream, shredded cheese, mayonnaise, onion and Tabasco sauce.
6. Add salmon to mixture and pour into pie crust. Sprinkle reserved crust crumbs over top.
7. Bake in a 400° F. oven for 45 minutes.
Yield: 6 servings

*Water may be substituted for fish stock.

HERBED SALMON RING

2 cups cooked, flaked salmon, or 1 15½-ounce can
½ cup wheat meal cracker crumbs
1 cup soft bread crumbs
3 tablespoons chopped pimiento-stuffed olives
¼ cup minced onion
¾ cup finely chopped celery
2 tablespoons chopped celery leaves

2 tablespoons chopped fresh parsley
1 teaspoon chopped fresh dill
1 tablespoon lemon juice
3 drops Tabasco or Worcestershire sauce
2 eggs, beaten
½ cup milk
Salt and freshly ground pepper, to taste

1. Preheat oven to 375° F.
2. Remove bones, if any, from salmon. No need to drain the canned salmon.
3. In a large bowl, combine salmon with all other ingredients. Mix well.

4. Put mixture in a buttered 5-cup ring mold and cover with heavy-duty aluminum foil. Place mold in a pan filled with 1″ hot water.
5. Bake in a 375° F. oven for 30 minutes.
6. Remove from oven, let stand for 5 minutes, and turn out onto a warmed serving platter.
7. Fill center of ring with cooked vegetables such as creamed peas or onions with chopped dill. Serve with dill sauce (Chapter 6).

Yield: 4 to 6 servings

In the late nineteenth century, horse teams—such as these on the Columbia River—were used to round up salmon at low tide in a method called drag seining.

Around the turn of the century, a booming salmon canning industry was producing over 60 million cans a year.

SALMON PORCUPINES

1 cup cooked, flaked salmon, or
1 7¾-ounce can
1 cup fish stock*, or liquid from
canned salmon
½ cup partially cooked rice
1 egg, well beaten
2 tablespoons minced onion

2 teaspoons minced celery
2 tablespoons butter
2 tablespoons flour
1 cup milk
Salt and freshly ground pepper,
to taste

1. Preheat oven to 325° F.
2. If using canned salmon, drain and reserve liquid. Add enough water to salmon liquid to make 1 cup. Set aside.
3. Mix salmon, rice, egg, onion and celery together. Shape into 1″ balls. Place the balls in a 1½-quart casserole.
4. Make a white sauce: in a saucepan, melt butter, add flour, mixing with a wire whisk, and cook over low heat for 1 minute. Stirring constantly, gradually add milk and cook over medium heat until slightly thickened and smooth. Season with salt and pepper.
5. Combine fish stock (or reserved liquid from the can) with white sauce and mix well. Pour over salmon balls.
6. Bake in a 325° F. oven for one hour, turning occasionally.

Yield: 4 to 6 servings

*Water may be substituted for fish stock.

SALMON LOAF

2 cups cooked, flaked salmon,
  or 1 15½-ounce can
½ cup wheat meal cracker
  crumbs
2 eggs, beaten
½ cup milk
2 tablespoons chopped celery
  leaves

2 tablespoons chopped fresh
  parsley
Salt and freshly ground pepper,
  to taste
1 tablespoon butter

1. Preheat oven to 350 °F.
2. Remove bones, if any, from salmon. No need to drain the canned salmon.
3. Add cracker crumbs, eggs, milk, celery leaves, parsley and salt and pepper.
4. Turn mixture into greased loaf pan, and dot top with butter. Bake in a 350° F. oven for 35 to 40 minutes.
5. Serve with celery-flavored white sauce (Chapter 6) or egg sauce (Chapter 6).

Yield: 4 servings

SALMON AND CABBAGE SOUP

This recipe may also be made with cooked haddock, pollock or other white fish.

2 potatoes, peeled and diced
2 carrots, thinly sliced
1½ cups water
1 small head cabbage, shredded
2 tablespoons butter
1 medium onion, coarsely
  chopped

1½ cups cooked, flaked salmon
Salt and freshly ground pepper,
  to taste
2 cups milk
1 cup medium cream

1. Cook potatoes and carrots in water until soft. Add cabbage and cook until slightly soft.
2. In a frying pan, melt the butter and sauté onion until soft.
3. Add onion to vegetables, then add salmon. Season with salt and pepper.
4. Stir in milk and simmer 5 minutes, until heated. Do not boil.
5. In separate saucepan, warm cream and add to soup mixture at last minute.
6. Serve in bowls, top with a pat of butter and sprinkle with parsley.

Yield: 6 servings

Note: A cup or two of heated fish stock (Chapter 6) may be added to expand the recipe.

"ROAST SALMON: Take a jole of salmon, or a rand, and divide it into four pieces. Season it with salt and grated nutmeg. Stick in it whole cloves and put it on a convenient spit, laying on it likewise a few bay leaves and sprigs of rosemary. Then baste it with butter and save the drippings to mingle with other butter, to be served in sauce, mixed with verjuice, the juice of oranges, and garnished with slices of orange."

—The Family Dictionary,
1705

GRAVLAX

This Swedish method of marinating salmon gives the fish a special pungent aroma. Once marinated, the salmon will keep for 10 days in the refrigerator.

2 whole salmon fillets (about 4 pounds)	3 tablespoons sugar
Needled twigs of pine or spruce	3 tablespoons salt
2 bunches fresh dill, coarsely chopped (about 1 cup)	1 teaspoon crushed white peppercorns
	4 tablespoons cognac

1. Wipe salmon fillets dry with paper toweling.
2. Spread needled pine or spruce twigs and one-third of dill on bottom of deep baking dish. Place one of the fillets, skin side down, on top of twigs.
3. Combine sugar, salt and peppercorns and spread on flesh side of fillet. Sprinkle one-third of the dill and all the cognac on top.
4. Cover with second fillet, skin side up, and sprinkle with the remaining one-third of the dill.
5. Cover and press with clean, weighted board. Let stand for two days in refrigerator or other cold place.
6. To serve, scrape seasonings off fish, and cut the salmon off the skin in thin, vertical slices. Garnish with dill and serve with mustard sauce (Chapter 6) or just a squeeze of lemon.

Yield: 6 main-course servings, 12 first-course servings, multiple hors-d'oeuvre servings

Variation: For a slightly different version of this, leave out the pine twigs and cognac, and use 4 tablespoons crushed black peppercorns instead of white peppercorns. The directions for preparation are the same.

Near the Celilo Falls on the Columbia River, Lewis and Clark made note of the Indian method of preserving salmon: "after [being] suffi(c)iently Dried it is pounded between two Stones fine, and put into a speces of basket neetly made of grass and rushes . . . lined with the Skin of Salmon Stretched and dried for the purpose, in this it is pressed down as hard as is possible, when full they Secure the open part with the fish Skins . . . thus preserved those fish may be kept Sound and sweet Several years, as those people inform me."

SMOKED SALMON KETCHIKAN

1 cup heavy cream	8 slices (½ to ¾ pound) smoked salmon, fresh* or canned
2 cups small cooked shrimp	
2 tablespoons horseradish	
Salt and freshly ground pepper, to taste	

1. Loosely whip cream. Add shrimp, horseradish and salt and pepper.
2. Lay smoked salmon slices out flat. Divide filling evenly among salmon slices and roll up into cornucopia shapes.
3. Serve on shredded lettuce bordered by thin lemon wedges.

Yield: 4 servings

*See Chapter 7 for smoking techniques.

SMOKED SALMON PÂTÉ I

This recipe may also be made with smoked trout or smoked mackerel.

4 ounces smoked salmon, fresh* **1 teaspoon lemon juice**
 or canned **3 ounces cream cheese**

1. Blend fish, lemon juice and cream cheese together in blender or with a fork until very dry. It may be difficult to mix.
2. Keep refrigerated until ready to serve. Serve at room temperature on unsalted crackers.

Yield: ¾ cup

Note: This pâté can be kept refrigerated for 4 to 6 days, but be sure it is well covered or the whole refrigerator will smell of smoked salmon.

*See Chapter 7 for smoking techniques.

When the salmon run begins on the Columbia River, Indians exercise their ancient and protected rights by spearing or netting the fish from small, precarious platforms built out over the rapids.

A fisherman known as Beaver Bill proudly poses with his gill net and a giant 75-pound Chinook salmon, a size once common to American waters.

SMOKED SALMON PÂTÉ II

This pâté is better if made a day in advance to allow mixture to firm up considerably. It can also be made with smoked trout or smoked mackerel.

4 ounces smoked salmon, fresh* or canned	2 tablespoons lemon juice
⅓ cup sour cream	Freshly ground pepper, to taste
½ cup cottage cheese	1 ounce salmon caviar, optional

1. Flake smoked salmon in a blender or food processor.
2. Add sour cream and cottage cheese, lemon juice and pepper. Blend to a puree.
3. Turn into small dish and chill for several hours or overnight. Garnish with salmon roe caviar, (if desired).

Yield: 1¼ cups

*See Chapter 7 for smoking techniques.

CAVIAR OF SALMON EGGS

Russian fishermen in Alaska, finding sturgeon in small supply in North American waters, looked for something to replace the caviar that ordinarily accompanied their vodka. This search reportedly led them to the discovery of salmon caviar, thus giving birth to a whole new industry—which spread not only along the northwest coast of America, but back to Siberia as well. Well prepared salmon caviar, according to most gourmet tastes, rivals all the finest sturgeon caviar imported from the Caspian Sea and the great rivers of Mother Russia.

½ cup salt   1 double sac salmon roe (about
2 cups water   2 cups red eggs)

1. Make a salt brine, mixing until salt is dissolved in water.
2. Break roe sac and empty red eggs into a large bowl. Remove as much of the membrane as possible.
3. Gently pour brine over eggs. Let stand for 30 minutes, allowing eggs to become slightly firm.
4. Drain eggs in a strainer and rinse gently with cold water. Remove any remaining white particles of the sac casing.
5. Store in refrigerator in a pint glass container with a tightly fitting lid. Caviar will keep indefinitely.

Yield: 2 cups

SALMON CAVIAR MOUSSE

8 ounces salmon caviar   ¼ cup water
¼ cup finely chopped parsley   1 clove mashed garlic, optional
1 tablespoon grated onion   ½ teaspoon freshly ground
1 teaspoon grated lemon peel   pepper
1 pint sour cream   1 cup heavy cream
1 envelope unflavored gelatin

1. Combine the caviar, parsley, onion and lemon peel. Stir in the sour cream.
2. Put the ¼ cup water in a small saucepan and sprinkle gelatin into the water. Cook over low heat, stirring, until gelatin dissolves. Stir gelatin into caviar and sour cream mixture.
3. Add mashed garlic (if desired) and pepper.
4. Whip cream until stiff. Fold whipped cream into mixture.
5. Turn into a lightly oiled 1½-quart mold and chill until firm.
6. Unmold and serve with small squares of thin pumpernickel bread spread with sweet butter.

Yield: 20 hors-d'oeuvre servings

If you catch a male, or cock, salmon, be sure to save the milt (which may half fill the fish's belly). Fried with the morning bacon, and with a few drops of lemon juice and a scattering of capers, milt is incredibly tender and delicious. If its marvelous taste weren't enough, some Scottish Highland fishermen swear that eating milt makes a man more virile.

SALMON CAVIAR OMELET

4 to 6 eggs	2 tablespoons butter
3 tablespoons milk	4 ounces salmon caviar
Salt and freshly ground pepper, to taste	

1. Beat the eggs with milk, salt and pepper until well mixed but not frothy.
2. In an omelet or frying pan, melt butter, rotating pan so butter coats bottom and lower sides. The pan will be ready for cooking when a drop of water sizzles, or the faintest bit of steam rises. Do not allow the butter to brown.
3. Turn heat to low and quickly pour in the egg mixture. Cook until the eggs thicken on the bottom. Then slide a spatula or fork under the edge of the omelet, lift up the edge of the cooked eggs, tilt the pan, and allow the uncooked egg to flow underneath the cooked part.
4. Spread salmon roe caviar on top of one half of the omelet.
5. When the entire mixture has just barely thickened, use a spatula to lift the plain half of the omelet and fold it over the caviar half, forming a half-moon shape. Slide out of pan onto a warmed platter.

Yield: 2 to 4 servings

Variation: In place of caviar use 3 slices of smoked salmon.

CHINOOK HORS D'OEUVRE

1 cup sour cream
2 ounces salmon caviar
1 teaspoon grated onion

1. Combine all ingredients.
2. Serve with crackers or chips.

Note: Try a spoonful of this in a baked potato.

Reef netters in Washington's San Juan Islands watch from their ladder platforms for tailing salmon to reveal their darting, silver schools.

QUICK SALMON CAVIAR

½ double sac salmon roe
2 teaspoons salt
1½ teaspoons freshly ground pepper
1 teaspoon sugar
1 tablespoon lemon juice

1. Break roe sac and empty eggs into a shallow bowl or deep plate. Remove as much of the membrane as possible.
2. Add salt, pepper, sugar and lemon juice, stirring carefully to avoid breaking the eggs.
3. Chill at least 3 hours.
4. Serve on buttered toast.

Yield: 4 to 6 servings, depending on size of salmon

3: Freshwater

The North American continent is dotted with lakes, rivers, streams, and ponds, a substantial number of which support a large variety of freshwater fish. There is lake and river fishing from the reedy muskellunge lakes of Minnesota, west to where giant white sturgeon cruise the Snake River in Idaho and blue catfish lurk in the broad Missouri, south to Hollow Lake, Kentucky, for fine fighting bass, and east to the bluegill ponds of Alabama, then north again for the smelt run in the Great Lakes.

Sauger

In America, most freshwater fish are still best known regionally, for until freezing techniques were developed, fresh fish were rarely shipped to distant markets. And with the exception of a few species, such as pike and lake whitefish, freshwater fish are still largely a regional commodity. However, trout farms, and commercial ponds of catfish and cold-water carp are changing the availability of these freshwater fish. Fish farming—which has been woefully slow in developing—may also become one of our most valuable sources of food, as overfishing, inadequate conservation efforts and pollution deplete wild fish stocks.

Freshwater fish vary enormously from one species to another, in both size and flavor. In general, though, those that are predators, such as bass and trout, have firmer, richer flesh because they feed on smaller fish and must develop and maintain swift, active body tone to survive as hunters. Fish that feed lower on the food chain are generally slower, and therefore softer, and sometimes have a less interesting flavor. Fishermen and cooks alike consider stock fish from hatcheries to be somewhat inferior to fish taken in their wild state, largely because of the cereal mixtures fed to hatchery fish.

Local fishermen have given their freshwater catches a vast number of regional names, which have enriched American folklore but left true identification difficult. Often precise Latin names are needed to distinguish, for example, catfish called madtoms or stonecats from bullheads or horned pouts or channel cats.

Sunfish

The sunfish family (*Centrarchidae*) outranks other fish families by sheer numbers, and counts among its members some of the most notable game and panfish in North America. Centrarchids are divided into three main groups: black bass (including largemouth, smallmouth and spotted bass), crappie, and sunfish (including bluegill, rock bass, and warmouth). Most fish known by the name sunfish (e.g., common sunfish, round sunfish, redear sunfish) rarely exceed six inches, and, though they are edible, are not considered game by anyone but children.

◄ *With the help of their Adirondacks fishing guide, this Herbert Hooveresque gentleman and his wife—both dressed in unlikely fishing costumes—have landed an impressive string of pickerel.*

LARGEMOUTH BASS: Largemouth bass (*Micropterus salmonides*) are the most broadly distributed freshwater bass in North America, occurring naturally in central and southern streams and lakes, and as stock fish in farm ponds. Largemouth are deep-bodied, flatish fish, greenish on the back with irregular

Largemouth Bass

side banding, rough scales and a sharp, thornlike forefin; and, as their name implies, they have large mouths. Widely respected as hard-fighting game fish, largemouth will readily take a variety of plugs and lures, as well as crayfish, minnows, and frogs cast with light tackle. Largemouth prefer fairly quiet waters and seek out shallow, weedy coves where they surface feed in the mornings and evenings. One to three pounds is the average size, but some have been caught weighing over 20 pounds. Those taken from cool waters have sweet, firm, smooth-textured flesh. The skin of the largemouth, like that of all freshwater bass, has a somewhat mossy flavor and, if possible, should be removed before cooking.

SMALLMOUTH BASS: Smallmouth bass (*Micropterus dolomieui*) prefer colder, swifter water and have a more northern range than largemouth, penetrating into mid-Canada; they are not found in the southern United States. Although smaller than the largemouth, the smallmouth puts up a good fight and will readily take live bait and a variety of plugs and lures. Smallmouth average about one pound, although some are caught weighing up to 10 pounds. They have pale, firm flesh and offer splendid table fare, but their skin, if possible, should be removed before cooking.

SPOTTED BASS: Spotted bass (*Micropterus punctulatus*) are found from Florida west into Texas, and north as far as Ohio. They are good sports fish, weighing from one-half to four pounds, and rank with largemouth as food fish. They should be prepared and cooked in the same manner as other bass.

CRAPPIE: Known by myriad local names, crappies live in lakes and ponds throughout the Mississippi River and Great Lakes systems. The two crappie species—**white crappie** (*Pomoxis annularis*) and the more common **black crappie** (*Pomoxis*

"In a shady narrow creek where the current glided perceptibly and the water looked deep we took to the skiff and, rowing along under the lee of one shelving bank of green, we cast for black bass. They did not run large and were of the big-mouthed variety, yet they afforded welcome change and sport. Besides, fresh water fish for the table was something new."
—*"Rivers of the Everglades,"*
Zane Grey

nigromaculatus)—are considered sporting fish that will take various lures as well as minnows and worms. Weighing an average of one-half to one pound, their flesh is sweet, although those caught in more southern waters may be somewhat soft.

BLUEGILL: Bluegill (*Lepomis macrochirus*), the best known and most widely distributed of the sunfish, are the small six-inch panfish that every little boy catches and takes home to his mother to be cooked. Flatish and thorny-finned, bluegill are easily identified by the prominent black spot behind each gill. Surprisingly quick, hard fighters, most weigh about one-quarter pound, but can weigh up to four. Their flesh is delicate and delicious.

ROCK BASS: The rock bass (*Amblopites rupestris*), which ranges from southern Canada throughout the eastern United States, is one of the largest of the sunfish, though it usually weighs no more than one-half pound. Easily identified by its bright red eye and dark spots below its lateral line, it has delicious, firm flesh.

WARMOUTH: Warmouth (*Lepomis gulosus*), are most commonly found in the warm waters of southeastern United States. They somewhat resemble rock bass, but have dark bands on their cheeks and no spots on their sides.

DEVILED BASS SALAD

1 cup cooked, flaked bass	1 teaspoon lemon juice
1 tablespoon minced green pepper	½ teaspoon dried mustard
⅓ cup minced celery	2½ tablespoons mayonnaise
5 hard-boiled eggs	¼ teaspoon salt
	⅛ teaspoon cayenne

1. Remove any bones from fish and add celery and green pepper.
2. Cut eggs in half lengthwise, remove yolks and set whites aside.
3. Combine lemon juice and mustard, add mayonnaise and blend well. Mash yolks and add to mayonnaise. Add salt and cayenne.
4. Add mayonnaise mixture to fish and toss.
5. Stuff hard-boiled egg whites with fish mixture. Arrange on lettuce leaves, placing remaining fish mixture in the center. Garnish with sliced tomatoes, green pepper rings and carrot sticks. Serve with extra mayonnaise, if desired.

Yield: 5 servings

"What a most beautiful creature is this fish before me! gliding to and fro and figuring in the still, clear waters, with his orient attendants and associates. It is the yellow bream [warmouth] or sun fish. It is about eight inches in length, nearly of the shape of the trout but rather larger in proportion over the shoulders and breast. . . . The whole fish is of a pale gold (or burnished brass) color. . . . He is a fish of prodigious strength and activity in the water, a warrior in a gilded coat of mail, and gives no rest or quarter to small fish, which he preys upon. They are delicious food and in great abundance."

—William Bartram

RHODE ISLAND BAKED BASS

2 2-pound bass, without heads
Salt and freshly ground pepper,
  to taste
Paprika

1 tablespoon butter
Juice of ½ lemon (2 tablespoons)
½ lemon, thinly sliced

1. Preheat oven to 350° F.
2. Rub each fish with salt, pepper, and paprika. Place in a well-buttered baking dish.
3. In a saucepan, melt the butter, add lemon juice and pour over fish.
4. Lay sliced lemons along top of each fish. Cover with aluminum foil and bake in a 350° F. oven until done, about 20 minutes. Fish is done when it flakes easily when tested with a fork.
5. Serve with mustard sauce (Chapter 6).

Yield: 4 servings

"In a curve between two of these level lanes there is a place where barefoot boys wade and fish for chubs and bask on the big boulders like turtles. It is a famous hole for chubs and bright-sided shiners and sunfish. And, perhaps because it is so known, and so shallow, so open to the sky, few fishermen ever learned that in its secret stony caverns hid a great golden-bronze treasure of a bass."
— *"The Lord of Lackawaxen Creek—1908," Zane Grey*

BASS BAKED WITH FENNEL

2 large tomatoes, peeled and
  diced
2 Spanish onions, cut into rings
1 cup dry white wine
1 cup water
Juice of ½ lemon (2 tablespoons)
2 2-pound bass, filleted and
  skinned

1 cup chopped celery and celery
  leaves
Several sprigs of fennel
1 bay leaf
Salt and freshly ground pepper,
  to taste
4 tablespoons butter

1. Preheat oven to 350° F.
2. On the bottom of a stove-to-oven baking dish (big enough to hold long fillets), lay tomatoes and onion rings. Add wine, water, and lemon juice and cook on stove top until tomatoes and onions start to soften. Remove from stove and let cool briefly.
3. Lay the fillets in the baking dish, and add celery, fennel, and bay leaf. Sprinkle fish with salt and pepper and dot with butter.
4. Cover the baking dish and bake in a 350° F. oven for 20 minutes. Remove cover, raise oven heat to 400° F. and cook for 10 more minutes.
5. With a slotted spatula, lift fish onto warmed serving platter. With a wooden spoon, force cooking liquid through a sieve into a bowl. Discard pulp. Season to taste and pour this tomato sauce over the fish. Decorate with fresh parsley.

Yield: 4 servings

SPICED BASS

1 cup lime juice
¼ cup white wine vinegar
1 teaspoon salt
8 black peppercorns

4 bass fillets (about 2 pounds), skinned
1 teaspoon turmeric
4 tablespoons peanut oil

Calvin Coolidge, one of our most enthusiastic presidential anglers, is shown here in 1928 on Wisconsin's Brule River.

1. In a deep dish, combine the lime juice, vinegar, ½ teaspoon of the salt, and the peppercorns. Place the fillets in the dish and marinate for 1 hour in a cool place.
2. Remove fish from the marinade. Strain marinade and reserve ¼ cup.
3. Rub the fillets with turmeric and the remaining ½ teaspoon of salt.
4. In a frying pan, heat oil over moderate heat. Add fillets and sauté for 4 to 5 minutes on each side.
5. Transfer the fillets to a warmed serving platter. Pour the reserved marinade over the fish.

Yield: 6 servings

GRILLED CRAPPIE

4 crappie (about ½ pound each)
½ cup lemon juice
¼ cup olive oil
1 teaspoon salt

1 teaspoon oregano
1 clove garlic, pressed
½ teaspoon freshly ground
   pepper

1. In an outdoor grill or fireplace, start a wood or charcoal fire and burn until there are hot coals.
2. Make 4 to 5 slits on both sides of each fish.
3. Combine lemon juice, olive oil, salt, oregano, garlic, and pepper. Brush fish inside and out with sauce.
4. Place fish in well-greased, hinged wire grill (see Chapter 7) and cook over moderately hot coals for 5 to 8 minutes. Baste with sauce, turn and cook for 5 to 8 minutes longer, or until fish flakes easily when tested with a fork.

Yield: 6 servings

BLUEGILL OVEN BAKED

Bluegill

4 bluegill (about 8″ and ¼
   pound each)
⅓ cup milk
¼ teaspoon salt

1 cup dried bread crumbs or
   cornmeal
2 tablespoons butter

1. Remove bluegills' heads and tails, if desired.
2. Preheat oven to 375° F.
3. In a small bowl, combine milk and salt. Dip each fish into seasoned milk. Then dredge in bread crumbs (or cornmeal) until evenly covered.
4. Place fish in single layer in a well-buttered baking dish. Melt the butter and pour over fish.
5. Bake in a 375° F. oven until done, about 8 minutes. Fish is done when it flakes easily when tested with a fork.

Yield: 2 servings

ROCK BASS SALAD

6 rock bass fillets, 6″ to 9″
1½ teaspoons salt
⅜ teaspoon freshly ground
   pepper
2 tablespoons chopped fresh dill
⅓ cup milk
½ cup sour cream

2 tablespoons lemon juice
½ teaspoon sugar
2 tablespoons chopped fresh
   chives
½ cup seeded and finely
   chopped cucumber

1. Preheat oven to 350° F.
2. Place the fillets in a baking dish and sprinkle them with 1 teaspoon of the salt, ¼ teaspoon of the pepper, and 1

tablespoon of the dill. Pour the milk over the fish and bake in 350° F. oven for 20 minutes. Let cool.
3. With a slotted spatula, remove fish to a serving platter. Cover and refrigerate at least 3 hours. Discard cooking liquid.
4. In a bowl, combine sour cream, lemon juice, sugar, the remaining ½ teaspoon salt, the remaining ⅛ teaspoon pepper, the remaining tablespoon of dill, chives, and cucumber. Refrigerate for at least 1 hour.
5. To serve, cover each fillet with sauce and garnish with additional dill. Serve remaining sauce in a sauce boat.
Yield: 6 servings

Perch

Although yellow perch, walleye, and sauger are among the most flavorful freshwater fish, many members of the perch family (*Percidae*) are too small to eat. All perch are long and slender, with two distinctly separate dorsal fins and heavy scales.

YELLOW PERCH: The yellow perch (*Perca flavescens*) is one of the most widely distributed game fish in America, found from the eastern United States and Canada west as far as Kansas. Perch survive well in both slow, warmish waters and cold, northern lakes. For their size—one-quarter to three pounds— they are swift, strong, fighting fish, with sweet, firm flesh, ranking them very high among America's best panfish. Adult yellow perch usually move about in small schools; catching one will often ensure the angler of more to come. Perch are commonly caught with worms and minnows, though they will readily take a variety of small spinning lures.

WALLEYE: Walleye (*Stizostedion vitreum*), the largest members of the perch family, prefer clear, cold waters and are found all across northern Canada and the northern United States as far west as Montana. They are also found in southern lakes (as far south as Alabama), where, with a year-round food supply, they often grow to weigh ten pounds or more. Walleye commonly measure up to 17 inches and weigh about two pounds. Sharp-toothed predators, walleye will take natural or artificial baits; because they usually feed in deep water, a deep troll spoon on wire is most effective. Walleye have pale, cloudy-blue eyes that glow if lights hits them at night; although the freshness of most fish can be judged by the clearness of the eyes, this rule of thumb will not work with walleye. Walleye, though not related to pike, are often marketed under the misnomers **walleyed pike** or **yellow pike.**

"What beautiful fishes these perches are! so silvery beneath, so deeply coloured above! What a fine eye too! But, friend, I cannot endure their gaspings. Pray put them on this short line, and place them in the water beside you, until you prepare to go home. In a few hours each fisher has obtained as many as he wishes. He rolls up his line, fastens five or six perches on each side of his saddle, mounts his horse, and merrily wends his way."

—Delineations of American Scenery and Character, John James Audubon

SAUGER: Sauger (*Stizostedion canadense*) closely resemble walleye both in habits and appearance, though they average only one pound and about 14 inches. Sauger live in lakes and slow rivers from Lake Champlain across northern New York State, eastern Canada west to Minnesota, and south into the Mississippi Valley. (They are also found in some central Canadian lakes.) Many knowledgeable fishermen consider the flesh of sauger the best flavored of all freshwater fish, especially when taken from cold waters from October through May. Sauger are often mistaken for pike, giving rise to its misnomer **sandpike.**

Straw hats, hammocks, ladies' bicycles, and ample strings of fish went hand in hand with leaf-green Wisconsin summers.

BRANDIED YELLOW PERCH

6 perch, about 10" each, heads
  removed
3 teaspoons salt
4 tablespoons butter, melted

3 fennel sprigs, coarsely
  chopped
½ cup brandy

1. In an outdoor grill or fireplace, start a wood or charcoal fire and burn until there are hot coals.
2. Sprinkle each perch with salt inside and out and roll in melted butter. Save the rest of the melted butter for basting.
3. Place fish in a hinged wire grill (see Chapter 7) and cook over hot coals for 6 to 8 minutes, turning and basting once. Perch are done when flesh turns opaque and flakes easily when tested with a fork.
4. Place perch side by side in shallow dish and sprinkle with chopped fennel. Warm the brandy, pour it over the fish and set aflame.

Yield: 6 servings

Amelia Simmons, author of America's first native cookbook, wrote in 1796: "Perch are noble pan fish, the deeper the water from whence taken, the finer are their flavors; if taken from shallow water, with muddy bottoms, they are impregnated therewith, and are unsavory."

PERCH FRIED IN SOUR CREAM SAUCE

6 pan-sized yellow perch, 8" to
  12", with or without heads
Flour seasoned with salt and
  freshly ground pepper, for
  dredging
½ cup (1 stick) butter
¼ pound mushrooms, thickly
  sliced

1 teaspoon lemon juice
1 cup sour cream
½ teaspoon salt
¼ teaspoon freshly ground
  pepper
1 teaspoon paprika

1. Dredge perch in seasoned flour.
2. In a large frying pan, heat 3 tablespoons of the butter. Fit 3 of the perch in the pan and sauté them about 4 minutes on one side and 3 minutes on the reverse until the skin turns light brown. Fish is done when it flakes easily when tested with a fork. Remove fish to a warmed serving platter and repeat with remaining perch, using another 3 tablespoons of butter.
3. In the same frying pan, melt the remaining 2 tablespoons butter. Add the mushrooms and sauté until they begin to soften.
4. Add the lemon juice, sour cream, salt, pepper, and paprika. Briefly heat the sauce, stirring constantly.
5. To serve, pour the sauce over the fish and garnish with parsley.

Yield: 6 servings

WALLEYE FILLETS COUNTRY STYLE

4 walleye fillets (about 2 pounds)
Flour seasoned with salt and
freshly ground pepper, for
dredging
Butter, for sautéing
1 onion, finely chopped
1 clove garlic, crushed
3 large tomatoes, peeled and
chopped

1 teaspoon oregano
1 teaspoon basil
Salt and freshly ground pepper,
to taste
¼ cup coarsely chopped black
olives
¼ cup white wine or dry
vermouth (optional)

1. Dredge the walleye fillets in seasoned flour.
2. In a frying pan, heat about 1½ tablespoons butter, add dredged fillets, and sauté fish until golden brown on both sides, about 8 minutes. Add more butter if necessary to keep fish from sticking. Fish is done when it flakes easily when tested with a fork.
3. With a slotted spatula, remove fish from pan and place in a serving dish. Keep fish warm in an oven set at lowest temperature.
4. In remaining butter in frying pan (at least 1 tablespoon, add more if necessary), sauté the onion until it begins to soften. Add garlic, tomatoes, and herbs and sauté about 3 minutes, until tomatoes become soft.
5. Season with salt and pepper, add olives and wine or vermouth (if desired), and stir to mix and warm.
6. Pour vegetable mixture over fish on serving dish and garnish with fresh parsley.

Yield: 4 servings

"Fishing is a chance to wash one's soul with pure air, with the rush of the brook, or with the shimmer of the sun on the blue water.

It brings meekness and inspiration from the scenery of nature, charity toward tackle makers, patience toward fish, a mockery of profits and egos, a quieting of hate, a rejoicing that you do not have to decide a darned thing until next week.

And it is discipline in the equality of man—for all men are equal before fish."

—Fishing for Fun—and to
Wash Your Soul,
Herbert Hoover

WALLEYE IN ASPIC

2 pounds walleye fillets
1 cup dry white wine
1 medium onion, quartered
1 stalk celery, cut into 4 pieces
2 bay leaves
1½ teaspoons salt
¼ teaspoon thyme
1 lemon
2 envelopes unflavored gelatin

¼ cup tarragon vinegar
2 tablespoons lemon juice
1 teaspoon dry mustard
¼ cup chopped celery
¼ cup chopped scallion
¼ cup chopped green pepper
2 tablespoons chopped pimiento
2 tablespoons chopped fresh
parsley

1. Place fish in greased 10″ frying pan. Add 2 cups boiling water, wine, onion, celery quarters, bay leaves, salt, and thyme. Cut lemon in half, squeeze in juice and drop in halves.
2. Cover and simmer for 5 to 10 minutes or until fish flakes easily when tested with a fork.

3. With a slotted spatula, remove fish and set aside to cool. Strain poaching liquid and reserve.
4. Put ½ cup cold water in a 1½-quart saucepan and sprinkle gelatin into the liquid. Add the reserved poaching liquid and cook over low heat, stirring, until gelatin dissolves. Add vinegar, lemon juice, and enough water to make 4 cups liquid.
5. Measure off enough of the gelatin mixture to make a paste of the dry mustard. Then return this paste to the gelatin and mix well. Chill gelatin until it reaches the consistency of raw egg whites.
6. Meanwhile, remove any skin or bones from the fillets and flake the fish. Add celery, scallion, green pepper, pimiento, and parsley and mix well.
7. When gelatin is chilled, fold fish mixture into it. Turn into a lightly oiled 1½-quart mold and chill until firm.
8. Unmold onto greens and serve with mayonnaise or green sauce (Chapter 6).

Yield: 6 servings

The mighty waters of Wagon Wheel Gap on the Rio Grande— which once knew only Indians, trappers, and traders—by the 1870s had come to know gentler fishing parties, such as these townfolk captured by photographer William Henry Jackson.

SAUGER IN CIDER

2 sauger fillets (about 1½
  pounds)
1 cup cider
2 medium onions, thinly sliced
1 green pepper, coarsely
  chopped
1 teaspoon marjoram

⅛ teaspoon cayenne
1½ teaspoons salt
½ teaspoon freshly ground
  pepper
3 tablespoons fine bread crumbs
¼ cup grated Parmesan cheese

1. Preheat oven to 350° F.
2. Cut fillets into strips about 1″ wide. Place in a stove-to-oven casserole.
3. In a saucepan, bring cider to a boil. Add onions and green pepper. Reduce heat and simmer until cider has reduced slightly and the vegetables have softened, about 5 minutes.
4. Remove from heat and add marjoram, cayenne, salt, and pepper. Pour the cider mixture over the fish.
5. Cover and bake in a 350° F. oven for 20 minutes.
6. Meanwhile, combine the bread crumbs and cheese. When the 20 minutes are up, sprinkle the bread-crumb mixture over the fish, turn the oven to broil and place under the broiler for 3 minutes, or until the cheese melts.

Yield: 4 servings

Minnows

Most people think of minnows as small, but the minnow family (Cyprinidae) includes a number of fairly large game and food fish, such as carp (which can weigh up to 80 pounds) and squawfish. The majority of the more than 1,500 minnow species, however, are quite small—no longer than six inches—including goldfish and shiners.

CARP: Carp (Cyprinus carpio), a native of Asian waters, were imported as early as the 4th century B.C. to Europe, where they were (and still are) considered an important food and game fish. Isaak Walton was even moved to call carp "the Queen of the Rivers." When carp were finally imported from Europe to America, in the late 19th century, bands played to celebrate the arrival; but carp soon lost in popularity as they began crowding the more highly regarded native game fish from their habitat. Today carp can be found wherever stocking has occurred—coast to coast and south from southern Canada, with a concentration in the Mississippi River drainage. Carp are cautious and powerful fish that rarely take artificial bait; they will, however, take an odd assortment of natural baits, from worms to balls of dough and cheese. The average carp weighs three pounds; 20 pounds is a prize and 55 pounds the record

"One time, in the spring, our grandmothers used to give us nasty brews from sulphur and herbs to purify our blood of the winter's corruption. They knew something was the matter with the boys. They could have saved trouble by giving them a pole, a string and a hook. Some wise ones—among them my own—did just that."

—Fishing for Fun—and to
Wash Your Soul,
Herbert Hoover

(taken with rod and reel). Carp taken from clean, clear, cold water (or those commercially farmed) are best. Many people feel that the carp's diet and bottom-feeding habits give its flesh and skin a slightly mossy or muddy flavor; but if skinned and bled as soon as possible after catching, any mossy flavor can be avoided. Their flavor can also be improved, if necessary, by soaking in fresh water or marinating with salt, onion, and vinegar. Carp are commercially available live in tanks for kosher killing, as fillets, and, most commonly, whole.

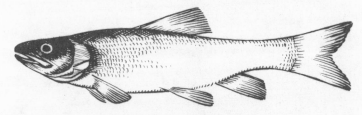

Northern Squawfish

NORTHERN SQUAWFISH: Northern squawfish (*Ptychocheilus oregonensis*) live in streams throughout the western United States and southwestern Canada. Salmon and trout fishermen sometimes go for squawfish because they fight well when taken on light tackle, and their flesh is delicate in flavor. Squawfish are often three feet long and may weigh up to 20 pounds.

BAKED CARP I

1 medium-sized carp (about 3 pounds), head and tail left on
3 tablespoons olive oil
1 tablespoon Worcestershire sauce
1 tablespoon lemon juice
1 tablespoon chopped fresh parsley
1 tablespoon minced onion
Salt and freshly ground pepper, to taste
Cayenne, to taste

1. Place carp in a stove-to-oven casserole, curling head and tail around inside of dish.
2. Combine olive oil, Worcestershire sauce, lemon juice, parsley, and onion. Season with salt, pepper, and cayenne.
3. Pour marinade over fish and marinate in a cool place for about 2 hours, basting at intervals.
4. Cover and bake in a 325° F. oven for 1 hour.
5. Place on a warmed serving platter and spoon pan juices over fish. Serve with a white sauce (Chapter 6) flavored with chopped sweet gherkins.

Yield: 6 servings

*Isaak Walton's recipe for carp:
"I will tell you how to make
this Carp, that is so curious to
be caught, so curious a dish of
meat as shall make him worth
all your labor and patience.
And though it is not without
some trouble and charges, yet
it will recompense both . . .
take sweet marjoram, thyme,
or parsley, of each a handful; a
sprig of rosemary, and moth-
er-of-savory; bind them into
two or three small bundles,
and put them to your Carp,
with four or five whole onions,
twenty pickled oysters, and
three anchovies. Then pour
upon your Carp as much claret wine as will only cover him;
and season your claret well
with salt, cloves and mace,
and the rind of oranges and
lemons. That done, cover your
pot, and set it on a quick fire
till it be sufficiently boiled.
Then take out the Carp, and
lay it with the broth into the
dish, and pour upon it a quarter of a pound of the best fresh
butter, melted and beaten with
a half-a-dozen spoonsful of the
broth, the yolks of two or
three eggs, and some of the
herbs shred; garnish your dish
with lemons, and so serve it
up, and much good to you."*

BAKED CARP II

1 medium-sized carp (about 3 pounds), head and tail left on	1 clove garlic, minced
Paprika	1 red pepper, seeded and coarsely chopped
Salt and freshly ground pepper, to taste	1 medium potato, thinly sliced
3 tablespoons butter	¼ cup medium cream
3 tomatoes, coarsely chopped	1 cup cooked and deveined shrimp
2 large onions, thinly sliced	

1. Preheat oven to 350° F.
2. Dust carp inside and out with paprika and salt.
3. In a frying pan, heat butter and sauté tomatoes, onions, garlic, red pepper, and potato until soft. Season with salt and pepper.
4. Place carp in a buttered baking dish and cover with vegetable mixture.
5. Bake in a 350° F. oven for about 30 minutes, basting twice with the cream.
6. Before serving, add shrimp to pan juices and serve as a sauce.

Yield: 6 servings

GEFILTE FISH

Carp is the traditional ingredient, but gefilte fish is also commonly made with whitefish. Northern pike and buffalo are good substitutes.

4 pounds carp fillets	6 cups water
2 medium onions, quartered	2 medium onions, coarsely chopped
½ cup matzoh or cracker meal	4 carrots, coarsely chopped
2 eggs	1 cup coarsely chopped celery
1 cup cold water	
Salt and freshly ground pepper, to taste	

1. In a blender or food processor, blend fish fillets and quartered onions. Add matzoh (or cracker) meal, eggs, 1 cup cold water, salt, and pepper. Mix until smooth.

2. Using two tablespoons, form the fish mixture into balls the size of small eggs.
3. In a large saucepan, place 6 cups water, chopped onions, carrots, and celery, and bring to a boil.
4. Add the balls, reduce the heat, and simmer for a little more than 1 hour. Cool the balls in the broth.
5. With a slotted spoon, remove fish balls, cover and refrigerate. Strain the broth and discard vegetables. Chill the broth overnight so that it has time to jell.
6. Serve the gefilte fish cold with the jellied broth as a sauce. Garnish with carrot sticks or horseradish sauce (Chapter 6).

Yield: 10 servings

SQUAWFISH CHOWDER

1 whole squawfish (about 3 pounds)
3 bay leaves, crushed
1 teaspoon basil
5 slices bacon, cut into small pieces
3 medium onions, thinly sliced

5 medium potatoes, diced
Salt and freshly ground pepper, to taste
3 cups milk
1 cup medium cream
2 tablespoons Worcestershire sauce

Garcia Abu

1. Cut fish into 3 equal sections. Place fish in a large pot with water to cover. Add bay leaves and basil. Bring to a boil, reduce heat and simmer about 10 minutes.
2. With a slotted spoon, remove fish and set aside to cool. Reserve 2 cups of cooking liquid.
3. Using fingers, remove meat from bones. Discard bones and set fish aside.
4. In a 4-quart Dutch oven, or stovetop casserole, fry bacon over low heat until crisp. Drain on paper towels, crumble and set aside.
5. Add onions to the bacon fat and cook until they begin to soften. Then add potatoes and water to cover. Season with salt and pepper. Cook until potatoes are soft, about 15 minutes.
6. Mash some of the potatoes with a fork to add thickness to the chowder, but leave at least half of the potatoes whole. Continue cooking until the mixture is quite thick, stirring frequently so it won't burn.
7. Add fish, the two cups of reserved cooking liquid, milk, and cream. Heat, but do not boil.
8. Remove from heat and add Worcestershire sauce. Sprinkle with bacon bits.
9. Serve in bowls with a pat of butter on top of each serving.

Yield: 6 servings

In the nineteenth century, catfish still came man-sized, and a catch such as this one was proudly paraded in the streets.

Catfish

More than three dozen species of freshwater catfish (family *Ictaluridae*) inhabit North America. They are strong fighters highly regarded by those who angle for them, and will take almost anything as bait, especially if it has a strong smell. They range in weight from one to 25 pounds, depending on the species. Catfish have a relatively simple skeletal structure and no scales. However all catfish, no matter the size, should be skinned before cooking, and if possible, immediately after catching. First-time catfish skinners should be warned, though, that catfish have a sharp spine on the leading edges of their dorsal and pectoral fins, which in some catfish such as **madtoms** and **stonecats** contains a numbing venom.

BROWN BULLHEAD: The most well-known of the catfish, bullhead are found coast to coast, with concentrations in the southeast. Able to survive in water so low in oxygen that they occasionally have to surface to take a gulp of air, bullhead live in waters too warm and still for most fish. Brown bullhead (*Ictalurus nebulosus*), the most common bullhead, average less than a pound, and taken from clear waters are good eating.

BLUE CATFISH: Found in clear, swift rivers in the Mississippi River system, blue catfish (*Ictalurus furcatus*) are larger than most catfish, with 25-pounders not uncommon. Some gourmets consider the firm, sweet, white flesh of blue catfish the most delicious of all freshwater fish.

CHANNEL CATFISH: The species most often grown in catfish farms, channel catfish (*Ictalurus punctatus*) prefer unpolluted, faster moving water. Strong fighters, averaging less than three pounds, channel catfish have firm, white, delicate flesh.

CATFISH MOCK SOUFFLÉ

2 tablespoons butter	¼ cup heavy cream
2 pounds catfish fillets, skinned	½ teaspoon salt
1 large green pepper, sliced	½ teaspoon freshly ground
2 cups mayonnaise	pepper
1½ cups grated Cheddar cheese	4 egg whites

1. Preheat oven to 350° F.
2. In a stove-to-oven casserole, heat butter and sauté catfish for 2 minutes on each side. Remove from heat. Arrange the pepper slices over the fish.
3. In a large bowl, combine the mayonnaise, cheese, cream, salt, and pepper.
4. Beat egg whites until stiff. Fold into the mayonnaise mixture. Pour the mixture over the fish.
5. Bake in a 350° F. oven for 20 minutes, or until top is golden brown.

Yield: 4 to 6 servings

SESAME CATFISH

1 pound catfish fillets or steaks, skinned	¾ cup flour
	2 teaspoons salt
1 egg	3 tablespoons sesame seeds
½ cup milk	½ cup oil

1. Cut fillets (or steaks) into serving portions.
2. Beat egg and milk together until well blended.
3. Season flour with salt and sesame seeds.
4. Dip fish in egg mixture, then seasoned flour.

Note: If heavier coating is desired, dip in egg and flour mixtures again.

5. In a heavy frying pan, heat oil so that it is hot but not smoking. Sauté fish over moderate heat for 7 to 8 minutes (depending on thickness of fish), turning once, until browned on both sides. Drain on paper towels.
6. Transfer to a warmed serving dish and serve immediately with cole slaw (Chapter 6).

Yield: 3 to 4 servings

"... about the first thing we done was to bait one of the big hooks with a skinned rabbit and set it and catch a cat-fish that was as big as a man, being six foot two inches long, and weighed over two hundred pounds. We couldn't handle him, of course; he would a flung us into Illinois. ... It was as big a fish as was ever catched in the Mississippi, I reckon. Jim said he hadn't ever seen a bigger one. He would a been worth a good deal over at the village. They peddle out such a fish as that by the pound in the market house there; everybody buys some of him; his meat's as white as snow and makes a good fry."
—Adventures of Huckleberry Finn, *Mark Twain*

CATFISH STEW

2 pounds catfish fillets, skinned
5 slices bacon
3 medium onions, thinly sliced
2 pounds tomatoes, skinned and coarsely chopped
1 cup tomato puree
5 medium potatoes, diced

2 tablespoons Worcestershire sauce
¼ teaspoon Tabasco sauce
2 teaspoons salt
¼ teaspoon freshly ground pepper

1. Cut fillets into 1½" pieces.
2. In a heavy 4- to 5-quart Dutch oven, fry bacon over low heat until crisp. Drain on paper towels, crumble and set aside.
3. Add onion to bacon fat in Dutch oven, cover and cook 5 minutes until soft.
4. Stir in tomatoes, tomato puree, potatoes, Worcestershire sauce, Tabasco sauce, salt, and pepper. Bring to a boil, then lower heat and simmer 30 minutes.
5. Add bacon and catfish. Cover and simmer 8 to 10 minutes or until fish flakes easily when tested with a fork.

Yield: 6 servings

In their time, these little steam launches shaded by green summer awnings were a fisherman's delight. Here in Chippewa County, Wisconsin, a well-dressed fisherman displays a muskie of proud proportions.

Pike

There are only five North American species in the pike family (*Esocidae*), northern pike, muskellunge, and three types of pickerel. All are aggressive predators with large mouths, sharp teeth, and long, slim bodies. Although they are somewhat bony fish, their flesh is sweet, firm and lean.

NORTHERN PIKE: Northern pike (*Esox lucius*) are the most widely distributed of the pike and are found throughout most of the forest lakes of Canada and many of the lakes and streams of the northern United States. Pike hunt in shallow reedy places and are most often lured to strike at wobblers and plugs in the early morning and the evening. Pike can weigh as much as 50 pounds, but average four to six pounds. Pike have always been considered splendid fare in Europe, but in America, where they are often improperly or over cooked, they have a poor reputation. Millions of pounds of northern pike from Canada are air shipped annually to Europe, while we continue to ignore this important natural resource. A freshly caught, carefully skinned and boned pike makes an excellent meal.

MUSKELLUNGE: The muskellunge (*Esox masquinongy*) takes its common name from a northeast Indian word, which historically has had a dozen different spellings. Most fishermen, however, simply call them "muskies" or, in Canada, "lunges." Muskellunge inhabit clear, reedy waters in the St. Lawrence River, the shallow lakes of lower Ontario, Wisconsin and Minnesota. Muskie are often taken in spring and summer by spin casting with spoons and plugs. An unusually long snout, piercing eyes and sharp teeth clearly identify muskie as hunters. Relentless predators, these lake giants lurking just beneath the surface may be as much as five feet long and weigh up to 80 pounds. They have appetites as fierce as barracudas and will snap down a young muskrat or kit beaver with a force that should make any swimmer grateful that muskie don't grow any bigger than they do. Their fierceness notwithstanding, muskie are fine flavored food fish, considered by many better than pike.

"When the waters are rising fast and have become muddy, a single line is used for catching Cat-fish. It is fastened to the elastic branch of some willow several feet above the water, and must be twenty or thirty feet in length. The entrails of a Wild Turkey, or a piece of fresh venison, furnish good bait; and if, when you visit your line the next morning after you have set it, the water has not risen too much, the swinging of the willow indicates that a fish has been hooked, and you have only to haul the prize ashore."

—Delineations of American Scenery and Character, John James Audubon

Chain Pickerel

PICKEREL: Compared with their two giant cousins, pike and muskellunge, pickerel are small—averaging less than two pounds. **Chain pickerel** (*Esox niger*) range from Florida and

Texas north to central Canada, but pickerel fishing today is by far the best in the northeastern section of Canada and the United States. Chain pickerel are so called because of the clear linklike pattern on their greenish sides. There are two other varieties of pickerel, the smaller **grass pickerel** (*Esox americanus vermiculatus*)—so called because of the grasslike vertical lines on their sides—and **redfin pickerel** (*Esox americanus*), identifiable by their orange fins, which redden during spawning. Walleye and sauger (see Perch) are sometimes marketed as pickerel.

"These fish [pike] were not only remarkably beautiful, but were excellent on the table, and differed utterly in both particulars from all other pickerel. They were taken in Summer among the water lilies, with the belly of a yellow perch. . . ."

—The Game Fish of the Northern United States and British Provinces, *1884*

NORTHERN PIKE AND WILD RICE

2 cups wild rice
2 pike fillets (about 2½ pounds)
1 cup fish stock (Chapter 6) or water
1 teaspoon salt
½ teaspoon freshly ground pepper
1 clove garlic, finely chopped
1 teaspoon rosemary

1 teaspoon marjoram
2 tablespoons chopped fresh parsley
3 tablespoons butter
1 onion, finely chopped
1 cup finely chopped celery
¼ pound mushrooms, thinly sliced
2 large tomatoes, sliced

1. Soak wild rice for at least 2 hours and then cook for 45 minutes, or follow package directions.
2. Preheat oven to 350° F.
3. Cut fillets into six 6″-long portions and place them in a buttered baking dish. Pour stock (or water) over fish and sprinkle with salt, pepper, garlic, rosemary, marjoram, and parsley. Dot with 1 tablespoon of the butter. Bake in a 350° F. oven for 15 minutes.
4. While the fish is baking, heat the remaining 2 tablespoons of butter in a frying pan and sauté onion, celery, and mushrooms, stirring occasionally, until onion is soft. With a slotted spoon, transfer vegetables to the cooked rice and mix well.
5. To the butter remaining in the frying pan, add the tomato slices and sauté for 1 minute on each side. Remove pan from heat.
6. Remove cooked fish from oven and transfer pike fillets to a warmed serving platter and arrange them around the edges of the platter. Place the wild rice-vegetable mixture in the center of the platter and top with the sautéed tomato slices.

Yield: 6 servings.

Note: On any good-sized pike, the long back fillets removed from both sides of the spinal column above the rib cage will be boneless.

Granny Turner, a Bear Island, Ontario, resident, hefts a pike with its dinner half swallowed— ample testimony to its reputation as a voracious predator.

Two ice fishermen ply their craft: the gentleman in the background has just landed his prey and has pulled it onto the ice, while his companion waits patiently for a strike.

CURRIED PIKE ATHABASCAN

2 pike fillets (about 2 pounds)
5 tablespoons lemon juice
2 teaspoons curry powder
4 tablespoons butter
4 scallions, chopped, including green tops
1 large tomato, peeled and chopped

2 tablespoons chopped fresh parsley
4 cups dried bread crumbs
½ teaspoon salt
Dash of paprika

1. Cut fillets into 4 equal portions and lay them in a flat dish. Combine lemon juice and curry powder and pour over fillets.
2. Cover and marinate in a cool place for 3 hours.
3. Preheat oven to 350° F.
4. Make stuffing: in a frying pan, heat butter, add scallions and sauté until tender. Add chopped tomato, parsley, bread crumbs and salt. Cook briefly and stir until mixture holds together.
5. Remove fillets from marinade, but reserve marinade. Lay fillets flat and spread stuffing on top of each. Roll up and fasten with toothpicks.

6. In a buttered baking dish place rolls upright, like crowns. Top each roll with any leftover stuffing and pour curry-lemon marinade over fish. Sprinkle with paprika.
7. Bake in a 350° F. oven for 25 minutes.
Yield: 4 servings

STUFFED MUSKELLUNGE WITH PRAWN SAUCE

1 muskellunge fillet (about 1½ pounds)	Salt and freshly ground pepper, to taste
2 cups soft bread crumbs, no crusts	1 cup fish stock
5 tablespoons milk	8 prawns or large shrimp
1 egg white	Butter, for sautéing
2 tablespoons heavy cream	1½ cups chopped mushrooms
	1 tablespoon flour

1. Skin and trim the fillet. Use skin and trimmings to make fish stock (Chapter 6). Set stock aside.
2. Preheat oven to 375° F.
3. Divide the fillet in half. Cut one half of the fillet into 2½″- to 3″-wide strips at least 6″ long and set aside. Take the other half of the fillet and finely grind in a blender, food processor or meat grinder.
4. Soften the bread crumbs in milk, add the ground fish and mix well.
5. Add the egg white and beat thoroughly until the mixture is light and fluffy. While beating, gradually add the cream, then season with salt and pepper.
6. Spread this mixture thickly on the strips of fish, roll up and secure with toothpicks.
7. Place the rolls in a buttered casserole and pour the fish stock over them. Cover tightly and bake in a 375° F. oven for 15 minutes.
8. While the fish rolls are cooking, clean the prawns (or shrimp) and chop coarsely. In a frying pan, heat about 1½ tablespoons butter and sauté prawns (or shrimp) for 3 minutes. Push them aside, add 2 tablespoons more butter and sauté the mushrooms until they begin to soften. Remove from heat.
9. With a slotted spoon, carefully remove the rolls to a warmed serving dish. Over moderate heat, thicken the pan juices in the casserole with the flour, stirring with a whisk to keep it smooth. Add the sautéed prawns (or shrimp) and mushrooms and heat briefly.
10. To serve, pour the prawn sauce over the fish rolls.
Yield: 4 servings

"Although all men are equal before fish, there are some class distinctions among them. The dry-fly devotees hold themselves a bit superior to the wet-fly fishermen; the wet-fly fishermen, superior to the spinner fishermen; and the spinners, superior to the bait fishermen. I have noticed, however, that toward the end of the day when there are no strikes, each social level collapses in turn down the scale until it gets some fish for supper."

—Fishing for Fun—and to Wash Your Soul, Herbert Hoover

PAN-POACHED MUSKELLUNGE

2 pounds muskellunge fillets or
 steaks
2 cups water
¼ cup lemon juice
1 small onion, thinly sliced

1 teaspoon salt
3 peppercorns
2 sprigs parsley
1 bay leaf

1. Cut fish into 6 equal serving portions.
2. In a greased frying pan, bring water to a boil. Reduce heat and add remaining ingredients.
3. Add fish, cover and simmer for 5 to 10 minutes, or until fish flakes easily when tested with a fork.
4. With a slotted spatula, carefully remove fish from pan and place on warmed serving platter. Serve with egg sauce (Chapter 6) and sprinkle with paprika.

Yield: 6 servings

For a Shaker community in northern Ohio, Lake Erie was an important source of food: "Last evening a number of the brethren went fishing in Lake Erie. Toward noon today they brought home their catch, except the small ones which they always cast into their mill-pond on the way home. They had enough fish for all three families [200 people]. There were several muskies, a fine haul of white fish, a number of pike along with a lot of catfish and yet other kinds. They are all splendid eating. This evening we had a good supper of boiled catfish with herb sauce, fried potatoes, boiled greens, pickled peppers, hot bread, and lemon pie and tea."

PICKEREL TART

Pastry:
1 cup flour
4 tablespoons butter
3 to 4 tablespoons cold water

Filling:
4 pickerel fillets (about 2
 pounds)
3 onions, sliced
4 slices bacon, cut into small
 pieces

½ teaspoon chopped fresh
 parsley
½ teaspoon thyme
Salt and freshly ground pepper,
 to taste
3 egg yolks
½ cup medium cream

1. Sift flour into large bowl. Rub or cut in butter. Add water and mix until dough forms a ball. Chill for at least 15 minutes.
2. Preheat oven to 350° F.
3. Divide pastry into 8 equal portions. Roll out into 8 rounds and press into individual tart tins. Prick bottoms and bake in 350° F. oven until lightly browned, about 5 minutes. Remove from oven and set aside.
4. Cut pickerel fillets into several smaller pieces.
5. In boiling water to cover, cook onion for 10 minutes. Reduce water to simmer, add pickerel pieces and cook for 3 minutes. With a slotted spoon, remove onion and fish and cool slightly. Discard cooking water. When the fish is cool, break it into flakes, removing any bones, and set aside.
6. In a frying pan, sauté bacon pieces until crisp. Remove pan from heat and drain off bacon grease. Add fish, onion, herbs, salt, and pepper and toss together with the bacon.

7. Beat yolks and cream together and add to bacon-fish mixture.
8. Pour filling into tart shells and bake in a 350° F. oven for 40 to 45 minutes.

Yield: 8 servings

PICKEREL MOLD

2 pounds pickerel fillets
Lemon slices
2 tablespoons butter
2 tablespoons flour
1 cup milk

1 tablespoon chopped fresh dill
Salt and freshly ground pepper,
 to taste
3 eggs

1. Preheat oven to 350° F.
2. Tie fillets in a piece of cheesecloth. Place in saucepan with boiling water to cover and several lemon slices, and cook until fish is done, about 6 minutes.
3. Remove fish from cheesecloth and pick out any skin and bones. Flake fish fine.
4. Make a white sauce: in a saucepan, melt butter, add flour, mixing with a wire whisk, and cook over low heat for 1 minute. Stirring constantly, gradually add milk and cook over medium heat until slightly thickened and smooth.
5. Add flaked fish and dill to white sauce, stirring until smooth and well mixed. Remove from heat and season with salt and pepper.
6. Beat eggs until light and stir into fish mixture.
7. Pour into well-buttered 1-quart mold and cover with aluminum foil. Place mold in pan filled with 1″ hot water and bake in a 350° F. oven for about 30 minutes, or until firm.
8. Unmold onto a warmed serving platter and serve with tomato sauce (Chapter 6) or shrimp sauce (Chapter 6).

Yield: 6 servings

Creel

Suckers

Members of the sucker family (*Catostomidae*) somewhat resemble minnows, but most have round protruding mouths used to suck up their food. Though somewhat bony, suckers taken from cool waters have firm, sweet flesh.

BIGMOUTH BUFFALO: Bigmouth buffalo (*Ictiobus cyprinellus*) look like carp, but are actually the largest members of the sucker family. Ranging from Texas and Alabama into southeastern Canada, buffalo are rarely taken by the angler, but are of some importance to commercial fishermen, who take these 30-

to 70-pound fish with open nets. Buffalo have sweet flesh, especially when taken from cold, clear water.

NORTHERN REDHORSE: Northern redhorse (*Maxostoma macrotepidotum*)—one of a dozen or so suckers called redhorse—can be found from the Mackenzie River system in western Canada south to Montana, through the Great Lakes to the Hudson River. They are commonly fished with worms and occasionally weigh two pounds, but are usually a pound or less. Because redhorse live in cold water, they have clear, firm flesh.

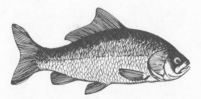

Bigmouth Buffalo

DEEP-FRIED BUFFALO

2 pounds buffalo fillets	¼ teaspoon freshly ground
1 egg	pepper
2 cups milk	½ cup cornmeal
1 teaspoon salt	Oil, for deep-frying

1. Cut the fillets into serving portions.
2. In a shallow bowl, beat together egg, milk, salt, and pepper.
3. Dip fish fillets into the egg mixture, then roll in cornmeal.
4. In a deep, heavy kettle, heat oil to 375° F. and drop the dredged fish into the hot oil. When fish is golden brown, lift it from the oil with a slotted spoon. Drain on paper towels.

Note: Do not add too much fish at once or the temperature of the oil will drop, causing the fish to cook more slowly and thus absorb too much oil.

5. Serve on a warmed serving platter garnished with lemon wedges.

Yield: 4 servings

BIGMOUTH BUFFALO LOAF

2 tablespoons butter, melted	2 teaspoons salt
4 slices whole wheat bread	2 teaspoons lemon juice
4 eggs, beaten	4 cups cooked, flaked bigmouth
1 tablespoon chopped fresh dill	buffalo
1 tablespoon chopped fresh	¼ cup grated Parmesan cheese
parsley	Paprika

1. Preheat oven to 350° F.
2. In a saucepan, melt butter and crumble in bread, and mix. Remove from heat and stir in eggs, herbs, salt, and lemon juice.
3. Add flaked fish and mix well.

4. Place in buttered loaf pan. Sprinkle top with grated cheese and paprika and bake in a 350° F. oven for 25 minutes.
5. To serve, garnish top with parsley and thin slices of hard-boiled egg.

Yield: 8 to 10 servings

REDHORSE IN SOURDOUGH

This recipe must be started 3 to 4 days ahead of time, unless you happen to have sourdough starter on hand, in which case it must be started a day in advance.

Sourdough starter:
1 package active dry yeast
1 quart lukewarm water
2 tablespoons sugar
4 cups flour

1. In a large crock or non-metal mixing bowl, dissolve yeast in water.
2. Add sugar and flour and beat until ingredients are well blended.
3. Cover and let stand at room temperature several days to develop slightly sour flavor. Refrigerate.

Note: Starter may be kept indefinitely. As it is used, add equal amounts of flour and water to replace the amount of starter used. If the starter is not used at least once every two weeks, add ½ teaspoon of sugar once a month to keep it active.

1 cup lukewarm water
1¼ cups flour
½ cup sourdough starter
¼ cup medium cream or milk
1 egg, beaten
1 tablespoon sugar
1 tablespoon vegetable oil
½ teaspoon baking soda
½ teaspoon salt
Oil, for frying
2 pounds redhorse fillets
Flour seasoned with salt and freshly ground pepper, for dredging

1. Add water and 1¼ cups flour to starter. Cover and let stand at room temperature overnight, then refrigerate.
2. When ready to cook, add cream (or milk), egg, sugar, oil, baking soda, and salt to sourdough mixture. Let stand and bubble 10 minutes.
3. In a large, deep frying pan, heat 2″ of oil.
4. While oil is heating, cut fish into 6 serving portions and dredge in seasoned flour. Then dip in the sourdough mixture. Add to the hot oil and fry, turning once, until both sides are brown and fish flakes easily when tested with a fork. Drain on paper towels.
5. Serve with tartar sauce (Chapter 6) and lemon wedges.

Yield: 6 servings

"The lines and circles in the slick water over yonder are a warning that that troublesome place is shoaling up dangerously; that silver streak in the shadow of the forest is the 'break' from a new snag, and he has located himself in the very best place he could have found to fish. . . .
—Life on the Mississippi,
    Mark Twain

In the good old days, on the Hood River in Oregon, sturgeon were sometimes caught weighing more than a thousand pounds. Their well-salted caviar was handed out free in Western barrooms to perk up drinkers' lagging taste for beer.

Sturgeon

Archaic fish, sturgeon (family *Acipenseridae*) have ranges of pointed, horny plates down their backs and sides, and look for all the world like prehistoric armored tanks. Although sturgeon grow to great age (some older than 150 years) and weight, the best and tastiest are the younger, smaller fish. Greatly prized for both their delicious flesh and roe, sturgeon have been vastly overfished and their rivers have been damned or polluted, greatly reducing their numbers. In addition to freshwater sturgeon, there are several marine species, including **Atlantic sturgeon** and two Pacific varieties: **green sturgeon** (taken mostly for their roe) and **white sturgeon.** Atlantic and white sturgeon spawn in fresh water, and some white sturgeon—in the upper Columbia River—are landlocked.

LAKE STURGEON: Lake sturgeon (*Acipenser fulvescens*) have a huge range in North America, from the Mississippi River system through all of the Great Lakes and along the St. Lawrence River, and rarely venture into brackish or salt water. Lake sturgeon spawn only once in every two or three years, laying a 12-pound mass of eggs numbering over 500 thousand. Sturgeon fight with slow and almost unbelievable tenacity; the record lake sturgeon caught with rod and reel was six feet long and weighed over 200 pounds. Most sturgeon taken, however, weigh under 50 pounds. Lake sturgeon have several freshwater relatives: the **pallid sturgeon,** found in the Mississippi River system, and the **shovelnose,** found everywhere lake sturgeon are except the Great Lakes system.

STURGEON IN WHITE WINE

6 1"-thick sturgeon steaks
Salt, to taste
Bouquet garni: 1 teaspoon each of rosemary, marjoram, basil, lemon balm
1 small onion, thinly sliced
1 cup dry white wine or dry vermouth
1 tablespoon butter
½ cup heavy cream
3 tablespoons chopped fresh dill

1. Preheat oven to 350° F.
2. Place steaks in a well-buttered baking dish and season with salt. Tie the bouquet garni herbs in a square of cheesecloth and add to the baking dish along with onion slices. Pour ½ cup of the wine (or vermouth) over the fish. Dot the fish with butter.
3. Cover the baking dish and place in a 350° F. oven. After 6 minutes pour remaining ½ cup of wine (or vermouth) over fish, remove cover and continue to bake until done, about 10 minutes, or until fish flakes easily when tested with a fork.
4. With a slotted spatula, remove fish to a warmed serving platter. Discard bouquet garni and onion.
5. To the pan juices in the baking dish, add cream and dill and serve this as a sauce. Sprinkle fish with capers and garnish with lemon wedges.

Yield: 6 servings

Meriwether Lewis recorded the Chinook method of steaming sturgeon: ". . . the sturgeon which had been previously cut into large fletches is now laid on the hot stones; a parsel of small boughs of bushes is next laid on a second course of the sturgeon thus rep(e)ating alternate layers of sturgeon and boughs untill the whole is put on which they design to cook. it is next covered closely with matts and water is poured in such a manner as to run in among the hot stones and vapor arrising being confined by the mats, cooks the fish. the whole process is performed in an hour, and the sturgeon thus cooked is much better than either boiled or roasted."

Two fishermen near Boise, Idaho, return home with a large catch of good-sized redhorse.

Whitefish

Closely related to trout and salmon, members of the whitefish family (*Coregonidae*) live in deep, cold, northern waters. But unlike trout and salmon, whitefish have large scales and their flesh is coarser grained and more delicately flavored.

LAKE WHITEFISH: The largest of the whitefish, lake whitefish (*Coregonus clupeaformis*) are widely distributed, from deep lakes in New England to British Columbia, north to Alaska and across subarctic Canada. Formerly taken only by commercial fishermen with gill nets or traps, whitefish are now considered notable game fish, a rare status granted only recently. Whitefish readily take an artificial surface fly, are astonishingly quick with swift, lunging habits, but have soft mouths and must be played with extreme care. By far the greatest numbers of lake whitefish, however, are taken by jigging through the ice in winter. Whitefish average two to three pounds. Whitefish taken in the winter or early spring taste best; and although they are completely scaled, the scales are easily removed. When properly cooked and boned, the flavor of lake whitefish is superior to most fish.

CISCO: Cisco, also called **lake herring** (*Coregonus artedii*), prefer the shallow waters of northern lakes and do not go as deep as lake whitefish. Like the whitefish, cisco are staunch fighters and will readily rise to a fly or other surface lure. Cisco are all too rarely offered fresh in North American markets, but are sold in great numbers as smoked fish; and in this form, they are especially delicious. They are generally smaller than whitefish—one-half to one pound average—and have fine bones. By slow smoking or lengthier cooking with low heat, the bones lose all their sharpness and become edible. In the United States these fish are marketed under the misnomer **chub,** and in Canada they are sold under the old fur traders' Indian name, **tullibee.** The cisco's small dark roe is sold as a delicious and inexpensive caviar substitute. Although cisco are still available commercially, there is some danger of their being overfished in north central America.

WHITEFISH IN ARTICHOKE SAUCE

2 pounds whitefish fillets
1½ cups fish stock (Chapter 6) or water
½ cup dry white wine
1 medium onion, coarsely chopped
½ cup coarsely chopped celery
½ teaspoon salt
6 peppercorns

½ teaspoon thyme
1 tablespoon lemon juice
2 tablespoons butter
3 tablespoons flour
Salt, to taste
¼ teaspoon cayenne
¼ cup heavy cream
6 artichoke hearts, cooked and coarsely chopped

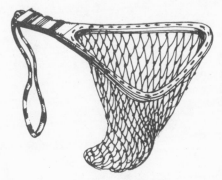

Landing Net

1. Cut each fillet into average serving portions.
2. In a large frying pan, make a court bouillon: combine fish stock (or water), wine, onion, celery, salt, peppercorns, thyme, and lemon juice. Bring to a boil, then lower heat.
3. Place the fish pieces in the liquid, which should cover the fish. If it doesn't, add more fish stock (or water). Simmer until fish is done, about 10 minutes. Remove from heat.
4. With a slotted spatula, remove fillets from court bouillon (reserve the liquid) and place them on a warmed serving platter. Keep fish warm in a 250° F. oven.
5. Strain the reserved court bouillon through a fine strainer. Discard the vegetables and spices. Pour off 1½ cups court bouillon and set aside.
6. In a saucepan, melt butter, add flour, mixing with a wire whisk, and cook over low heat for 1 minute. Stirring constantly, gradually add the reserved court bouillon and cook over medium heat until slightly thickened and smooth. Add salt and cayenne.
7. Reduce heat to low and, still stirring, add the cream and artichoke pieces. Do not allow to boil.
8. To serve, pour the artichoke sauce over the poached fillets and sprinkle with chopped parsley.

Yield: 6 servings

WHITEFISH IN MUSHROOM SAUCE

2 whitefish fillets (about 1 pound each)
3 tablespoons butter
2 tablespoons flour
1½ cups milk

Butter, for sautéing
½ pound mushrooms, sliced
½ cup finely chopped celery and celery leaves
Paprika

1. Preheat oven to 350° F.
2. Cut each fish fillet into four serving pieces of equal size and place in a buttered baking dish.
3. Make a white sauce: in a saucepan, melt butter, add flour, mixing with a wire whisk, and cook over low heat for 1 minute. Stirring constantly, gradually add milk and cook over medium heat until slightly thickened and smooth.
4. In a frying pan, heat 2 to 3 tablespoons butter and sauté mushrooms until they begin to soften. Add celery and stir. Add white sauce and stir.
5. Pour sauce over fish and sprinkle top with paprika. Bake in a 350° F. oven for 20 minutes.

Yield: 4 servings

Variation: Before baking, top with grated Parmesan cheese or cooked bacon bits.

King Jig

WISCONSIN FISH BOIL

This can be done outdoors over hot coals, or indoors.

20 small potatoes, or new potatoes
8 quarts water
2 cups salt

10 whitefish steaks (about ½ pound each)
Melted butter
Lemon wedges

1. Scrub potatoes well, but do not peel. Slice a small piece off the ends of potatoes so flavor will penetrate.
2. In a large 10-quart pot (preferably one with a removable basket insert), bring water to a boil. Add salt, then potatoes. After 15 to 20 minutes, depending on size of potatoes, pierce potato with a fork to test for doneness.
3. When potatoes are almost done, add fish steaks, cooking for about 7 to 8 minutes. Skim off fish oils while cooking. When the fish is done, it should flake when tested with a fork, but should not fall apart.
4. Remove potatoes and fish, place on serving platter, and serve with melted butter and lemon wedges.

Yield: 10 servings

Variation: Add 10 small onions, peeled but whole, when the potatoes are added.

CISCO IN MUSTARD SAUCE

6 cisco fillets (about 2 pounds)
1 tablespoon lemon juice
2 eggs
3 teaspoons dry mustard
Flour seasoned with salt and
   freshly ground pepper, for
   dredging

1 cup (2 sticks) butter,
   approximately
½ teaspoon cayenne

*A fine fish breakfast is ser-
iously prepared and eaten
on the West Branch of the
Penobscot River in Maine,
September 5, 1885.*

1. Sprinkle the cisco fillets with lemon juice and set aside.
2. In a shallow bowl, beat together eggs and 2 teaspoons of the
   dry mustard. Dip each fillet first in the egg mixture and then
   dredge in the seasoned flour.
3. In a frying pan, heat about 4 tablespoons of the butter and
   cook one half of the fillets until done, about 3 minutes on
   each side. Transfer to a warmed serving platter. Repeat until
   all fillets are cooked. Keep warm in a low oven.
4. Melt ½ cup (1 stick) butter. Stirring constantly, add the
   remaining teaspoon of mustard and cayenne and mix well.
5. To serve, pour the mustard sauce over the cisco and garnish
   with lemon wedges.

Yield: 6 servings

Mooneye

Both the **mooneye** (*Hiodon tergisus*) and its cousin the **goldeye** (*Hiodon alosoides*) are herringlike members of the mooneye family (*Hiodontidae*), living in large rivers and lakes in eastern North America. Both fish fight when taken on light tackle, and will take flies and other artificial lures. They commonly weigh between one and two pounds. Goldeye are fairly undistinguished, flavorless fish, and would have remained so had it not been for the arrival in Winnipeg, in 1886, of a young Englishman named Robert Firth. After an unsuccessful turn as a butcher, Firth decided to try selling smoked fish. He built a smokehouse and bought baskets of goldeye, which then cost only five cents a dozen, and resold smoked goldeye for 25 cents a dozen. Then one day, by mistake, he smoked the fish for too long, which not only smoked but also cooked them. The results were spectacular. With the addition of some vegetable dye to make the fish golden, Firth had invented the now famous Winnipeg goldeye. Ranked among Winnipeg goldeye's devotees have been Woodrow Wilson and Sinclair Lewis. Unfortunately, its popularity proved its downfall. Overfishing has seriously reduced the goldeye population, and mooneye are being used as a supplement.

Net menders—such as these photographed in 1906 in Charlevoix, Michigan—were an indispensable part of the Great Lakes fishing industry.

Saltwater Relatives

The following fish are freshwater members of predominantly saltwater fish families:

WHITE BASS: A freshwater member of the sea bass family, and a close relative of striped bass, white bass (*Morone chrysaps*) range from Texas to the Mississippi River, north into the Great Lakes and east along the St. Lawrence River, and are widely stocked in manmade lakes. White bass—with an average weight of one to two pounds, but a record weight of six—have firm and tasty flesh.

BURBOT: Burbot (*Lota lota*) are freshwater members of the cod family and are found in deep, cold lakes and streams in Alaska, Canada, and the northern United States. Because of some similarities in appearance, they are occasionally mistaken for catfish. Burbot feed throughout the winter and may be caught on a deep troll in open water or jig-hooked through the ice. Burbot are often two and a half feet long and commonly weigh six to eight pounds.

SMELT: Most of the nine species of smelt in North American waters are anadromous: going from the sea to spawn in fresh water. The main species of landlocked smelt (*Osmerus mordax*) range from Maine across southern Ontario to the farthest end of the Great Lakes, with a concentration in Lake Superior. During a two-week spawning period in late April, smelt swarm in the millions. They are similar to salmon in their habits and structure but rarely exceed nine inches, and average four to five inches. They have a very delicate flavor (thought by some to resemble cucumbers), a fragrant oil, and are excellent fried.

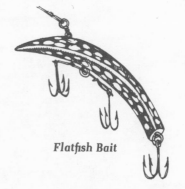

Flatfish Bait

BURBOT WITH PARSLEY

1 2-pound burbot
Salt and freshly ground pepper, to taste
½ cup soft bread crumbs
½ cup chopped fresh parsley
1 tablespoon butter

1. Preheat oven to 450° F.
2. Season fish with salt and pepper. Place on buttered aluminum foil and cover with bread crumbs and parsley. Dot with butter.
3. Fold foil together and seal. Bake in 450° F. oven until done, allowing 10 minutes for every inch of the burbot's thickness (see Canadian fish cooking rule, Chapter 1). Fish is done when it flakes easily when tested with a fork.
4. Serve with parsley sauce (Chapter 6).

Yield: 4 servings

On a sparkling morning in mid-July, 1898, fishermen work their dip nets as they pole through the rapids at Sault Ste. Marie.

NUTTED WHITE BASS

4 white bass, 9″ to 10″, with or
  without heads
Salt and freshly ground pepper,
  to taste
1 cup cottage cheese
½ cup chopped fresh parsley
1 clove garlic, finely chopped
⅓ cup slivered almonds
1 tablespoon cornstarch

1 medium onion, coarsely
  chopped
½ teaspoon chervil
1 teaspoon chopped fresh dill or
  ½ teaspoon dried
1 teaspoon salt
¼ teaspoon paprika
1 cup dark beer
1 cup dried bread crumbs

1. Preheat oven to 375° F.
2. Season fish with salt and pepper. Combine cottage cheese, parsley, and garlic. Stuff fish beginning at tail end and sew up with heavy thread and large darning needle, or use skewers (see Chapter 7).
3. Place fish in a single layer in a baking dish.
4. Place almonds, cornstarch, onion, chervil, dill, salt, paprika, and beer in a blender or food processor and mix.
5. Cover fish with sauce and sprinkle with bread crumbs.
6. Bake in a 375° F. oven for 25 minutes.
Yield: 4 servings

LAKE SUPERIOR SMELT

2 pounds smelt	Flour seasoned with salt and
1 egg	freshly ground pepper, for
1 tablespoon lemon juice	dredging
½ cup cracker crumbs	Oil or butter for frying (about ½
⅓ cup grated Parmesan cheese	cup)

1. Split the smelt and remove the bones, butterfly-style (see Chapter 7).
2. In a shallow bowl, combine egg and lemon juice. In a shallow bowl or plate, combine cracker crumbs and cheese.
3. Dredge each fish in seasoned flour, then dip in egg-lemon mixture. Finally, roll each fish in cracker crumb and cheese mixture.
4. In a frying pan, heat ¼ " of oil (or butter). Add fish and sauté over high heat until golden brown on one side, about 3 to 4 minutes. Turn and brown the other side.

Yield: 6 servings

Variation: Spread boned smelt with prepared mustard, then dip in cheese-crumb mixture to which has been added 2 teaspoons dry mustard.

4: Saltwater

The vast continent of North America is surrounded by ocean and penetrated by countless saltwater estuaries, sheltered bays, and sounds, from which millions of tons of fish are captured each year. And although there are more than 20,000 known species of fish in the world's waters, most sea life is concentrated along the continental shelves; for in mid-ocean, the waters are relatively void of nutrients.

Red Snapper

Fisherfolk along North American coasts have for centuries depended on this nearby abundance for their livelihood. But beyond their importance to commercial fishermen, saltwater fish have long held powerful sway over sports fishermen—those who are drawn to the sea hoping to lure a hard-fighting bluefish or a striped bass from the breaking surf, or others who chum the blue-green waters of the Gulf Stream for a giant swordfish, or do battle with a wahoo off the coast of California. There is something primordial about the act of trying to snatch a fish from the sea, an ancient human reflex that does not seem to want to go away.

Sea Bass

The sea bass family (*Serranidae*) includes more than 300 species (many of them important foodfish), some weighing as much as 1,200 pounds and others only a few ounces.

STRIPED BASS: Striped bass (*Morone saxatilis*), also known as **striper, rockfish,** or **rock bass,** range from the St. Lawrence to northern Florida, with concentrations from Cape Cod to South Carolina. They have also been successfully transplanted to the Pacific, off California. Striped bass spawn in brackish water and are often caught during runs to or from their spawning grounds. Averaging 10 pounds, with record weights of over 100 pounds, these splendid fighting fish are best for the table in smaller sizes, from six to eight pounds.

BLACK SEA BASS: Black sea bass (*Centropristis striata*) are most common from the Carolinas to New York. Hard fighters, sought by anglers using live bait, they average one to three pounds but can weigh up to six pounds. They have delicious firm, white flesh.

GIANT SEA BASS: Giant sea bass (*Stereolepis gigas*) range from southern California to Baja and can grow to more than 500 pounds. They are sometimes mistakenly called **jewfish** or **black sea bass,** but are only loosely related to those fish. Their flesh is lean and white, and tastes somewhat like grouper.

GROUPER: Grouper are warmwater reef fish found in the Atlantic from North Carolina to Florida, and along the Gulf

◀ *Entrepreneur and frequent fishing companion of Thomas Edison, Capt. John Lake Young instituted one of Atlantic City's most popular attractions: the daily net-haul at Young's Pier.*

Coast. The largest of the grouper are **jewfish** (*Epinephelus itajara*), which reach enormous size and can weigh 800 pounds or more. Jewfish readily take bait and large ones should be taken with shark equipment (stiff hooks and strong steel wire or chain leaders). Another large grouper, **Warsaw grouper** weigh up to 300 pounds and are marketed as jewfish. **Nassau grouper** (*Epinephelus striatus*), one of the best textured of the grouper, weigh six to 12 pounds, and **red grouper** (*Epinephelus morio*) weigh eight to 10 pounds. Although grouper are caught commercially, most of the catch is consumed locally, usually in delicious fish chowders. Grouper have sweet, lean, white flesh and are easily filleted. They should be skinned before cooking, and their roe is not worth eating. Other grouper include **rock hind** (*Epinephelus adscencionis*)—scaleless fish weighing up to 10 pounds—**red hind** (*Epinephelus guttatus*)—sometimes called **strawberry grouper**—and **speckled hind** (*Epinephelus drummondhayi*). All are sold commercially, but they are best in chowders.

"The Basse is an Excellent Fish, both fresh & salt. They are so large the head of one will give a good eater a dinner, and for daintiness of diet they excell the Marybones of beef. There are such multitudes that I have seen stopped into the river with a sand at one tide, so many as well loade a ship of one hundred tonnes."
—New English Canaan, 1632

BAKED STUFFED SEA BASS

2 to 3 tablespoons butter
1 medium onion, thinly sliced
½ cup soft bread crumbs (about 2 slices bread)
1 tablespoon chopped fresh parsley
2 anchovy fillets, roughly chopped
1 teaspoon grated lemon rind

½ teaspoon sage
Salt and freshly ground pepper, to taste
Milk
1 3- to 4-pound sea bass, with or without head and tail
Juice of 2 oranges
1 cup red wine

1. Preheat oven to 350°F.
2. In a frying pan, heat 1 tablespoon of the butter and sauté onion until soft.
3. In a bowl, combine the sautéed onion, bread crumbs, parsley, anchovy, lemon rind, sage, salt, and pepper. Add just enough milk to hold stuffing together, but keep it fairly dry.

4. Stuff fish beginning at tail end. Sew up with heavy thread and large darning needle, or use skewers (see Chapter 7).
5. Warm a tablespoon or two of butter in the palm of a hand and spread over fish's skin. Place the bass in a baking dish and add the orange juice and wine. Sprinkle with some salt and freshly ground pepper.
6. Bake in a 350° F. oven, basting occasionally, for about 25 minutes. Test for doneness with a knife point in flesh around backbone. Fish is done when flesh is opaque, no longer translucent.
7. Serve garnished with parsley and lemon wedges.

Yield: 8 to 10 servings

Fisherman Edward Llewellen stands beside the impossibly large, 425-pound giant sea bass he caught off Catalina Island, California, on August 29, 1903. Although this may have been the world's record at the time, it has since been eclipsed by a 575-pound catch taken off Anacapa Island, California, in 1968.

PORTUGUESE STRIPED BASS

3½ to 4 pounds striped bass fillets	½ pound mushrooms, coarsely chopped
6 tablespoons olive oil	½ cup (1 stick) butter
1 large green pepper, coarsely chopped	½ cup dried bread crumbs
1 large onion, coarsely chopped	2 cups tomato sauce (Chapter 6)
	¼ pound Cheddar, cut in slices

1. Preheat oven to 350° F.
2. Cut fillets into pieces 3″ to 4″ long. Place in ovenproof baking dish with 4 tablespoons (¼ cup) of the olive oil.
3. In a frying pan, heat the remaining 2 tablespoons of the olive oil and sauté pepper, onion, and mushrooms until soft.
4. Melt butter and stir into bread crumbs.
5. Cover bass with vegetables and tomato sauce. Top with buttered bread crumbs.
6. Cut cheese slices into strips and lay over bread crumbs in a criss-cross pattern.
7. Bake in a 350° F. oven for 30 minutes.

Yield: 8 servings

"The Striped Bass, it is said, is known to attain the weight of a hundred pounds; but such giants are rare, though up to forty or fifty pounds they are no rarities. The largest fish are taken in deep, rapid tideways, such as Hellgate or the Haerlem river, by trolling from the stern of a rowboat with a strong hand-line and a large hook baited with the hideous piscine reptile, or insect rather, the real squid, or with the artificial squid of tin or pewter."

—Frank Forester's Fish and Fishing of the United States and British Provinces of North America, 1864

BASS WITH CRAYFISH PILAF

1 cup rice	1 teaspoon freshly ground pepper
2 tablespoons butter	½ teaspoon cayenne
1 medium onion, chopped	1 cup heavy cream
1 dozen crayfish, cleaned and cooked	4 quarts court bouillon (Chapter 6)
2 medium tomatoes, skinned, seeded, and chopped	1 striped bass (about 3½ pounds), with head and tail
1 teaspoon salt	

1. Cook rice according to package directions.
2. Preheat oven to 350° F.
3. In a frying pan, heat butter and sauté onion until golden.
4. Set 6 crayfish aside for garnish, and chop remaining 6 coarsely.
5. Combine cooked rice, onion, chopped crayfish, tomatoes, salt, pepper, cayenne, and heavy cream. Place mixture in a buttered 3-quart casserole and bake in a 350° F. oven for 25 minutes.
6. While rice is baking, bring court bouillon (in a fish poacher) to a boil, then lower heat and simmer for 10 minutes.
7. Lower fish into simmering liquid and poach until fish is done, allowing 10 minutes for every inch of thickness (see Canadian fish cooking rule, Chapter 1).

8. Remove fish to a warmed serving platter and serve with pilaf garnished with 6 reserved crayfish. Serve shrimp sauce (Chapter 6) in sauce boat.

Yield: 6 servings

Variation: Remove cooked fish from bones in bite-sized chunks and arrange on top of pilaf.

FLORIDA GROUPER CHOWDER

¼ pound salt pork, diced
2 large onions, sliced
2 pounds skinned and boned
  grouper
3 cups water

1 cup clam juice
2 potatoes, diced
Salt and freshly ground pepper,
  to taste
1 cup heavy cream

1. In a large saucepan, cook salt pork until crisp and brown. Remove and reserve.
2. Add onions to the fat and sauté gently until they start to turn golden. Then add grouper, water, clam juice, potatoes, salt, and pepper.
3. Cook gently until fish is tender, about 30 minutes. If necessary, break the fish into bite-sized pieces.
4. Add cream and sprinkle salt pork croutons on top. Serve with pilot or other crackers.

Note: This chowder can be prepared through Step 3 ahead of time. When ready to serve, reheat fish and potato mixture and then add cream and croutons.

Yield: 4 servings

Codfish

The codfish family (*Gadidae*) includes among its five dozen or so species some of the Northern hemisphere's prime foodfish: cod, haddock, hake, and pollock. The abundance of these coldwater fish played a major role in the survival of colonial America. All members of the codfish family live in saltwater except **burbot** (see page 95).

ATLANTIC CODFISH: The Atlantic codfish (*Gadus morhua*) was of such value to the New England fishing industry that it was constantly commemorated on coins, stamps, and seals—and is still a part of the Massachusetts state seal. Cod range all along the New England coast north as far as Newfoundland and

"In the summer I saw two men fishing for Bass hereabouts. Their bait was a bullfrog, or several small frogs in a bunch, for want of squid. They followed a retiring wave, and whirling their lines round and round their heads with increasing rapidity, threw them as far as they could into the sea; then retreating, sat down flat on the sand, and waited for a bite. . . . And they knew by experience that it would be a Striped Bass, or perhaps a Cod, for these fishes play along near the shore."

—Cape Cod,
Henry David Thoreau

Labrador, but will stray as far south as North Carolina when the water is cool enough. They are most abundant off the Georges and Grand Banks. Perhaps the world's greatest commercial fish (eight billion pounds are harvested annually), cod should seriously be considered a sporting fish as well. Cod average under 10 pounds and 60-pounders today are rare, but the record net catch was a six-foot giant weighing 211½ pounds. Almost identical to Atlantic cod are **Pacific cod** (*Gadus macrocephalus*), found from Oregon north. Cod have delicious, tender, white flesh and are marketed in many forms (fresh, frozen, smoked, canned), the most famous of which is salt cod—a staple in the diet of Portuguese-American cod fishermen. Young cod—between 1½ and 2½ pounds—are marketed as **scrod.**

Haddock

HADDOCK: Haddock (*Melanogrammus aeglefinus*)—traveling in large, densely packed schools—rarely move south of Cape Hatteras or north of Newfoundland. An important commercial fish, haddock stocks off the American coast have been seriously depleted in recent years by heavy foreign fishing. Most haddock stay in deep water, but those that school in shallow waters will occasionally take an artificial lure and trolling spoon, and are now appreciated as worthwhile gamefish. Smaller than cod, most haddock caught weigh two to four pounds. Young haddock, like cod, are marketed as **scrod.** Haddock are too soft to be salted like cod, but are sold smoked, especially as **finnan haddie** (haddie is Scottish slang for haddock). In North America, however, haddock are most often sold fresh or frozen.

POLLOCK: Caught in commercially important numbers from New Jersey north to the Grand Banks off Newfoundland, pollock (*Pollachius virens*) remain closer to shore than either cod or haddock. Pollock will take artificial lures and are now considered a good sporting fish. They average three to nine pounds, but may reach over 30 pounds. Pollock are sometimes marketed under the name **green cod.**

HAKE: There are about a half dozen hake species in North American waters—including **red hake** and **white hake**—but only **silver hake** (*Merluccius bilinearis*) are of any significance

on the American table. Silver hake are found from Florida to the coast of Labrador. Hake are high in protein with soft, white flesh and are commonly marketed under the name **whiting.**

The codfishing industry was nothing if not practical: here— in a photograph by Albert Cook Church—a dory does double duty as a wash tub for split cod.

SCROD HARVARD-STYLE

2 tablespoons white wine
   vinegar
2 teaspoons olive oil
1 tablespoon lemon juice
2 tablespoons finely chopped
   fresh parsley
1 teaspoon chopped fresh dill
Salt and freshly ground pepper,
   to taste

4 medium potatoes, peeled
1 tablespoon butter
¼ pound mushrooms, coarsely
   chopped
Dash of paprika
1 cup cooked scrod, broken into
   chunks
Coarsely chopped walnuts

1. Combine vinegar, olive oil, lemon juice, parsley, dill, salt, and pepper. Set aside.
2. Boil potatoes until tender, drain, and cut into dice. While still hot, pour dressing over them.
3. In a frying pan, heat butter. Add mushrooms and sauté lightly. Sprinkle with paprika and let cool.
4. Add mushrooms to potatoes. Add fish and toss. Garnish with chopped walnuts.

Yield: 4 servings

DILL-PICKLED POLLOCK

2 pounds pollock fillets	2 tablespoons flour
2 tablespoons dill-pickle liquid*	3 tablespoons dry white wine
3 dill pickles	Salt and freshly ground pepper,
3 tablespoons butter	to taste
¼ cup chopped mushrooms	

1. In a large saucepan, simmer fillets in at least 1½ cups water with the dill-pickle liquid for about 3 minutes.
2. Peel pickles, seed, quarter lengthwise and add to fish, simmering about 5 more minutes. Remove from heat.
3. In a frying pan, heat 1 tablespoon of the butter and sauté mushrooms until they begin to soften. Push mushrooms to a corner of the pan.
4. Add remaining 2 tablespoons of butter, add flour and cook for 1 minute, stirring constantly with a whisk. Pour off 1¼ cups of the reserved poaching liquid and add to pan. Add white wine, salt, and pepper. Cook over low heat, stirring constantly, until sauce begins to thicken, about 2 minutes.
5. With a slotted spoon, remove fillets from saucepan and place on a warmed serving platter. Remove pickles and place on top of each fillet. Cover the whole with the mushroom sauce and sprinkle with chopped parsley.

Yield: 4 to 6 servings

*If pickles are from the delicatessen and not a jar, be sure to ask for some of the brine. If this is inconvenient, substitute lemon juice or white vinegar for the dill-pickle liquid.

Daniel Webster, in 1842, sent his recipe for fish chowder to biographer S. P. Lyman: "1. Fry a large bit of well-salted pork in the kettle over the fire. Fry it thoroughly. 2. Pour in a sufficient quantity of water, and then put in the head and shoulders of a cod-fish, and a fine, well-dressed haddock, both recently caught. 3. Put in three or four good Irish potatoes, for which none better can be found than at Marshfield, and then boil them well together. An old fisherman generally puts in two or three onions. 4. When they are about done, throw in a few of the largest Boston crackers, and then apply the pepper and salt to suit the fancy. Such a dish, smoking hot, placed before you, after a long morning spent in the most exhilarating sport, will make you no longer envy the gods."
—The Public and Private Life of Daniel Webster, General S. P. Lyman, 1852

BRANDADE OF SALT COD

2 pounds salt cod	1¼ cups hot milk or light cream
3 to 3½ cups olive oil	Salt and freshly ground pepper,
1 clove garlic, crushed	to taste

1. Soak salt cod in water for 10 minutes and rinse to remove salt. Cut into pieces, place in a saucepan and cook in water to cover, 7 to 8 minutes, no longer. Drain the cod. Remove skin and bones, if any, and flake.
2. In a heavy saucepan, heat 1 cup of the olive oil until it begins to smoke. Add cod, then garlic. Cooking over medium heat, press fish flakes with a wooden spoon until they are reduced to a smooth paste.
3. Turn the heat very low and keep working the mixture with the wooden spoon, adding 2 to 2½ cups more oil, a little at a

time. Alternating with the oil, and stirring constantly, add the milk (or cream) a little at a time. Mash until the brandade has the consistency of mashed potatoes. Season with salt and pepper.
4. Serve the brandade in a deep dish, molding it into a dome shape. Garnish with triangles of sandwich bread fried in oil or butter.

Yield: 6 servings

HADDOCK ROLLS WITH CAPER SAUCE

2 haddock fillets (about 2 pounds)
1 cup fish stock (Chapter 6) or water
1 cup dry white wine
¼ teaspoon grated nutmeg
½ teaspoon salt
¼ teaspoon freshly ground pepper

8 medium shrimp
1 teaspoon cornstarch
1 tablespoon water
1 cup heavy cream
3 tablespoons capers
Paprika

"For dressing Codfish. Put the fish first into cold water and wash it, then hang it over the fire and soak it six hours in scalding water, then shift it into clean warm water, and let it scald for one hour, it will be much better than to boil."
—American Cookery, Amelia Simmons, 1796

1. Cut the haddock fillets into 8 serving portions, each at least 6″ long. Roll up each piece of fish and tie in a roll with a piece of string. Place the rolled fillets around the bottom of a saucepan.
2. Add the fish stock (or water), wine, nutmeg, salt, and pepper. Bring the liquid just to the boil and reduce the heat to low. Cover the saucepan and simmer for 10 minutes.
3. Add the shrimp to the poaching liquid and poach all together for no longer than 5 minutes, until shrimp are cooked but not tightly curled.
4. Remove the saucepan from the heat and with a slotted spoon remove the shrimp and fillet rolls from the pan. Cut off and discard the string ties from the fish rolls. Place the fish on a deep, warmed serving dish and keep hot. Shell and devein the shrimp and keep warm together with the fish.
5. Return the saucepan with the poaching liquid to moderate heat and bring to a boil. Dissolve the cornstarch in 1 tablespoon water. Stir the cornstarch mixture into the liquid and cook to thicken (about 5 minutes) stirring constantly.
6. Lower the heat and add the cream and capers. Stir together until warm. Do not allow the sauce to boil.
7. Pour the sauce over the fish rolls. Sprinkle each with a dash of paprika and top with a shrimp.

Yield: 4 servings

KEDGEREE

2 finnan haddie (about 1 pound)
or 2 cups cooked, flaked
haddock
Milk
6 tablespoons butter
2 cups cooked rice
1 tablespoon chopped fresh
parsley

1 tablespoon chopped fresh
chives
½ teaspoon freshly ground
pepper
Dash of nutmeg
4 hard-boiled eggs, finely
chopped

1. Poach the finnan haddie in milk to cover for about 5 minutes. Drain fish, remove skin and bones, and flake.
2. In a frying pan, heat butter. Add fish, rice, parsley, chives, pepper, and nutmeg. When hot, add three-quarters of the chopped egg.
3. Turn onto a hot serving platter and garnish top with remaining egg. Serve with tomato sauce (Chapter 6) and lemon wedges.

Yield: 6 servings

Variation I: Use sautéed onions in place of chives.
Variation II: Add 2 teaspoons curry powder, but not if making kedgeree with smoked fish or salmon, fresh or smoked.

*"BOILED FINNAN
HADDIE
Select a thick fish. Take half
of it. Put flesh side down in a
saucepan, cover with cold water, and set to cook on the
back of the range. In about
half an hour draw to a hotter
part of the range, and gradually heat the water to the sim-
mering-point. Let simmer
from five to ten minutes, then
drain the fish carefully. Serve
on a hot platter. Pass at the
same time hot, boiled potatoes
and egg sauce."*
—Cooking For Two, A
Handbook for Young
Housekeepers, *1916*

GINGERED HAKE CROQUETTES

2 cups cooked, flaked hake
¾ cup soft bread crumbs
2 tablespoons chopped fresh
parsley
1 teaspoon salt
½ teaspoon freshly ground
pepper
1 egg, beaten
3 tablespoons flour

4 tablespoons butter
½ teaspoon ground ginger
½ teaspoon ground coriander
¼ teaspoon ground turmeric
⅛ teaspoon hot chili powder
1 onion, finely chopped
¾ cup fish stock (Chapter 6)
¾ cup dry white wine

1. Combine the fish, bread crumbs, parsley, salt, and pepper. Add the beaten egg and mix thoroughly.
2. Patting spoonfuls of the mixture in the palms of the hands, shape about 10 small croquettes. Spread the flour in a shallow dish or plate, and dredge the croquettes in the flour. Chill the croquettes in the refrigerator for 45 minutes.
3. In a large frying pan, heat the butter and add the ginger, coriander, turmeric, and chili powder. Then add the onion and stir to coat the onion evenly. Sauté until the onion is soft.
4. Pour in the fish stock and wine. Bring the liquid to a boil,

stirring constantly, then lower heat and allow sauce to simmer for about 2 minutes. Season to taste.

5. With a spoon, gently place croquettes in the simmering liquid and baste them with sauce. Cook for 6 to 8 minutes on each side, or until they are evenly done, basting frequently.

6. Transfer cooked croquettes onto a warmed serving platter. Pour the sauce over croquettes and garnish with parsley and lemon wedges.

Yield: 4 servings

Flounder & Sole

Flounder and sole can actually be divided into three separate families of flatfish (*Bothidae, Pleuronectidae,* and *Soleidae*) but are so interchangeable in the marketplace and in the kitchen that they have been lumped together here under one heading.

WINTER FLOUNDER: Winter flounder (*Pseudopleuronectes americanus*) may be the most abundant and popular flatfish on the East Coast, occurring from Arctic waters south to Georgia. Winter flounder, averaging two pounds, have fine-textured white flesh and delicious roe. The smaller winter flounder are marketed under the name **lemon sole.**

SUMMER FLOUNDER: Best known by the market name **fluke,** summer flounder (*Paralichthys dentatus*) occur from the Carolinas to Maine. Averaging three pounds, fluke are comparable in taste to winter flounder.

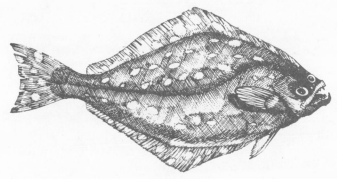

Atlantic Halibut

HALIBUT: Atlantic halibut (*Hippoglossus hippoglossus*) are the largest of the flatfish, occasionally weighing as much as 600 pounds. Coldwater fish, they range from New Jersey north. Almost identical to Atlantic halibut are **Pacific halibut** (*Hippo-*

"A vessel of one hundred tons or so, is provided with a crew of twelve men, who are equally expert as sailors and fishers, and for every couple of these hardy tars [cod fishermen], a Hampton boat is provided, which is lashed on the deck, or hung in stays. . . . The men are supplied with warm clothing, water-proof oiled jackets and trowsers, large boots, broad-brimmed hats with a round crown, and stout mittens, with a few shirts. The owner or captain furnishes them with lines, hooks, and nets, and also provides the boat best adapted to ensure success. The hold of the vessel is filled with casks of various dimensions, some containing salt, and others for the oil that may be procured."

—Delineations of American Scenery and Character, John James Audubon

glossus stenolepsis), ranging from California to Alaska (most halibut come from Alaska and northern British Columbia). The flesh of both halibut is firm, white, and delicate; and halibut cheeks are considered a great delicacy.

AMERICAN PLAICE: American plaice (*Hippoglossoides platessoides*)—also known as **sanddab, dab** or **Canadian plaice**—are northern fish found from south Labrador to Cape Cod. Commonly weighing two to three pounds, these are important commercial fish with substantial amounts shipped annually to Europe. They have close-grained flesh and a splendid flavor.

TURBOT: There are no turbot native to American waters that are of particular value as foodfish. However, many markets carry imported, frozen **Greenland turbot,** which have soft, flaky flesh and average around five pounds. Greenland turbot should not be confused with the Eastern Atlantic turbot, which are so highly esteemed in European cuisine.

SOLE: There are only two true sole to be found off the American coast, neither of much interest as foodfish. The true sole of culinary fame—such as Dover sole—are all European fish. There are, however, a number of fine flavored Pacific flounder called sole, including **butter sole, rex sole,** and **petrale sole.** In addition, young flounder on both coasts are often marketed under the name sole.

"TO BOIL TURBOT *The turbot kettle must be of proper size and in the nicest order. Set the fish in cold water to cover it completely. Throw a handful of salt and one glass of vinegar into it; let it gradually boil. Be very careful that there fall no blacks, but skim it well, and preserve the beauty of the colour. Serve it garnished with a complete fringe of curled parsley, lemon and horseradish."*
—A New System of Domestic Cookery, 1807

TURBANS OF FLOUNDER

4 flounder fillets (about 1½ pounds)
3 tablespoons butter
¾ cup chopped mushrooms
2 tablespoons finely chopped celery and leaves
1 cup dried bread crumbs
½ cup dry white wine, fish stock (Chapter 6) or water

1 tablespoon chopped fresh parsley
Dash of nutmeg
¾ teaspoon salt
⅛ teaspoon freshly ground pepper
Dash of cayenne

1. Cut flounder fillets in half lengthwise. Line 8 individual buttered ramekins or muffin tins with strips, facing the "whiter" side out.
2. Preheat oven to 375° F.
3. In a frying pan, heat butter and sauté mushrooms and celery until they just begin to soften.
4. Add bread crumbs, wine (fish stock, or water), parsley,

nutmeg, salt, pepper, and cayenne, and mix, scraping melted butter from pan.

5. Fill center of fish forms with mushroom stuffing and bake in a 375° F. oven for 20 minutes.

6. Unmold onto a warmed serving dish. Serve with Hollandaise sauce (Chapter 6) or lemon butter.

Yield: 4 main-course servings, 8 first-course servings

CROWNED FLOUNDER

8 flounder fillets (about 2½ pounds)
Salt and freshly ground pepper, to taste
1 egg
½ cup heavy cream
4 tablespoons butter

1 tablespoon flour
1 cup fish stock (Chapter 6)
6 to 8 shrimp, shelled, deveined, and chopped
½ cup chopped mushrooms
4 artichoke hearts, chopped

1. Make a mousseline stuffing: in a blender or food processor grind ½ pound of the fillets. Add salt, pepper, and egg, and mix well. Blending slowly, gradually add cream. Set aside.

2. Preheat oven to 350° F.

3. Into a buttered, 2-quart ring mold, place the remaining fillets, their sides slightly overlapping, their ends hanging over the mold's center and outside edges.

4. Spoon mousseline into the mold on top of fillets, and fold ends of fish over the stuffing.

Winter Flounder

5. Cover mold with buttered waxed paper or foil. Put mold in a baking tin and pour in boiling water to halfway up the sides of mold.

6. While mold is in oven, make a velouté sauce: in a saucepan, melt 1 tablespoon of the butter, add flour, mixing with a wire whisk, and cook over low heat for 1 minute. Stirring constantly, gradually add fish stock and cook over medium heat until slightly thickened and smooth.

7. In a frying pan, heat remaining 3 tablespoons butter. Add shrimp and mushrooms and sauté for 5 minutes. Add artichoke hearts and heat through.

8. When mold is done, take out of oven, remove waxed paper and allow to rest about 5 minutes. Using a cooling rack to keep fish in place, invert mold briefly to drain off any excess liquid. Then unmold onto a warm serving dish.

9. Into center of mold spoon shrimp, mushrooms, and artichoke hearts. Pour velouté sauce over entire dish.

Yield: 8 servings

Thousands of split and salted fish sun-dry in the flake yards of Gloucester, Massachusetts, the birthplace of the New England fishing industry.

SHRIMPER'S SOLE

Sole is one of the most adaptable and delectable of fish. In *Madame Prunier's Fish Cookery Book* (1939), there are no fewer than 161 recipes for sole alone. Flounder, the closely related flatfish commonly available in North America, is similar in texture and flavor and can be used in any recipe calling for sole.

½ cup dried bread crumbs, plus some for topping
6 tablespoons butter
1 tablespoon chopped fresh parsley
1 cup chopped, cooked shrimp

2 eggs, beaten separately
Dash of nutmeg
Salt and freshly ground pepper, to taste
4 small whole sole (about 1 pound each)

1. Preheat oven to 350° F.
2. Combine bread crumbs, butter, parsley, shrimp, 1 of the eggs, nutmeg, salt, and pepper.
3. Make an incision along either side of each fish's backbone (see Chapter 7). Lay the stuffing along the bone, under the fillets, leaving the center open.
4. Place the fish in a buttered baking dish. Brush fish with the remaining beaten egg, sprinkle with bread crumbs and bake in a 350° F. oven for 20 minutes, until well browned.

Yield: 4 servings

HEAVENLY SOLE

1 cup (2 sticks) butter
⅓ pound mushrooms, finely
 chopped
2 teaspoons chopped fresh
 chives
4 tablespoons chopped fresh
 fennel
6 cooked shrimp, finely chopped
¾ cup heavy cream
Salt and freshly ground pepper,
 to taste
4 tablespoons flour

2 eggs and 1 egg yolk
8 small sole fillets (about 2
 pounds)
½ cup vegetable oil (peanut or
 corn)
¼ cup water
Flour seasoned with salt and
 freshly ground pepper, for
 dredging
3 cups dried bread crumbs
¼ cup lemon juice

1. In a frying pan, heat 3 tablespoons of the butter. Add mushrooms, chives, and fennel and sauté until mushrooms begin to soften.
2. Add shrimp and sauté about 1 minute. Reduce heat and add cream, salt, and pepper. Stirring constantly, cook briefly until cream is absorbed.
3. In a saucepan, heat 4 tablespoons of the butter and add the 4 tablespoons of flour, stirring with a whisk until smooth. Add a spoonful at a time to shrimp and mushroom mixture, stirring to mix. When thickened and smooth, stir 1 egg yolk into mixture. Season with salt and pepper. Remove from heat and let cool.
4. Slice fillets in half lengthwise. Place half of them on a platter. Place mushroom-shrimp mixture on each fillet, then place a matching fillet on top of mixture. Refrigerate at least 10 minutes.
5. In a shallow bowl, combine whole eggs, 2 tablespoons of the vegetable oil, water, salt, and pepper, and blend well.
6. Dip filled sole, one at a time, first in seasoned flour, then in egg mixture, then in bread crumbs, pressing crumbs down to adhere.
7. Heat about 2 tablespoons of oil and 2 tablespoons of butter in each of two skillets. Add as many fish fillets as the skillets will hold. Cook about 5 minutes on one side; turn and cook 5 minutes on other side. Remove to warm platter in a 250° F. oven. Wipe out skillets, add more oil and butter as necessary, and cook remaining sole.
8. Heat remaining butter (4 tablespoons) and add the lemon juice. Pour this over fish. Serve garnished with lemon slices.

Yield: 8 servings

Variation: 1 cup of finely chopped lobster meat may be combined with the shrimp.

Robert Beverley, a planter and historian, described Indian fishing methods in seventeenth-century Virginia: "The Indian Invention of Weirs in Fishing, is mightily improved by the English besides which, they make use of Seins, Trolls, Casting-Netts, Setting-Netts, Hand-fishing, and Angling, and in each find abundance of Diversion. I have set in the shade, at the Heads of Rivers Angling, and spent as much time in taking the Fish off the Hook, as in waiting for their taking it."

SOLE EN PAPILLOTE

1 3- to 4-pound sole, head and tail left on	1 stalk of celery, sliced
Salt	3 tablespoons chopped fresh tarragon
1 lemon plus 3 teaspoons lemon juice	2 tablespoons chopped fresh parsley
7 tablespoons butter	1 clove garlic, sliced
1 shallot, finely chopped	Freshly ground pepper, to taste

1. Preheat oven to 350° F.
2. Rub sole with salt, then rinse in cold water to which the juice of 1 lemon has been added. (Save the lemon rind.)
3. Make 3 to 4 incisions down the back (the dark side) of the sole to act as steam vents. Place sole on a large piece of buttered aluminum foil.
4. In a frying pan, heat 3 tablespoons of the butter and sauté the shallot and celery. Add 1 tablespoon chopped tarragon, the parsley, garlic, and pepper. Remove from heat, add 2 teaspoons lemon juice and grate in a little of the reserved lemon rind.
5. Pour vegetable mixture over fish and seal foil. Bake in a 350° oven for 25 minutes.
6. Meanwhile, in a small saucepan, melt the remaining 4 tablespoons of butter. Add 2 tablespoons (or more, if desired) chopped tarragon. Season with salt, pepper, and 1 teaspoon lemon juice.
7. When the fish is cooked, garnish with more tarragon and serve with the hot tarragon butter.

Yield: 6 servings

Halibut Hook

HALIBUT WASHINGTON

4 halibut steaks, 1″ thick (about 2 pounds), skinned	½ teaspoon chopped fresh tarragon
1 small onion, chopped	Salt and freshly ground pepper, to taste
4 tomatoes, skinned, chopped, and seeded	1 tablespoon lemon juice
2 tablespoons chopped fresh parsley	½ cup dry white wine
½ teaspoon chopped fresh thyme	½ cup heavy cream
	2 tablespoons butter

1. Preheat oven to 350° F.
2. Place steaks in shallow buttered baking dish. Add onion,

tomatoes, parsley, thyme, tarragon, salt, pepper, lemon juice, and wine.

3. Cover with buttered foil and bake in a 350° F. oven until halibut is cooked, about 10 minutes.
4. Drain the stock off into a saucepan and keep fish steaks warm. Boil the stock to reduce it by about one-quarter. Add heavy cream. Cook 2 to 3 minutes to thicken. Add butter a little at a time and shake pan to mix. Pour sauce over fish.

Yield: 4 servings

Wrasse

Although the wrasse family (*Labridae*) is large—over 400 species—only a handful of its members are commonly caught as foodfish. **Tautog** (*Tautoga onitis*)—also called **blackfish** or **oysterfish**—range from New Brunswick to the Carolinas and average three pounds, but can weigh up to 12 or 15 pounds. **Hogfish** (*Lachnolaimas maximus*) are found from the Carolinas south, with a concentration in the Florida Keys. Slightly larger than tautog, they average four to six pounds. Pacific wrasse, **California sheephead** (*Pimelometopon pulchrum*)—no relation to the porgy called sheepshead—range from central California south and average four to five pounds. These wrasse have firm, white flesh and are the ideal ingredient for chowders.

"Fishiest of all fishy places was the Try Pots, which well deserved its name; for the pots there were always boiling chowders. Chowder for breakfast, and chowder for dinner, and chowder for supper, till you began to look for fish-bones coming through your clothes."

—Moby Dick,
Herman Melville

TAUTOG GOULASH

4 tablespoons butter
2 medium onions, cubed
1 pound tautog fillets, cut into large cubes
3 medium potatoes, peeled and cut into quarters

2 cloves garlic, crushed
1 tablespoon paprika
Salt and freshly ground pepper, to taste
2 tablespoons tomato puree

1. Preheat oven to 375° F.
2. In a frying pan, heat butter, add onions and sauté until they begin to soften. Off the heat, add fish, potatoes, garlic, paprika, salt, and pepper. Stir to mix.
3. Place mixture in a well-buttered baking dish. Stir tomato puree into enough warm water to just cover fish mixture and pour over fish.
4. Cover dish and bake in a 375° F. oven for 30 minutes.

Yield: 4 servings

Mullet

Mullet (family *Mugilidae*) are warmwater fish with a half dozen species in North American waters, the most common of which are **white mullet** (*Mugil curema*), found in the Caribbean and in Florida bayous. In the Pacific, larger **striped mullet** (*Mugil cephalus*) commonly weigh under two pounds. Mullet are firm, oily-fleshed fish that take well to smoking. They are, however, quite bony and should be carefully filleted. Mullet are also prized for their delicious roe.

FLORIDA SMOKED MULLET

4 tablespoons butter
2 tablespoons flour
2 cups milk
2 cups flaked smoked mullet*

2 tablespoons grated onion
Salt and freshly ground pepper, to taste
¾ cup soft bread crumbs

1. Preheat oven to 350° F.
2. Make a white sauce: in a saucepan, melt 2 tablespoons of the butter, add flour, mixing with a wire whisk, and cook over low heat for 1 minute. Stirring constantly, gradually add milk and cook over medium heat until slightly thickened and smooth.

In commercial smokehouses such as this one, fish were hung on racks and air-dried through open, barn-style windows before being smoked. The smoked fish were then packed in wooden crates (lower left) and shipped to market.

3. Place fish in a buttered baking dish. Cover with sauce, onion, salt, and pepper. Top with bread crumbs and dot with remaining 2 tablespoons of butter.
4. Bake in a 350° F. oven for 30 minutes.
Yield: 6 servings

*See Chapter 7 for smoking techniques.

Butterfish

Butterfish (*Boronotus triacanthus*)—the most common member of the butterfish family (*Stromateidae*)—are known as **pumpkin seed** in Connecticut, **dollar fish** in Maine, but as butterfish over much of the Atlantic coast from Florida to Canada. Butterfish are valiant fighters for their size—eight inches average—and will readily take a feathered lure or natural bait. Butterfish flesh is dark and has a buttery taste. The scales are fine and will come off with the slightest scrubbing of a brush.

SAUTÉED BUTTERFISH

8 butterfish (about 2 pounds)	2 tablespoons milk
Salt and freshly ground pepper, to taste	1½ cups cornmeal
2 eggs, beaten	Butter, for sautéing

1. Sprinkle fish on both sides with salt and pepper.
2. In a bowl, combine eggs and milk. Dip fish in egg mixture, then roll in cornmeal.
3. In a heavy frying pan, heat about 1 or 2 tablespoons butter. Add fish and sauté over moderate heat, 5 minutes on each side. Add more butter as needed to keep fish from sticking.
4. Serve immediately on a hot platter, with lemon wedges, and tartar sauce (Chapter 6).
Yield: 4 servings

Captain John Smith in 1614 visited New England and recorded in his journal: "What pleasure can be more than to recreate themselves before their owne doores, in their owne boates, upon the Sea, where man, woman, and childe, with a small hooke and line by angling, may take diverse sorts of excellent fish, at their pleasure?"

Drum

Members of the drum family (*Sciaenidae*) are noted, and named, for a drumming, purring, or croaking sound they make with their air bladders. All of the smaller drum are popular commercial fish, though gourmet cooks give them only a fair rating.

ATLANTIC CROAKER: Atlantic croaker (*Micropogon undulatus*) range from the Gulf of Mexico to New Jersey, but are most common south of the Carolinas. Lean, proteinaceous fish, croaker average one to three pounds. In the Pacific, **spotfin croaker** (*Roncador stearnsi*), averaging under a pound, are popular gamefish.

DRUM: **Black drum** (*Pogonias cromis*), the largest of the drum, average eight to 12 pounds, but can weigh up to 100 pounds. **Red drum** (*Sciaenops ocellata*), also known as **redfish** or **channel bass,** have firm, coarse-flaked flesh—as do black drum.

WEAKFISH: Weakfish (*Cynoscion regalis*), also called **sea trout** or **squeteague,** range from Cape Cod to the Gulf of Mexico. Called weakfish because their mouths are soft and will easily shed a hook, they fight well, if briefly, and will take natural bait or artificial lures. Averaging one pound, weakfish have lean, sweet flesh, and delicious roe, and were a dish often ordered by George Washington at New York's Fraunces Tavern. Weakfish should be kept iced as soon as they are caught to keep their flavor from fading. Relatives of weakfish with a more southern range and of comparable table quality are **spotted sea trout** (*Cynoscion nebulosus*).

WHITE SEA BASS: White sea bass (*Cynoscion nobilis*) are Pacific relatives of weakfish, ranging from California north into Canadian and Alaskan waters. Often taken by anglers with artificial bait, spin casting, trolling, or still fishing, white sea bass average 10 pounds, but may weigh over 50 pounds. Important commercial fish much sought after in summer and autumn by West Coast fish fanciers, white sea bass are firm fleshed and good to eat.

> *"Immediately around the Battery, and even from the Castle Garden bridge, good sport is frequently had with this fish. . . . It is said that the afternoon tides are the most favorable for taking the Squeteague, until a short time before sun-set, but that so soon as the peculiar drumming or croaking sound, which is ascribed to this fish, is heard, it is useless to fish longer, as he then ceases to bite."*
> —Frank Forester's Fish and Fishing of the United States and British Provinces of North America, 1864

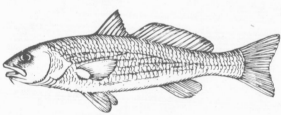

California Corbina

CALIFORNIA CORBINA: California corbina (*Menticirrhus undulatus*) are usually taken by surf fishing off the beaches of California. They are strong fighting fish that will take both natural and artificial lures, and commonly weigh from two to eight pounds. Corbina, protected gamefish, may not be taken or sold commercially. Delicious fish with close-grained white meat, corbina should be skinned and filleted.

CROAKER CAKES

1½ cups cooked, flaked croaker
¼ pound potatoes, peeled,
    cooked, and mashed
1 tablespoon butter
Salt and freshly ground pepper,
    to taste

¼ cup white sauce (Chapter 6)
    or beaten egg, to bind
1 egg, beaten
½ cup fine bread crumbs
Oil or butter, for frying

1. In a large saucepan, combine fish, potatoes, butter, salt, and pepper, and heat through. Remove from heat and add white sauce (or beaten egg) to bind. Spread the mixture on a large plate to cool, then divide into 8 cakes of equal size.
2. Dip cakes in beaten egg and then bread crumbs.
3. In a frying pan, heat enough oil (or butter) to fry cakes without sticking. Cook until golden brown and drain on paper toweling.
4. Serve with lemon wedges and garnish with parsley.

Yield: 4 servings

DRUM PIE

2 pounds drum fillets or steaks
6 to 12 shrimp, shelled and
    deveined (optional)
1 medium onion, finely chopped
3 tablespoons chopped fresh dill
3 tablespoons butter
3 tablespoons flour

2 cups fish stock (Chapter 6)
Salt and freshly ground pepper,
    to taste
¼ cup dry sherry
Dough for 1 9″ pie crust
1 egg yolk, beaten

1. Cut fish into pieces, removing any skin and bones.
2. Into a buttered baking dish, place fish, shrimp (if desired), onion, and dill. With a spoon, mound fish mixture so that it is higher in the center of the dish.
3. Preheat oven to 400° F.
4. Make a velouté: in a saucepan, melt butter, add flour, mixing with a wire whisk, and cook over low heat for 1 minute. Stirring constantly, gradually add fish stock and cook over medium heat until slightly thickened and smooth. Season with salt and pepper.
5. Add the sherry to the sauce and pour over the fish.
6. Roll out prepared, chilled pie dough. Lay on top of fish and crimp edges onto baking dish. Brush crust with beaten egg yolk.
7. Bake in a 400° F. oven for 15 minutes. Reduce heat to 350° F. and bake an additional 15 minutes.

Yield: 6 servings

"Florida possesses a coast line of about twelve hundred miles, of which greatly the larger half is washed by the Gulf of Mexico. . . . The most marvelous stories are told . . . of the hosts of fish, even to the stoppage of vessels that have sailed into shoals of them. . . . Here are the black-fish, white-fish, yellow bream, blue bream, silver bream, grouper, porgy, barracooter, trout, perch, eel, mullet, herring, flounder, gar, sheep-head, bass, grunt, yellow-tail, jew-fish, king-fish, pompino, amber-fish, angel-fish, red-snapper, drum, whiting, sturgeon, whipperee (whip-jack), skate, and one knows not how many more."

—Florida, Its Scenery,
Climate, and History,
Sidney Lanier

Massachusetts fishermen pose for a photograph (taken around 1870) in front of their fishing lodge on Cuttyhunk Island.

SEA TROUT AND AVOCADO CASSEROLE

1 pound sea trout fillets	3 tablespoons flour
1½ cups milk	2 teaspoons dry mustard
Salt and freshly ground pepper, to taste	1 teaspoon Worcestershire sauce
6 tablespoons butter	1 avocado
	½ cup slivered almonds

1. Preheat oven to 400° F.
2. In a large frying pan, poach fish in milk seasoned with salt and pepper. When fish is barely tender, remove to a shallow casserole. Reserve milk.
3. In a saucepan, melt butter, add flour and dry mustard, mixing with a whisk, and cook over low heat for 1 minute. Stirring constantly, gradually add reserved milk and Worcestershire sauce. Season with salt and pepper, if needed. Cook over medium heat until slightly thickened and smooth. Pour sauce over fish.
4. Peel and slice avocado and arrange slices on top of fish. Sprinkle with almonds.
5. Bake in a 400° F. oven for 15 to 20 minutes.

Yield: 4 servings

CALIFORNIA CORBINA IN WHITE WINE

2 pounds corbina fillets
Salt and freshly ground pepper,
  to taste
2 teaspoons lemon juice
¼ cup dry white wine
1½ tablespoons chopped fresh
  dill

3 tablespoons butter
1 tablespoon minced scallion or
  shallot
2 tablespoons flour
½ cup hot water

1. Preheat oven to 400° F.
2. Sprinkle fillets with salt, pepper, and lemon juice. Place in a
   buttered baking dish. Add wine and dill, cover and bake in a
   400° F. oven for 15 to 20 minutes. Remove to hot platter and
   keep warm.
3. In a frying pan, heat butter. Add scallion (or shallot) and
   sauté about 2 minutes. Add flour and blend in. Add water
   and stir to form a sauce. Cook over low heat, stirring until
   sauce thickens.
4. To serve, pour sauce over fillets and garnish with chopped
   parsley.
Yield: 4 to 6 servings

WHITE SEA BASS WITH OYSTER STUFFING

1 white sea bass (about 10 pounds), with head and tail
Salt and freshly ground pepper, to taste
1 cup soft bread crumbs
3 tablespoons butter, softened
2 tablespoons lemon juice
2 tablespoons chopped fresh parsley

1 dozen oysters, shucked and minced
1 egg yolk
Liquid from oysters
1 cup dry white wine
½ onion, finely chopped
1 teaspoon Cognac

1. Preheat oven to 425° F.
2. Wipe body cavity of fish and sprinkle lightly with salt and pepper, inside and out.
3. Make the stuffing: combine bread crumbs, butter, lemon juice, parsley, salt, and pepper. Add minced oysters and mix well. Add egg yolk and enough oyster liquid to hold mixture together.
4. Stuff fish beginning at tail end and sew up with heavy thread and large darning needle, or use skewers (Chapter 7).
5. Place stuffed fish in a buttered stove-to-oven casserole. Add ½ cup of the wine and all of the onion and bake in a 425° F. oven for 10 minutes. Baste with remaining ½ cup of wine. Lower temperature to 375° F. and continue baking for another 20 minutes.
6. Remove fish to a warmed serving platter. Place casserole on stove and cook at a simmer for 5 minutes to thicken sauce. Add Cognac at last moment. Garnish with chopped parsley and chives.

Yield: 4 servings

"See those clouds; how they hang! That's the greatest thing I have seen to-day. I thought, I might go a-fishing. That's the true industry for poets. It's the only trade I have learned. Come, let's along."

—Walden,
Henry David Thoreau

Porgy

Porgy (family *Sparidae*) are small, sheep-nosed fish—a dozen species of which are found in the Atlantic—that take their name from a Narraganset Indian word. Outside of America, porgy are known as **sea bream**. Usually taken with shrimp or small crabs, porgy put up a good brief fight, but are noted bait stealers. Although they are somewhat bony, porgy have firm, white flesh. **Jolthead porgy** (*Calamus bajonado*), **whitebone porgy** (*Calamus leucosteus*), and **red porgy** (*Pagrus sedecim*) are all good foodfish. **Scup** (*Stenotomus chrysops*) are more northern than the other porgy, ranging from the Carolinas to Cape Cod and are commonly taken at one pound. **Sheepshead** (*Archosargus probatocephalus*) occur as far north as Nova Scotia, but are most common from the Chesapeake to the Gulf of Mexico. Their skin is tough and should be removed before cooking.

SEA BREAM SUPREME

1 3-pound sea bream, with or without head and tail	1 onion, sliced
Salt, to taste	3 tomatoes, sliced
Hot paprika, to taste	1 green pepper, sliced
6 slices bacon	1 tablespoon flour
	½ cup sour cream

1. Preheat oven to 400° F.
2. Wipe body cavity of fish and sprinkle lightly with salt and paprika, inside and out. Make small slits diagonally across skin with a sharp knife and place bacon inside slits.
3. Lay fish in a well-buttered baking dish. Arrange onion, tomato, and pepper slices over it.
4. Bake in a 400° F. oven for 15 minutes. Blend flour and sour cream together and pour over fish and continue baking for another 15 minutes or so depending on thickness of fish (see Canadian fish cooking rule, Chapter 1).

Yield: 6 servings

SHEEPSHEAD PIE

5 tablespoons butter	1 teaspoon lemon juice
3 tablespoons chopped onion	Salt and freshly ground pepper, to taste
4 tomatoes, skinned, seeded, and chopped	½ cup water
1 clove garlic, finely chopped	1 teaspoon cornstarch
2 tablespoons chopped fresh parsley	2 cups cooked, flaked sheepshead
	1 cup flour

1. Preheat oven to 350° F.
2. In a frying pan, heat 1 tablespoon of the butter. Add onion and sauté until it just begins to soften. Add tomatoes and cook 3 more minutes.
3. Add garlic, 1 tablespoon of the parsley, and lemon juice. Season with salt and pepper. Boil for 5 minutes.
4. Mix water with cornstarch, add to sauce, and cook briefly, allowing to thicken.
5. Place fish in a buttered baking dish, cover with sauce, and stir to mix.
6. Cut the remaining 4 tablespoons of butter into flour until it forms crumbs the size of peas and add remaining parsley. Sprinkle mixture over fish.
7. Bake in a 350° F. oven for 15 minutes.

Yield: 4 to 6 servings

Variation: In place of crumb topping, cover with spoonfuls of biscuit dough and bake in a 450° F. oven for 10 to 12 minutes.

"Innumerable bands of fish are seen, some clothed in the most brilliant colors . . . inimical trout, and all the varieties of gilded, painted bream; the barbed catfish, dreaded stingray, skate, and flounder, spotted bass, sheepshead and ominous drum; all in their separate bands and communities, with free and unsuspicious intercourse performing their evolutions. There are no signs of enmity, no attempt to devour each other."

—William Bartram

SANDWICHED SCUP WITH ANCHOVIES

8 scup fillets (about 2 pounds)
Salt and freshly ground pepper,
  to taste
2 cups cooked rice
6 anchovy fillets, chopped
3 hard-boiled eggs, chopped

1 teaspoon chopped fresh
  parsley
2 egg yolks, beaten
½ cup soft bread crumbs
2 tablespoons butter
½ cup dry white wine or water

1. Preheat oven to 350° F.
2. Arrange 4 fillets on bottom of buttered baking dish. Season with salt and pepper.
3. Combine rice, anchovies, chopped eggs, parsley, and egg yolks. Spoon this mixture over the fillets and cover with remaining fillets.
4. Sprinkle with bread crumbs and dot with butter. Add wine (or water) to baking dish, and bake in a 350° F. oven for 25 minutes.

Yield: 4 to 6 servings

In New York harbor, the lean, hard men who put out after bluefish were notorious for being just as strong, wild, and quick tempered as the fish they sought—a reputation that no doubt pleased this jaunty crew.

Bluefish

Bluefish (*Pomatomus saltatrix*) are the only members of their family (*Pomatomidae*). Atlantic fish, they winter off Florida and spend the summer off Massachusetts. But the bluefish population historically has fluctuated, with bluefish all but disappearing for several years, then reappearing in great numbers. Hard-fighting fish that, when hungry, will take any lure presented, bluefish are noted for being viciously aggressive with prominent razor-sharp teeth. Baby bluefish are called **snappers** for the noise their teeth make clacking together. Bluefish, which are commonly caught at 10 pounds, have soft-textured flesh with a distinctive, natural smoky taste.

BROILED BLUEFISH

2 bluefish fillets (about 1½ pounds)
3 tablespoons mayonnaise

1 teaspoon prepared mustard
Salt and cayenne, to taste
1 medium tomato, sliced

1. Preheat oven to 350° F.
2. Place fillets in an ovenproof pan. Combine mayonnaise and mustard and season with salt and cayenne. Spread mixture evenly over fillets.
3. Bake in a 350° F. oven for 6 minutes.
4. Remove and place tomato slices on top of fillets. Place under broiler for 4 minutes.

Yield: 4 servings

RED, WHITE, AND BLUEFISH

2 tablespoons oil
2 medium onions, finely chopped
1 clove garlic, crushed
1 pound tomatoes, skinned and seeded

2 tablespoons chopped fresh parsley
Salt and freshly ground pepper, to taste
1½ pounds bluefish fillets

1. Preheat oven to 350° F.
2. In a frying pan, heat the oil, add the onions and garlic and sauté until they just begin to soften.
3. Add tomatoes, parsley, salt, and pepper, and remove from heat.
4. Place fish in a buttered baking dish. Cover with the sauce and bake in a 350° F. oven for 20 minutes.

Yield: 4 servings

"Daniel Webster, in one of his letters describing blue-fishing off Martha's Vineyard, referring to those smooth places, which fishermen and sailors call 'slicks,' says: 'We met with them yesterday, and our boatman made for them, whenever discovered. He said they were caused by the blue-fish chopping up their prey. That is to say, those voracious fellows get into a school of menhaden, which are too large to swallow whole, and they bite them into pieces to suit their tastes. And the oil from this butchery, rising to the surface, makes the slick.'"

—Cape Cod,
Henry David Thoreau

Tilefish

Common tilefish (*Lopholatilus chamaeleonticeps*) are the only members of their family (*Branchiostegidae*) of any culinary significance. They are deepwater fish, ranging from the northern Carolinas to Cape Cod. Long important as foodfish, they suddenly disappeared just before the turn of this century, and

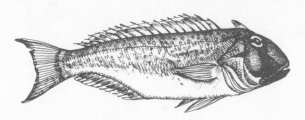

Tilefish

have only recently reappeared in great numbers. Tilefish sometimes weigh 20 to 30 pounds, but are commonly marketed in smaller sizes, six to eight pounds. Their flesh is firm and similar in taste, some say, to lobster.

"FRESH FISH BALLS
With a silver fork pick remnants of cooked fish into bits and sprinkle with salt and pepper. Pass through a vegetable ricer a few hot, boiled potatoes; to those add a little fish sauce, if at hand, or cream or butter, also salt and pepper, and beat as for mashed potato. To the fish add just enough of the hot potato to hold the fish together. Shape the mixture into balls; roll these in fine crumbs, then cover them with an egg, beaten and diluted with its bulk of milk or water, and again roll them in crumbs. Fry in deep fat; serve with Philadelphia relish or tomato catsup."

—Cooking For Two, A Handbook For Young Housekeepers, *1916*

ALICE'S TILEFISH QUENELLES

1½ pounds tilefish fillets	**2 eggs**
Salt and freshly ground pepper,	**¼ teaspoon nutmeg**
to taste	**1½ cups heavy cream**

1. Cut fish into cubes and place in blender or food processor. Add salt and pepper and grind until just barely smooth. This may have to be done in two batches.
2. Add eggs and blend. Add nutmeg. Gradually add cream, continuing to blend. Scrape mixture from sides to prevent lumps. Chill for at least 45 minutes.
3. Form quenelles by using two large tablespoons to make elongated egg shapes, and place in a large, buttered frying pan big enough to hold 24 or so quenelles without touching. Use two frying pans if necessary.

Note: Rinse spoons in hot water after making each quenelle. Keeping the spoons smooth and clean will make it easier to form quenelles.

4. In a large saucepan, bring well salted water to a boil, and pour gently over quenelles, almost, but not quite, covering them. Simmer for 3 to 4 minutes, turn the quenelles and simmer for a bare 1 minute longer.

5. Using a slotted spoon, remove quenelles to a warmed serving dish and top with warm shrimp sauce (Chapter 6).
Yield: 24 quenelles

BAKED TILEFISH

½ cup olive oil	¼ teaspoon paprika
¼ cup tomato puree	2 tablespoons lemon juice
1½ cups water	½ teaspoon chopped fresh
2 onions, thinly sliced	parsley
¼ cup chopped celery	Salt and freshly ground pepper,
3 carrots, thinly sliced	to taste
2 cloves garlic, minced	2 pounds tilefish fillets or steaks

1. Preheat oven to 375° F.
2. In a frying pan, heat 1 tablespoon of the olive oil. Add rest of olive oil, tomato puree, water, onions, celery, carrots, garlic, paprika, lemon juice, and parsley. Cover and simmer for 20 minutes, stirring occasionally. Season with salt and pepper.
3. Place fish in well-buttered baking dish, cover with sauce, and bake in a 375° F. oven for 15 minutes.
Yield: 6 servings

Sablefish

Members of the *Anoplopomatidae* family, sablefish (*Anoplopoma fimbria*) range from Alaska to southern California and grow to 3 feet and weigh 40 pounds. Although they are often called **black cod** or **black Alaskan cod,** sablefish, unlike cod, are very oily. They are delicious when smoked.

SMOKED PACIFIC SABLE

1 2-pound piece smoked sable*	1 tablespoon butter
1 onion, finely chopped	1 cup milk (approximately)

1. Preheat oven to 325° F.
2. Place sable in a well-buttered baking dish. Sprinkle with onion and dot with butter. Add milk to just cover fish, to protect it from drying out.
3. Bake in a 325° F. oven for 40 to 45 minutes.
4. Serve with egg-and-shrimp sauce (Chapter 6).
Yield: 4 servings

*See Chapter 7 for smoking techniques.

"There is no way of preparing salt fish for breakfast, so nice as to roll it up in little balls, after it is mixed with mashed potatoes; dip it into an egg, and fry it brown."
—The American Frugal Housewife, *Mrs. Child*

Snook

Snook (*Centropomus undecimalis*), sometimes called **robalo,** are warmwater inshore fish rarely found north of central Florida. Now classed as gamefish, they are no longer caught and sold commercially. Snook will take artificial or natural baits when they are feeding and when they strike give the angler a sudden thrill. Snook average six pounds, but have been netted weighing over 60 pounds. Their flesh is white, finely textured, and flavorful (snook have occasionally been marketed as **red snapper**), with the smaller snook—two to five pounds—tasting best. Snook should be skinned before cooking.

SNOOK AND SUMMER SQUASH

4 cups sliced summer squash	2 cups cooked, flaked snook
2 eggs	1 teaspoon chervil
2 tablespoons butter	2 tablespoons chopped fresh dill
4 tablespoons sour cream	1/3 cup finely chopped celery
1½ teaspoons salt	2 tomatoes, thinly sliced
½ teaspoon freshly ground pepper	1 cup soft bread crumbs

1. Preheat oven to 350° F.
2. Steam squash, drain and mash along with eggs, 1 tablespoon of the butter, sour cream, salt, and pepper.
3. In a large bowl, combine fish, squash mixture, chervil, dill, and celery, and mix together until blended. Turn mixture into a buttered 2-quart baking dish. Top with tomato slices.
4. Sprinkle bread crumbs on top of casserole and dot with remaining tablespoon of butter. Bake in a 350° F. oven for 25 minutes.

Yield: 6 servings

Rockfish

There are a dozen or so rockfish (family *Scorpaenidae*) of some interest to the cook, the most prominent of which are **ocean perch** (*Sebastes marinus*)—also called **redfish** because they turn brilliant red during spawning. The only rockfish in the Atlantic, ocean perch range from Cape Cod to Labrador, and weigh about 10 pounds. Taken in the millions of pounds by commercial trawlers, ocean perch are marketed as fish sticks or frozen fillets under a number of names, including **sea perch, Norwegian haddock,** and **rosefish.** Other rockfish of interest are **bocaccio** (*Sebastes paucispinis*)—found from San Diego to Alaska and weighing up to 20 pounds—and **chilipepper** (*Sebastes goodei*), found where bocaccio are.

"You might make a curious list of articles which fishes have swallowed—. . . open clasp-knives, and bright tin snuff-boxes, not knowing what was in them,—and jugs, and jewels, and Jonah. The other day I came across the following scrap in a newspaper. 'A RELIGIOUS FISH.—A short time ago, mine host Stewart, of the Denton, Hotel, purchased a rock-fish, weighing about sixty pounds. On opening it, he found in it a certificate of membership of the M. E. Church. . . . The paper was, of course, in a crumpled and wet condition, but on exposing it to the sun, and ironing the kinks out of it, it became quite legible.—Denton (Md.) Journal.'"

—Cape Cod,
Henry David Thoreau

OCEAN PERCH IN RED WINE

1 sprig fresh parsley	½ cup dry red wine
1 onion, chopped	1 cup fish stock (Chapter 6) or
4 cloves	water
½ bay leaf	1½ tablespoons flour
Salt and freshly ground pepper, to taste	4 tablespoons butter
8 ocean perch fillets (about 2 pounds)	

1. Into a large frying pan, place parsley, onion, cloves, bay leaf, and pepper, to taste.
2. Season the fish with salt, cut each fillet in half and lay on top of the seasonings in the pan. Add red wine and stock (or water), cover the pan and simmer for 10 minutes.
3. With a slotted spatula, remove fish to a warmed serving platter and keep warm. Strain the poaching liquid into a saucepan and reduce the liquid by half over high heat. Discard spices.
4. Rub flour and butter together, add this to the reduced liquid and simmer, stirring constantly, for 3 minutes, until thickened.
5. Remove sauce from heat. Season to taste and pour over fish.

Yield: 4 servings

Pompano & Jack

A large family of warmwater fish, *Carangidae* include jack, amberjack, yellowtail, and—the culinary stars of the group—pompano.

"It was an amberjack, and twice as large as any I had ever seen before. As I drew up the captain's snapper this amberjack came to the surface, and I certainly yelled. One hundred and fifty pounds seemed a conservative estimate of its weight. It had a tail over a foot broad, and eyes as large as a teacup."
—Tales of Fishing Virgin Seas, Zane Grey

POMPANO: Florida pompano (*Trachinotus carolinus*), found in some abundance from the Gulf of Mexico to the Carolinas, are on the small side, averaging 1½ to 3½ pounds, with five pounds not unknown. Their firm, delicate, white flesh makes them a gourmet prize. Close relatives to pompano are the larger **permit** (*Trachinotus falcatus*)—averaging nine pounds—whose range is the same as pompano. Permit, like pompano, are excellent fighting fish. Small permit are best, but large permit makes delicious chowder. Pacific relatives of Florida pompano are **paloma pompano** (*Trachinotus paitensis*), found as far north as central California.

JACK **Yellow jack** (*Caranx bartholomaei*), most commonly found in southern Florida, are small jack with a sweet, white, delicious flesh. **Yellowtail** (*Seriola dorsalis*) range from southern California to Washington state. Usually taken by casting or trolling, yellowtail are hard-fighting, deep diving fish, averaging 10 pounds but occasionally weighing up to 50. Yellowtail are important commercial fish with good flavor. **Rainbow runner** (*Elagatis bipinnulata*) are swift swimming jack, averaging four pounds, with netted weights of up to 40 pounds. One of the better flavored jack, rainbow runner have flaky, whitish flesh. **Amberjack** (*Seriola dumerili*), the largest of the jack, range from the Gulf of Mexico to Massachusetts. Sometimes netted, like the other jack, these fish are hard fighters when taken with rod and reel. Record amberjack may weigh over 150 pounds but small amberjack weighing 10 to 15 pounds are the most common and most flavorful. When caught, amberjack (in fact, all large jack) should be bled to improve their flavor and are best if skinned before cooking. In addition, amberjack flesh has strongly flavored red muscle, which should be removed.

POMPANO FLORENTINE

1½ pounds pompano fillets	1 tablespoon butter
1 cup dry white wine	1 tablespoon flour
½ cup water	½ cup shredded Gruyère or
2 slices lemon	Parmesan cheese
1 pound spinach	

1. Place fillets in fish poacher or frying pan and add ½ cup of the wine, water, and lemon slices and poach for 5 minutes. Drain, reserving poaching liquid, and cool.
2. Wash spinach and steam it in a large pan, about 5 minutes, using the wash water left on spinach leaves as moisture enough to prevent burning. Drain and chop coarsely. Set aside.
3. Preheat oven to 350° F.
4. Reduce reserved court bouillon by one-third by quick boiling.
5. In a saucepan, melt butter, add flour, mixing with a wire whisk, and cook over low heat for 1 minute. Stirring constantly, add reduced poaching liquid, the remaining ½

cup of wine, and cheese. Cook sauce over medium heat until slightly thickened and smooth.

6. Place spinach in bottom of buttered baking dish, lay in fish, and cover with sauce. Bake in a 350° F. oven for 10 minutes.

Yield: 4 servings

Variation: Pour a layer of sauce on bottom of baking dish, arrange fish on top, and cover with more sauce. Sprinkle with more grated cheese and brown under broiler.

Florida's Gulf Stream waters have long provided sports fishermen with both quantity and variety, as in this mixed catch taken around Indian River.

PINEAPPLE AMBERJACK

4 amberjack fillets (about ¾ pound each)
Salt and freshly ground pepper, to taste
2 tablespoons lemon juice
Flour, for dredging
2 eggs, beaten

Oil, for sautéing
2 tablespoons butter
4 tablespoons sliced almonds
½ fresh pineapple, trimmed and cut into thin strips
¼ cup dry white wine

1. Season fish with salt, pepper, and lemon juice.
2. Dredge fish in flour, then in beaten eggs.
3. In a frying pan, heat a thin layer of oil. Sauté fish 5 minutes on one side and 3 minutes on reverse. With a slotted spatula, remove fish to serving platter and keep warm in a low oven. Discard oil.
4. In the frying pan, heat butter, add almonds and pineapple strips and sauté gently until golden brown. Add wine. To serve, pour sauce over fish.

Yield: 4 servings

Directions for making a
CHOUDER

First lay some Onions to keep the Pork from burning,
Because in Chouder there can be no turning;
Then lay some Pork in Slices very thin,
Thus you in Chouder always must begin.
Next lay some Fish cut cross-ways very nice
Then season well with Pepper, Salt and Spice;
Parsley, Sweet-Marjoram, Savory and Thyme,
Then Biscuit next which must be soak'd some Time.
Thus your Foundation laid, you will be able
To raise a Chouder, high as Tower of Babel;
For by repeating o're the Same again,
You may make Chouder for a thousand Men.
Last Bottle of Claret, with Water eno' to smother 'em,
You'l have a Mess which some call Omnium gather 'em.
—The Boston Evening Post, September 23, 1751

YELLOWTAIL OVEN CHOWDER

2 pounds yellowtail fillets
4 potatoes, peeled and sliced
3 onions, sliced
1 clove garlic, crushed
2 tablespoons chopped celery leaves
1 bay leaf
4 whole cloves or to taste
¼ teaspoon dill seed

2½ teaspoons salt
¼ teaspoon freshly ground pepper
½ cup (1 stick) butter
½ cup dry white wine or vermouth
½ cup boiling water
2 cups light cream

1. Place all ingredients except cream in a large casserole. Cover and bake in a 375° F. oven for 1 hour.
2. Heat cream to scalding and add to chowder. Stir to blend, and garnish with dill.

Yield: 8 to 10 servings

PUFFED PERMIT

2 pounds permit fillets
Salt and freshly ground pepper, to taste
Lemon juice, to taste

½ cup tartar sauce (Chapter 6)
1 teaspoon capers
Dash of paprika
2 egg whites

1. Place fillets skin side down on a buttered broiler pan. Season with salt and pepper and sprinkle with lemon juice.

2. Combine tartar sauce, capers, and paprika. Beat egg whites until stiff and fold into tartar sauce mixture.
3. Place fish under broiler and broil about 3 minutes. When fillets begin to get flaky, spread sauce over them. Broil until covering becomes puffed and brown.
4. Serve with additional tartar sauce and lemon wedges.

Yield: 4 servings

Snapper

The most well known of the snapper family (*Lutjanidae*), **red snapper** (*Lutjanus campechanus*) rival pompano in popularity. Commonly taken at five pounds, some weigh up to 30 pounds. **Yellowtail snapper** (*Ocyurus chrysurus*) are smaller, rarely weighing more than two to three pounds. Traditionally these fish are difficult to keep fresh and have earned their reputation as a breakfast fish because they are usually caught at night and bought at market early in the morning. Other snapper of culinary interest are **silk snapper, vermillion snapper, mutton snapper,** and **schoolmaster snapper.** All snapper should be scaled as soon as possible. They are bony but the skeleton is easily removed, especially after cooking.

SAVANNAH SNAPPER

1 4- or 5-pound red snapper, without head and tail	1 cup sour cream
½ cup lemon juice (approximately)	½ teaspoon dry mustard
Salt and freshly ground pepper, to taste	1 tablespoon Worcestershire sauce
	½ cup soft bread crumbs

1. Preheat oven to 350° F.
2. Cut fish in half lengthwise, butterfly style, and place halves skin side down on a large buttered sheet of aluminum foil. Brush with lemon juice, and season with salt and pepper. Fold the edges of foil to seal securely and bake in a 350° F. oven for 30 minutes.
3. While fish is baking, combine sour cream, mustard, Worcestershire sauce, and 1 tablespoon of the lemon juice.
4. Remove fish from oven, open foil, spread fish evenly with sauce and sprinkle with bread crumbs.
5. Leaving foil open, return to oven for about 15 minutes, or until bread crumbs are brown and sauce is thoroughly warmed.

Yield: 6 servings

"The result was a foaming maelstrom, and in the boiling water below shone a great crimson patch a hundred feet long and half as wide. Fish! Redsnapper! There were thousands of them. And when we ran into that current the crimson patch disintegrated and appeared to string out after our boats. The redsnapper followed us. Each angler was playing a fish at the same time, and that, while hundreds of great red-golden fish, hungry and fierce, almost charged the boats."

—Tales of Fishing Virgin Seas, Zane Grey

RED SNAPPER MOLD

1 red snapper (about 2 pounds)   3 eggs, separated
2 cups court bouillon (Chapter 6) 1 teaspoon salt
4 tablespoons butter   ¼ teaspoon cayenne
1 cup cream

1. Poach fish in court bouillon for 10 minutes. Drain fish. Skin and remove all bones.
2. Preheat oven to 350° F.
3. In a food processor or electric blender chop fish until light. Add butter, cream, egg yolks, salt, and cayenne and mix until well blended.
4. Beat egg whites until stiff and fold into fish mixture.
5. Pour fish mixture into a buttered 2-quart mold. Cover with aluminum foil, place mold in pan of water and bake in a 350° F. oven for 30 minutes, until set.
6. Serve with mushroom sauce (Chapter 6).

Yield: 4 servings

Rack upon rack of the Pacific smelt called eulachon dry in a Tsimshian village near Fishery Bay in British Columbia.

Smelt

Smelt (family *Osmeridae*) are popular table fish that live primarily in saltwater and spawn in fresh water; some are landlocked (see page 95) and some strictly marine. **American** or **rainbow smelt** (*Osmerus mordax*), the most widely distributed of the nine North American species, range from Florida north to the St. Lawrence (as well as in inland lakes). They grow to just under a pound, and are most often dipnetted out of fresh water as they run upstream to spawn, or are taken through the ice in winter. **Eulachon** (*Thaleichthys pacificus*), or **hooligan fish** as they are sometimes called in Alaska, run in great numbers in Northwest Coast rivers. The Indians used these extremely oily fish as candles (sometimes with a cedar wick drawn through them), giving rise to the name **candlefish.** Indians also prized the fish's oil as a condiment. No feast was considered complete without a serving of smoked or dried salmon, or other food, topped with eulachon oil.

Lewis and Clark were introduced to the Pacific smelt known as eulachon (or candlefish) by Comowool, chief of the Clatsop: "The Chief and his party had brought . . . a species of small fish which . . . are taken in great quantities in the Columbia R. . . . by means of skimming or scooping nets . . . I find them best when cooked in Indian stile, which is by roasting a number of them together on a wooden spit without any previous preparation whatever, they are so fat they require no additional sauce, and I think them superior to any fish I ever tasted, even more delicate and lussious than the white fish of the lakes which have heretofore formed my standart of excellence among fishes."

SIMPLE SMELT PIE

4 tablespoons butter
1 cup cooked, flaked smelt
1 cup mashed potatoes
1 egg, beaten
Salt and freshly ground pepper, to taste

¼ cup dry sherry (optional)
4 tablespoons dried bread crumbs

1. Preheat oven to 375° F.
2. In a stove-to-oven casserole, melt 2 tablespoons of the butter. Add fish, mashed potatoes, and egg. Season well with salt and pepper. Add sherry (if desired).
3. Cover with bread crumbs and dot with remaining 2 tablespoons of butter.
4. Bake in a 375° F. oven for 20 minutes, or until golden brown.

Yield: 2 servings

Herring

Members of the herring family (*Clupeidae*) are generally small (few species exceed 10 pounds), silvery fish including herring, sardines, and shad.

HERRING: Atlantic herring (*Clupea harengus*) swim in schools of countless billions from the Carolinas to Labrador. **Pacific herring** (*Clupea harengus pallasi*) are found from San

Diego north. **Alewives,** or **spring herring** (*Alosa pseudoharengus*), are a small Atlantic Coast species that spawn in freshwater streams. Herring grow to 1½ pounds, but are commonly taken in smaller sizes. Fresh herring and their roe are delicious, but most herring are marketed in cured form, either pickled, salted, or smoked (as **kippers**). On the Northwest coast of America, Indians steam or eat dried a delicacy they call *gow*, which is herring roe attached by the fish to seaweed.

SHAD: Shad are anadromous (leaving saltwater to spawn in fresh water) members of the herring family with several species, the most important of which is the **American shad** (*Alosa sapidissima*). Found on both coasts, from Florida to the St. Lawrence River in the East and in the West from central California to Alaska, the shad population has steadily decreased as their spawning rivers have become more polluted. Shad will take an artificial fly when properly presented and fight with the vigor of a lively trout. American shad, the largest of the herring, average three pounds, but can grow to 12 pounds and up to two feet in length. Shad flesh is delicate in texture and taste, but must be carefully boned. And shad roe is a springtime treat and a gourmet prize.

SARDINES: Though there are several members of the herring family that are true sardines, none of them is of any commercial importance. **Pacific sardines,** once abundant, have been heavily overfished and are now nearly extinct. In the marketplace, however, the term **sardine** is used to describe any of several members of the herring family when they are very small.

Eighteenth-century Tidewater aristocrat William Byrd II marveled at Virginia's piscine wealth: "Herring are not as large as the European ones, but better and more delicious. . . . If one prepares them with vinegar and olive oil, they then taste like anchovies or sardines. . . . When they spawn, all streams and waters are completely filled with them, and one might believe, when he sees such terrible amounts of them, that there was as great a supply of herring as there is water. In a word, it is unbelievable, indeed, indescribable, as also incomprehensible, what quantity is found there. One must behold oneself."

HERRING IN ALE

3 onions, finely chopped	Pinch of saffron
2 cups ale	4 fresh herring (½ pound each),
2 tablespoons raisins	filleted
1 teaspoon dry mustard	2 tablespoons fine bread crumbs

1. Preheat oven to 350° F.
2. In a saucepan, cook onions in 1 cup of the ale for 10 minutes. Add remaining cup of ale, raisins, mustard, and saffron and remove from heat.
3. Place fillets in a buttered casserole. Pour sauce over them and bake in a 350° F. oven for 30 minutes.
4. To serve, remove fish to a warmed serving platter. Thicken sauce with bread crumbs and pour over fish.

Yield: 4 servings

MARINATED HERRING

4 fresh herring (about 8″ each)	2 leaves chopped fresh sage
Flour seasoned with salt and freshly ground pepper, for dredging	Sprig of fresh rosemary
	1 bay leaf
	4 peppercorns
Olive oil, for sautéing	1 to 2 chilies (optional)
1 medium onion, thinly sliced	2 tablespoons red wine vinegar
1 clove garlic, crushed	5 tablespoons water

1. Clean fish through gills, keeping fish whole (Chapter 7). Dredge fish in seasoned flour and sauté in about 1 tablespoon olive oil (or just enough to keep fish from sticking) for 5 minutes on each side. Place fish side by side in a deep, flat, non-metallic dish.
2. In a frying pan, heat another tablespoon of olive oil and sauté onion for 10 minutes. Add remaining ingredients and heat through.
3. Pour the mixture, while still hot, over the fish. Marinate for 12 hours in a cool place. Turn herring and marinate for another 12 hours.
4. Remove garlic. Serve each fish with a spoonful of marinade.

Yield: 4 servings

SHAD PIE

4 tablespoons butter	⅓ cup grated Parmesan cheese
3 tablespoons flour	1½ teaspoons dry mustard
2 cups milk	3 hard-boiled eggs, chopped
Salt and freshly ground pepper, to taste	½ cup soft bread crumbs
2 cups cooked and carefully boned shad	

1. Preheat oven to 350° F.
2. Make a white sauce: in a saucepan, melt 3 tablespoons of the butter, add flour, mixing with a wire whisk, and cook over low heat for 1 minute. Stirring constantly, gradually add milk and cook over medium heat until slightly thickened and smooth. Season with salt and pepper.
3. Add fish, cheese, mustard, and eggs. Place mixture in a buttered baking dish. Sprinkle bread crumbs over the mixture. Dot with remaining tablespoon of butter.
5. Bake in a 350° F. oven for 25 to 30 minutes.

Yield: 4 to 6 servings

Receipt for Roasted Shad
Split your fish down the back after he is cleaned and washed, nail the halves on shingles or short board; stick them erect in the sand round a large fire; as soon as they are well-browned, serve on whatever you have got; eat with cold butter, black pepper, salt, and a good appetite."

—Frank Forester's Fish and Fishing of the United States and British Provinces of North America, 1864

MOUNT VERNON SHAD ROE

1 double sac shad roe
4 tablespoons lemon juice
2 tablespoons butter
Salt and freshly ground pepper, to taste
½ teaspoon chopped fresh parsley

½ teaspoon chopped fresh chervil
½ teaspoon chopped fresh chives (optional)

1. With the sharp tip of a knife, gently prick the outer membrane of the roe in 3 or 4 places to prevent bursting.
2. Place the roe in a pan and cover with boiling water mixed with 2 tablespoons of the lemon juice. Simmer briefly, about 3 to 7 minutes depending on size. Drain and discard poaching liquid.
3. In a frying pan, heat butter and sauté shad roe briefly, turning once to brown on both sides. Season with salt and pepper. Remove roe to a warmed serving platter and keep warm.
4. To the drippings in the frying pan, add remaining 2 tablespoons of the lemon juice, parsley, chervil, and chives (if desired). Stir to mix and warm. Pour the butter sauce over the roe and serve.

Yield: 2 servings

As new master of Mount Vernon, George Washington wrote, in 1759: "A river [the Potomac] well-stocked with various kinds of fish at all seasons of the year, and in the spring with shad, herrings, bass, carp, perch, sturgeon, etc., in great abundance. The borders of the estate are washed by more than ten miles of tidewater, the whole shore, in fact, is one entire fishery." Washington did in fact profit from the Potomac's marine life, setting out nets every spring to capture shad and herring on their way upstream to spawn.

KIPPER MOUSSE

2 tablespoons butter
2 tablespoons flour
1 cup milk
2 eggs, separated
2 teaspoons lemon juice

¼ teaspoon nutmeg
3 tablespoons water
1 envelope unflavored gelatin
2 cups flaked kippers
⅔ cup mayonnaise

1. Make a white sauce: in a saucepan, melt butter, add flour, mixing with a wire whisk, and cook over low heat for 1 minute. Stirring constantly, gradually add milk and cook over medium heat until slightly thickened and smooth. Remove from heat.
2. Whip the yolks with a whisk. Pour a small amount of the hot white sauce into the beaten yolks and stir, then return the yolk mixture to the white sauce and mix well. Add the lemon juice and nutmeg, and mix.
3. Put the water in a small saucepan and sprinkle gelatin into the water. Cook over low heat, stirring, until gelatin dissolves. Stir gelatin into sauce mixture.
4. Add the flaked fish and mayonnaise, and mix. Allow to set for a few minutes.

5. Whip the egg whites until stiff. Fold into the fish mixture. Pour the mixture into a lightly-oiled, shallow, 1-quart mold. Refrigerate and allow to set for several hours.
6. Turn out onto a serving dish, surround with lettuce leaves, and garnish with stuffed olives and tomato slices.

Yield: 8 servings

By the turn of the century, alewives still ran so tightly packed that their spawning rivers turned silver with their flashing sides. Here, at Mattapoisett, Massachusetts, a group of well-dressed women have turned out to watch alewife dipnetters at work.

SARDINE PÂTÉ

1 cup (2 sticks) butter
8 ounces canned sardines, skinned and chopped
¼ cup minced celery
¼ cup minced black olives

3 hard-boiled eggs, finely chopped
Dash of freshly ground pepper
¼ cup lemon juice

1. Cream butter until light and fluffy.
2. Add sardines, celery, olives, eggs, pepper, and lemon juice to butter. Mix thoroughly. Chill.

Yield: 2 cups

Whitebait

Whitebait is not a scientific fish category but a popular generic term for any of a number of juvenile saltwater fish, such as **herring, anchovies,** and **silversides.** One of the more well-known sources of whitebait is a silverside called a **grunion.** On the famous moonlight grunion runs in California, fishermen work by flashlight to load their buckets with these fish, which swarm by the millions to spawn in the wet sand. Whitebait—a traditional favorite in England—are served whole, sautéed, or deep-fried.

WHITEBAIT DEEP-FRIED

1 pound whitebait   Oil, for deep-frying
Flour seasoned with salt and
  freshly ground pepper, for
  dredging

1. Leave whitebait whole. Rinse and dry with paper toweling.
2. Place seasoned flour on a large plate or in a paper bag. Roll or shake whitebait in the flour, coating thoroughly.
3. In a large deep pan, heat enough oil for deep-frying, over moderate heat, until it reaches 360° F. (or until a cube of bread turns golden in 45 seconds). A handful at a time, carefully lower the small fish into the oil and fry them for 2 to 3 minutes, until they turn light brown and crisp. Occasionally shake the pan gently to prevent fish from sticking together.
4. With a slotted spoon, remove whitebait from the oil and drain on paper toweling. Keep hot while frying remaining fish.
5. When all fish are cooked, serve on a warm serving platter with lemon wedges.

Yield: 4 servings

"It is no mean sport to stand upon the old worm-eaten, weather-stained bridge, and wield the long rod, playing your allurement over the water to the music of the rushing current and the steady clack of the mill-wheel, and see one after another of the green-backed, silvery snappers [mackerel] dart from under the accumulated froth, chase and swallow your bait, and no slight satisfaction to observe the increasing number in your basket, and think of how your friends will enjoy their supper that night."

—The Game Fish of the Northern States and British Provinces, *1884*

Mackerel & Tuna

The fast-moving, predatory members of the *Scombridae* family are firm-fleshed and delicious foodfish as well as much sought after gamefish.

MACKEREL: Atlantic mackerel (*Scomber scombrus*) range the coastline from Canada to the Carolinas. Sports fishermen usually troll for these hardy fighting fish with feathered lures or spoons. They average one pound and their flesh has a strong, distinctive flavor, which is much enhanced by lemon juice. **Kingfish** or **king mackerel** (*Scomberomorus cavalla*) range from the Gulf of Mexico almost to New England. These frantic gamefish, with an average weight of six to 16 pounds, will take a number of different feathered lures and spoons and put up a spectacular fight. Their firm, white flesh has a stronger, oilier flavor than most other mackerel, which can be reduced by marinating in lime juice for an hour before cooking. Less oily and more delicately flavored are **Spanish mackerel** (*Scomberomorus maculatus*), which range as far north as Chesapeake Bay. Spanish mackerel average under two pounds, but can weigh as much as 15 to 20 pounds. Another more delicately flavored species is **cero** (*Scomberomorus regalis*), found from Cape Cod south and weighing an average five to 10 pounds. In general, mackerel are considered oily fish, which means they are best eaten absolutely fresh; but this same oiliness makes mackerel well suited to smoking. Some have described the more reasonably priced smoked mackerel as poor man's smoked salmon.

Wahoo

WAHOO: **Wahoo** (*Acanthocybium solanderi*), considered one of the most delicious ocean fish, are found off southern California and around Hawaii where they are locally known as **ono.** When feeding, wahoo will take natural baits or artificial lures and, when hooked, leap like salmon, giving the sports fisherman a challenging and exciting fight. Wahoo average 12 to 24 pounds, but occasionally weigh up to 140. Wahoo have lean, white, finely flaked flesh.

TUNA: Tuna, the largest of the *Scombridae*, have long been considered one of the sea's most treasured prizes, for both sports and commercial fishermen. Unfortunately, heavy overfishing by foreign fishing fleets has threatened the tuna's future. Sports fishermen take tuna—extremely hardfighting fish—by trolling with live bait, feathered lures, or jigs. The smaller tuna (those under 100 pounds) swim in schools, but larger tuna are often solitary. **Bluefin tuna** (*Thunnus thynnus*) summer in the cold waters off Nova Scotia and winter in the warmer waters of Florida and farther south. The largest of the tuna, bluefin are commonly caught weighing 300 pounds, but the record taken on

"An instant later I had the same kind of a strike, and let the fish run a few yards before I hooked him. . . . This fish got slack line on me several times, making me incline to the conviction that I had hooked a wahoo. But I certainly never had hold of a wahoo as heavy as this. I was using heavy tackle and worked my limit on him. He came in stubbornly, then suddenly shot for the boat. I knew what that meant. Reeling frantically, I took up the slack line, and presently saw a flash in the blue water. The next instant I had a perfect view of a huge wahoo, fully six feet long, round as a telegraph pole, barred in silver across his green-purple side."

—Tales of Fishing Virgin Seas, Zane Grey

rod and reel is 1,120 pounds. Their somewhat strongly-flavored, dark meat should be soaked in a salt brine before cooking. **Yellowfin tuna** (*Thunnus albacares*), the mainstay of the West Coast tuna fishing industry, spend much of their time in the tropics but in the East come as far north as Cape Cod in the summer months. They average 12 to 24 pounds, with 80-pounders fairly common and a record weight of over 300 pounds. Yellowfin have firm, rich flesh that is sold in cans as "light meat" tuna. **Albacore tuna** (*Thunnus alalunga*) are found primarily in the Pacific, migrating between Japan and North America, where they remain from July until early November. Splendid gamefish, albacore commonly weigh eight to 12 pounds, with a record netting of over 80 pounds. Albacore are the only tuna marketed in cans as "white meat" tuna, but are rarely available fresh. **Blackfin tuna** (*Thunnus atlanticus*) range as far north as Cape Cod and are often taken off Florida. They average six to 10 pounds, but can weigh up to 50 or 60 pounds. They have firm, light-colored flesh, but are rarely sold commercially in North America.

SKIPJACK TUNA: Skipjack tuna (*Euthynnus pelamis*)—which are not true tuna, but belong to the same family—got their name from their habit of skipping over the water in pursuit of prey. Skipjack tuna are southern Atlantic fish but in the summer can range as far north as Massachusetts. Like their close relatives, **little tunny** (*Euthynnus alletteratus*) and **black skipjack** (*Euthynnus lineatus*), skipjack tuna have fairly strong flavored flesh that should be brined before cooking.

"When you are buying mackerel, pinch the belly to ascertain whether it is good. If it gives under your finger, like a bladder half filled with wind, the fish is poor; if it feels hard like butter, the fish is good. It is cheaper to buy one large mackerel for ninepence, than two for four pence half-penny each."

—The American Frugal Housewife, *Mrs. Child*

MACKEREL TETRAZZINI

1½ cups uncooked egg noodles
2 tablespoons butter
1 tablespoon flour
1 cup milk
Salt and freshly ground pepper, to taste
2 cups cooked, flaked mackerel

¼ cup sliced black olives
2 tablespoons grated Parmesan cheese
2 tablespoons dry sherry
½ cup soft bread crumbs
1 tablespoon chopped fresh parsley

1. Preheat oven to 350° F.
2. Cook noodles and drain. Rinse with hot water and drain again.
3. Make a white sauce: in a large saucepan melt 1 tablespoon of the butter, add flour, mixing with a wire whisk, and cook over low heat for 1 minute. Stirring constantly, gradually add milk and cook over medium heat until slightly thickened and smooth. Season with salt and pepper.
4. Add fish, noodles, olives, cheese, and sherry. Mix well.

5. Pour mixture into a buttered 1½-quart casserole.
6. Mix bread crumbs and parsley, sprinkle on top of casserole and dot with remaining tablespoon of butter.
7. Bake in a 350° oven for 35 to 40 minutes.

Yield: 4 to 6 servings

BAKED SPANISH MACKEREL

2 pounds Spanish mackerel fillets
½ cup vegetable oil
2 tablespoons lemon juice
1 clove garlic, crushed
1 cup dried bread crumbs
½ cup grated Parmesan cheese
3 tablespoons chopped fresh parsley
½ teaspoon basil
½ teaspoon thyme

1. Divide fillets into 6 portions and place in a shallow baking dish.
2. Combine oil, lemon juice, and garlic. Pour marinade over fish and let stand for 30 minutes in a cool place, turning once.
3. Preheat oven to 375° F.
4. Remove fish from marinade and reserve liquid. Combine bread crumbs, cheese, and herbs. Roll fillets in bread crumb mixture and return to the baking dish.
5. Sprinkle any leftover bread crumbs on top of the fish and moisten with 2 tablespoons of the marinade.
6. Bake in a 375° F. oven for 10 to 15 minutes, or until fish flakes easily when tested with a fork.

Yield: 6 servings

KING GEORGE'S WAHOO

2 pounds wahoo steaks or fillets
Salt and freshly ground pepper, to taste
2 tablespoons lemon juice
1 teaspoon grated onion
4 tablespoons butter, melted

1. Preheat oven to 350° F.
2. Cut fish into serving-sized portions. Sprinkle both sides with salt and pepper.
3. Combine lemon juice, onion, and butter. Dip each piece of fish into the mixture and place in a buttered baking dish. Pour the rest of the mixture over the fish.
4. Bake in a 350° F. oven for 30 minutes, or until the fish flakes easily when tested with a fork.

Yield: 4 servings

"In the old days it was all daylight fishing, but with the later and harder driving captains, night fishing came into vogue. On dark moonless nights, lookouts aloft spot mackerel by the phosphorescent trail they leave on the sea. It is like white fire. On such nights the seine boat and the dory men will be towing astern of the vessel to a short painter. The vessel will be close hauled, and if the sea be choppy and the vessel doing eleven or twelve knots close hauled, the men in the seine boat and dory are in for a lively evening. Or a whole night of it maybe, those seiners being great ones for sticking to it while a hope of a fish is before them."

—American Fishermen,
Albert Cook Church

BROILED YELLOWFIN

Although this recipe is fairly spicy, most fresh tuna can be prepared very simply. See recipes for swordfish.

3-pound yellowfin fillet	2 cloves garlic, crushed
1 cup soy sauce	1 small piece ginger root, grated
¼ cup sugar	1 scallion, thinly sliced

1. Place fillet in baking dish. Combine soy sauce, sugar, garlic, ginger, and scallion. Pour mixture over fish. Marinate for 1 hour in a cool place. Drain off marinade.
2. Place under broiler and broil until flesh is firm and flakes easily. Allow 10 minutes for every inch of the fish's thickness (see Canadian fish cooking rule, Chapter 1).
3. Serve with caper sauce (Chapter 6).

Yield: 8 servings

"That was when we took to the tuna tackle. I trolled a bait about twenty feet. A school of beautiful turbot, velvet dark in color with blue stripes, churned the water back of my bait. Blue gleams, green flashes! Then a broad bar of bronze! Smash! A shark hit that bait as clean and hard as any tarpon or marlin I ever saw. He made a long run and cut my line."

—Tales of Fishing Virgin Seas, Zane Grey

ORIENTAL TUNA

2 6½-ounce cans white-meat tuna, packed in oil	2 teaspoons minced ginger root
1 tablespoon butter	2 cups sour cream
½ cup chopped onion	Salt and freshly ground pepper, to taste
½ cup sliced water chestnuts	

1. Drain tuna oil into a frying pan. Add butter, heat, then add onion and sauté until soft.
2. Break tuna into large flakes and add to frying pan along with water chestnuts, ginger, sour cream, salt, and pepper. Heat gently. Serve over rice.

Yield: 6 servings

Swordfish

Swordfish (*Xiphias gladius*), the only members of the family *Xiphidae*, are found in the warmer waters of the world's oceans, although in the Atlantic their summer range extends from the Gulf of Mexico to Newfoundland. Swift, torpedo-shaped predators, swordfish race through close-packed schools of smaller fish, using their long, hard-edged bill like a swordsman with a sabre, slashing to right and left, stunning numerous fish then swimming back to consume them. Sports fishermen take them with a stout rod and reel using mackerel or herring or other similar baits and may fight one for five hours or more before boating a good-sized fish. Swordfish average more than 100 pounds, but may weigh as much as 1,200 pounds. Robustflavored swordfish flesh turns cream colored when cooked. Mako shark steaks are occasionally sold as swordfish, which have recently been overfished by foreign fishing concerns.

BAKED SWORDFISH

2 pounds swordfish steaks, 1"
 thick
6 tablespoons butter

2 tablespoons lemon juice
Salt and freshly ground pepper,
 to taste

1. Preheat oven to 400° F.
2. Place steaks in buttered baking dish. In a saucepan, heat butter until golden brown and baste fish with melted butter to seal all juices.
3. Bake in a 400° F. oven for about 5 minutes. Baste fish with butter. Sprinkle with lemon juice, season with a dash of salt and pepper, and bake for another 5 minutes. Fish is done when it flakes easily when tested with a fork.
4. Serve with dill sauce (Chapter 6).
Yield: 6 servings

Thomas C. Weston, photographer and amateur paleontologist with Canada's Geological Survey, holds up an enormous bluefin tuna he harpooned off Nova Scotia in this photograph (possibly a self-portrait) taken in 1879.

BROILED SWORDFISH

2 pounds swordfish steaks, 1″ thick	Salt and freshly ground pepper, to taste
2 tablespoons butter	1 tablespoon lemon juice
1 tablespoon chopped fresh dill	

1. Place swordfish in a well-buttered baking dish. Dot with butter and sprinkle with dill. Season with a dash of salt and pepper.
2. Place under hot broiler and broil for 5 minutes. Turn steaks over, sprinkle with lemon juice and baste with pan drippings. Broil second side another 5 minutes or so. Fish is done when flesh turns opaque in center.
3. Serve garnished with lemon wedges and dill sauce (Chapter 6).

Yield: 6 servings

SKEWERED SWORDFISH

3 pounds swordfish steaks, 1″ thick	½ pound cherry tomatoes
3 tablespoons butter	1 small green pepper, cut into wedges
1 tablespoon lemon juice	
Salt and freshly ground pepper, to taste	

1. Cut swordfish into 1″ cubes.
2. In a small saucepan melt butter and add lemon juice.
3. Dip cubes in melted butter. Season with salt and pepper, and spear onto skewers. Place a cherry tomato and wedge of green pepper on the tip of each skewer.
4. Cook in the broiler or on a barbecue grill. Baste frequently with remaining melted butter. Fish is cooked when it turns opaque. Serve with lemon wedges.

Yield: 8 servings

"In the excitement of the moment I hardly had time to look at the marlin, although I never lost sight of him for a moment. . . . He was as quick as a flash. He sheered to and fro, weaved back and forth, then glided toward us to rap the teaser. He knocked it out of water. Then he dropped back a few rods, only to loom up again, colorful and beautiful. Somehow he resembled a wild species of bird underwater."

—Tales of Southern Rivers, Zane Grey

Dolphin

One of the ocean's most remarkable fish, **dolphin** (*Coryphaena hippurus*) range through all the world's tropical and subtropical seas (occasionally travelling, in summer, as far north as Cape Hatteras). Averaging about six pounds, these beautiful gamefish seem to light up when caught, subtly flashing all the colors of the rainbow, graying only as they die. Called **mahimahi** in Hawaii—the only place where they are readily available commercially—dolphin are one of the sea's great gifts to both cook and fisherman. Their sweet, moist flesh is delicious, as is their orange roe. But most experts agree that dolphin should be bled and chilled as soon as possible to enhance the flavor. In addition, the tough skin should be removed before cooking.

SEVICHE

2 pounds dolphin fillets or steaks, cut into bite-sized pieces	Salt and coarsely ground pepper, to taste
1 medium onion, thinly sliced	Lime juice
	Dash of Tabasco sauce (optional)

1. In a medium-sized bowl, alternate layers of fish and onion slices. Season with salt and pepper.
2. Pour enough lime juice over fish-onion mixture to almost cover it. Cover bowl tightly and marinate in a cool place for 2 hours. Turn bowl upside down or stir to redistribute juice. Add Tabasco (if desired). Cover tightly and marinate 2 more hours. Fish is finished "cooking" (marinating) when it is all opaque.
3. Serve chilled with crackers or cucumber slices.

Yield: 10 to 12 hors-d'oeuvre servings

AMBASSADOR'S STEW

1 cup water or vegetable bouillon	Salt and coarsely ground pepper, to taste
2 to 3 medium potatoes, sliced	6 tomatoes, coarsely chopped
1 to 2 green peppers, sliced	1 pound dolphin fillets or steaks, cut into chunks
1 medium onion, sliced	
1 bay leaf	

1. In a heavy Dutch oven, bring water (or bouillon) to a boil. Reduce heat to moderate, add potatoes and cook about 10 minutes. Then add green peppers, onion, bay leaf, salt, and pepper and cook 5 minutes longer.
2. Reduce heat to low and add tomatoes and fish. Simmer about 5 minutes, or until fish flakes when tested with a fork.

Yield: 4 servings

"Vast numbers of beautiful dolphins glided by the side of the vessel, glancing like burnished gold through the day, and gleaming like meteors by night. . . . When just caught, the upper fin, which reaches from the forehead to within a short distance of the tail, is of fine dark blue. The upper part of the body in its whole length is azure, and the lower parts are of a golden hue, mottled irregularly with deep blue spots. The flesh of the Dolphin is rather firm, very white, and lies in flakes when cooked. The first caught are generally eaten with great pleasure."

—Delineations of American Scenery and Character, John James Audubon

Shark

Because of their unfortunate personalities and eating habits, shark have not been popular foodfish in America, at least not under their own name. **Mako shark** (*Isurus oxyrhynchus*) are often sold as swordfish steaks. **Atlantic porbeagle** (*Lamna nasus*) and **spiny dogfish** (*Squalus acanthias*) are used in English fish and chips, and spiny dogfish are occasionally marketed fresh as **grayfish.** Shark meat is also salted and sold as salt cod

Mako Shark

or cut into plugs with a round cookie-cutter device and sold as sea scallops. **Blue shark** (*Prionace glauca*), **blacktip shark** (*Carcharhinus limbatus*), **soupfin shark** (*Galeorhinus zyopterus*), and **Atlantic nurse shark** (*Ginglymostoma cirratum*) are other sharks used as foodfish. In spite of all their bad press, shark have delicious, flavorful flesh. However, their flesh *does* have a fairly high urea (an ammonia compound) content that should be neutralized by soaking in brine, vinegar, lemon juice, or milk.

"TO SERVE THORNBACK OR SKATE *Should be hung one day at least, before it be dressed and may be served either boiled, or fried in crumbs, being first dipped in egg.*"
—A New System of Domestic Cookery, *1807*

ROYAL MAKO

1 mako shark steak (about 1 pound)
1 tablespoon butter
Salt and freshly ground pepper, to taste
1 teaspoon tarragon
½ teaspoon chopped fresh chives
½ cup sour cream
½ teaspoon paprika

1. Preheat oven to 375° F.
2. Wipe shark with a damp cloth. Place fish in a well-buttered baking dish, dot with butter, and season with salt and pepper.
3. Bake in a 375° F. oven for 5 minutes.
4. Combine tarragon, chives, and sour cream. Turn fish over and cover with sour-cream mixture. Continue to bake for 15 minutes.
5. Sprinkle with paprika, then brown under broiler for 5 minutes.

Yield: 3 servings

Two Italian fishermen head out for the open sea from San Francisco's old Fisherman's Wharf. Italian immigrants, who began supplying San Francisco with fish in the 1850s, were still fishing with handlines from their lateen-rigged feluccas well into the twentieth century.

Skate & Ray

Flat-bodied, winged, creatures with whiplike tails, skate and ray—like their relatives the shark—are generally overlooked as a source of food in North America. However, as with shark, meat from the wings of skate and ray are punched out and sold as ersatz sea scallops. Skate and ray belong to the same order (*Rajiformes*), but to different families. As commercial or culinary terms, however, the names are interchangeable. Like shark, skate and ray flesh should be soaked in brine, vinegar, lemon juice, or milk before cooking.

SEAMAN'S SKATE

2 pounds ray wings, cut into
  strips
6 cups fish stock (Chapter 6)
3 eggs, beaten
¼ cup lemon juice

½ teaspoon salt
¼ teaspoon freshly ground
  pepper
2 tablespoons chopped fresh
  parsley

1. Place the ray in a shallow frying pan, add fish stock and bring to a boil. Lower heat and simmer fish for about 15 minutes, until fish flakes easily when tested with a fork. With a slotted spatula, remove cooked fish to a warmed serving platter and reserve the poaching liquid.
2. In the top of a double boiler, combine eggs, lemon juice, salt, pepper, and ¼ cup of reserved poaching liquid. Over boiling water, stirring constantly, cook sauce until it thickens, about 5 minutes. If sauce gets too thick, add 1 or more tablespoons poaching liquid.
3. Pour sauce over cooked ray and garnish with parsley and lemon wedges.

Yield: 6 servings

Variation: Serve a Hollandaise sauce (Chapter 6) in place of the egg and lemon sauce.

"At eleven we dressed our dinner, and found an Indian by the river side resting himself. All his provision was a dried eel. This he made us a present of, and we gave him a share of our dinner.

"Their way of roasting eels is thus: They cut a stick about three foot long and as thick as one's thumb. They split it about a foot down, and when the eel is gutted, they coil it between the two sides of the stick and bind the top close, which keeps the eel flat, and then stick one end in the ground before a good fire. . . ."

—John Bartram

Eel

The opposite of such anadromous fish as trout and salmon, eels (family *Anguillidae*) are born in saltwater, mature in fresh water, then return to saltwater to spawn and die. **American eels**

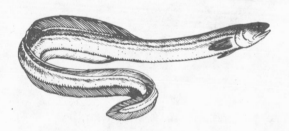

American Eel

(*Anguilla rostrata*) leave their birthplace to enter freshwater rivers along the Gulf and Atlantic coasts, as far north as Labrador. Averaging two to three feet in length, eels are sold live, fresh-killed, or smoked. They have extremely rich, firm flesh and must be skinned before cooking.

MINCED EEL

A fisherman repairs his nets as they hang in the sun to dry.

1 2-pound eel, skinned
4 cups soft bread crumbs
2 tablespoons butter
1 onion, finely chopped
Salt and freshly ground pepper,
  to taste

2 small eggs, beaten
1 cup minced mushrooms
2 tablespoons sour cream
Fine bread crumbs, for dredging
Melted butter, for basting

1. Preheat oven to 400° F.
2. Carefully remove flesh from eel's backbone, leaving backbone intact. Set backbone aside. Mince the eel flesh in a blender or food processor.
3. Moisten the bread crumbs with a little water, then squeeze water out until bread is almost dry. Add minced eel and blend.
4. In a frying pan, heat butter and sauté onion until just soft. Add to eel mixture and season with salt and pepper. Add eggs, mushrooms, and sour cream.
5. Pack this mixture around the backbone in the shape of an eel.
6. Carefully roll the eel form in fine bread crumbs. Then lay carefully in a buttered baking dish and bake in a 400° F. oven for 15 to 20 minutes. Baste frequently with melted butter.
7. Serve with Hollandaise sauce (Chapter 6) and lemon wedges.

Yield: 4 servings

5: Shellfish

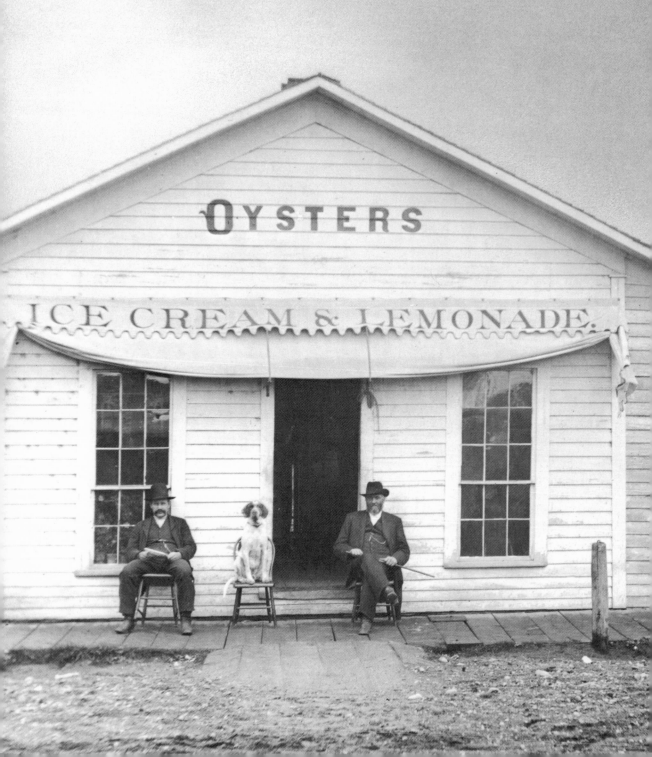

Unlike their finny relatives, who must be chased and fought to be won, shellfish are fairly easy game; most lead sedentary lives and are simply there for the plucking—or, as the Northwest Coast Indians say, "When the tide goes out, the feast begins." Shellfish are found in both salt and fresh water along all of North America's coasts and throughout many of its inland waters. They are low in calories and cholesterol, high in protein, and delicious.

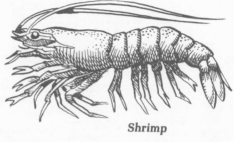

Shrimp

All shellfish are invertebrates and fall into two main categories: crustaceans and mollusks. Crustaceans include lobsters, crabs, shrimp, and crayfish. All crustaceans have an external or exoskeleton (commonly called a shell), which must be shed occasionally in order for them to grow. Mollusks are divided into three classes: bivalves (those with two shells), gastropods (those with one shell who move by means of a footlike muscle), and cephalopods (those who usually have an internal shell and a foot elongated into tentacles or arms). Bivalves include scallops, clams, and oysters; gastropods, popularly called univalves, include abalones and conchs; and octopus and squid are cephalopods.

Fishing for shallow-water shellfish can be fun, yet also somewhat risky. For example, oysters, clams, and mussels filter the water in which they live and therefore may retain any toxins in their fat or organs, making it essential to consult a local health department to ensure that these shellfish are safe to eat. In addition, there are often local regulations governing when and how many shellfish can be harvested by non-commercial fishermen.

In general, shellfish require very little cooking, and, in fact, become tough and rubbery if they are cooked too long. Some varieties, such as oysters and clams, are best eaten raw.

Lobster

The name lobster is applied to two different shellfish, both crustaceans, that are similar in taste and appearance: the American lobster and the spiny lobster.

AMERICAN LOBSTER: The most popular lobster, these large-clawed, marine creatures can be found from northern Canada to North Carolina, but are most abundant around Maine, Nova Scotia, and Newfoundland. The average American lobster (*Homarus americanus*) measures about 10 inches long and weighs from one and one-half to two pounds, but one record holder measured 34 inches. Lobsters range in color from dark green to yellow orange to reddish brown, but when cooked all turn bright red.

◀ *In the nineteenth century, Americans were consumed by a passion for oysters, and, in turn, consumed the objects of their passion at the annual rate of several pounds per person. Express wagons (and later the railroad) delivered barrels of the coveted shellfish to oyster houses—such as this one in Black River Falls, Wisconsin—all across the country.*

Lobster can be purchased year round, but the best seasons are from mid-May to late June and mid-October through November. At those times, the choicest lobsters at the most reasonable prices are available. Lobsters are most commonly purchased live, but are also available cooked in the shell, or cooked with meat removed from the shell—fresh, frozen, or canned. When buying a live lobster, do not accept one that is relaxed. Look for active movement of the legs. The tail should readily curl. Also, a fresh-cooked lobster should have spring in its tail. Test it: the fresher the creature, the stronger the spring back of the tail. Lobsters are sold from chicks at one-half pound to jumbos weighing two and one-half pounds or more. Allow one pound of live lobster per serving. Live lobster should be cooked the same day it is purchased.

Some cooks believe that the meat of the male lobster is finer and firmer in texture than that of the female lobster. But the female lobster is prized because it usually contains spawn, or roe, which can be made into delicious lobster butter and fine sauces. The grass-green liver in both male and female is called tomalley, and is also edible.

> "The end of a lobster is surrounded with what children call 'purses,' edged with a little fringe. If you put your hand under these to raise it, and find it springs back hard and firm, it is a sign the lobster is fresh; if they move flabbily, it is not a good omen."
>
> —The American Frugal Housewife, by Mrs. Child

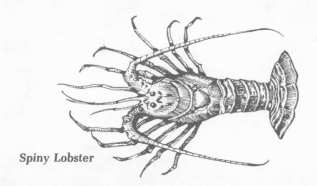

Spiny Lobster

SPINY LOBSTER: Unlike the American lobster, the spiny lobster (*Panulirus argus*) has no claws. Also mistakenly called **sea crawfish** or **crayfish,** the spiny lobster is found in warm water, on coral reefs or under rocks in coral lagoons, from North Carolina to Florida, in the Caribbean, and off southern California. Spiny lobster flesh is slightly coarser than the American lobster's, and usually only the tail meat is sold, as a frozen product. Spiny lobster is also marketed as **rock lobster.** So-called cold-water tails, imported from South Africa and Australia, are said to be superior to the warm-water tails.

LOBSTERETTE: Closely related to American lobsters are a miniature variety called lobsterettes or **langostinos.** Three kinds of these tiny lobsters are commercially fished in the Caribbean and Atlantic: **red lobsterettes, Caribbean lobsterettes,** and **Flori-**

da lobsterettes. Only the tails are eaten and they are very similar in appearance and taste to rock shrimp. In the Mediterranean, the tail portions of lobsterettes are called **scampi**—a term that in this country is used to describe a shrimp dish prepared with garlic and butter (or oil). Lobsterettes are most often sold frozen, tail portions only.

BOILED LOBSTER

1. In a large kettle, place enough salted water (1 tablespoon for every quart of water) to cover the lobsters. Bring to a boil.

Note: Seasonings or lemon juice can be added to the cooking water for extra flavor.

2. Grasp each lobster behind the head and plunge it head first into the rapidly boiling water.
3. Cover. When water returns to the boil, lower the heat. Simmer 5 minutes for 1-pound lobsters, 10 minutes for 2-pound lobsters.
4. Remove from water and drain. Serve hot, in the shell, with lemon wedges and melted butter, or lemon butter. Or, to serve cold, cool quickly under running water after removing from pot, and drain. Serve with mayonnaise.

MAINE LOBSTER SALAD

3 medium tomatoes
2 cups cooked, chilled rice
1 cup diced cucumber
1 cup cooked, minced green beans
1 cup cooked, minced carrots
2 tablespoons chopped fresh parsley
½ cup seafood salad dressing (Chapter 6)
10 to 12 ounces cooked lobster meat, cut into chunks
1 teaspoon lemon juice
½ cup mayonnaise

1. Cut 1 tomato in half, finely chop one of the halves, and set aside. Dice the remaining 2½ tomatoes.
2. Toss rice, tomatoes, cucumber, beans, carrots, and parsley with the salad dressing.
3. Place the rice-vegetable mixture on serving platter and arrange lobster on top.
4. Blend the reserved chopped tomato, lemon juice, and mayonnaise and pour over lobster. Serve chilled, garnished with parsley and capers.

Yield: 6 servings

"You would have been amused to see the manner in which these men, and their families on shore, cooked the lobsters; they threw them alive into a great wood-fire; and, as soon as they were broiled, devoured them while yet so hot that any of us could not have touched them. When properly cooled, I tasted these roasted lobsters, and found them infinitely better flavoured than boiled ones."

—Delineations of American Scenery and Character, John James Audubon

Posed in the doorway of a Massachusetts lobsterman's shack, two women show off their Sunday finery as the gentleman in the foreground holds his catboat in check for the photographer.

LOBSTER-STUFFED EGGPLANT

1 large eggplant	1 cup soft bread crumbs
6 tablespoons butter	2 teaspoons chili powder
1 clove garlic, finely chopped	1 teaspoon salt
1 cup cooked, chopped lobster meat	¼ teaspoon freshly ground pepper
1 egg, beaten	

1. Cut eggplant in half. With a spoon scoop out the center of each half, leaving side walls ½″ thick. Coarsely chop center pieces.
2. Parboil the outer shells of eggplant in boiling water for 15 minutes.
3. Preheat oven to 350° F.
4. In a frying pan, melt half the butter and sauté chopped eggplant and garlic briefly. Remove from heat. Add lobster pieces, egg, ¼ cup of the bread crumbs, chili powder, salt, and pepper.
5. Fill eggplant shells with mixture. Top with remaining bread crumbs and dot with remaining butter.
6. Bake in a 350° F. oven for 35 minutes. Serve with a tomato sauce (Chapter 6).

Yield: 4 to 5 servings

LOBSTER WITH BERCY SAUCE

¼ cup fish stock (Chapter 6) or water
½ cup dry white wine
2 teaspoons chopped shallots
1 cup velouté (Chapter 6)
1 teaspoon dry mustard
3 tablespoons butter

1 teaspoon chopped fresh parsley
½ pound mushrooms, chopped
1½ cups cooked lobster meat, cut into sections
6 tablespoons grated Gruyère cheese

1. Preheat oven to 400° F.
2. Make Bercy sauce: in a saucepan, combine fish stock (or water), ¼ cup of the wine, and shallots and reduce by ⅓ by boiling rapidly. Add velouté and mustard and bring to a boil. Add 1 tablespoon of the butter and parsley, stirring constantly to mix.
3. In a frying pan, heat remaining 2 tablespoons of butter, add mushrooms and sauté until just soft. Add lobster and remaining ¼ cup of wine. Cook another 5 minutes.
4. Divide lobster mixture evenly among 6 buttered ramekins and spoon sauce into them. Sprinkle with grated cheese.
5. Bake in a 400° F. oven until hot, about 10 minutes, and place under broiler for a few minutes, until browned.

Yield: 6 servings

"LOBSTER A LA NEW-BURG. Heat a spoonful of butter, cut lobster in small pieces and put into butter while hot. Add pinch of salt, little white and red pepper, and a wine glass of sherry. Cook all down to one-half the amount. Beat three eggs with one cup cream. Pour in with lobster and the rest. Simmer on stove five to ten minutes. If liked, add a few mushrooms and serve on toast."
—Ladies Auxiliary Cookbook, 1900

LOBSTER BISQUE

4 cups milk	1 tablespoon chopped pimiento
1 medium onion, sliced	½ cup heavy cream
4 tablespoons butter	Dash of cayenne
4 tablespoons flour	1 teaspoon salt
10 to 12 ounces cooked lobster meat (from 2 1-pound lobsters)	Dry sherry (optional)

1. In top of double boiler, heat milk and add onion. Cook over medium heat until thoroughly heated. Strain milk, remove onions and discard.
2. In a saucepan, melt butter, add flour, mixing with a wire whisk, and cook over low heat for 1 minute. Stirring constantly, gradually add milk and cook over medium heat until slightly thickened and smooth.
3. Add lobster meat and pimiento and simmer 10 minutes.
4. Add cream, cayenne, and salt. Heat briefly. Serve with a spoonful of sherry (if desired) in each bowl.

Yield: 6 servings

Crayfish

Crayfish (*Astacidae*) look like miniature lobsters and live in freshwater streams, ponds, and lakes. Louisiana, its neighboring states, and the inland waters of Oregon, Washington, and California yield the most abundant supply of crayfish. Less popular are the **northern crayfish** found from Wisconsin to Maine, and the **Allegheny crayfish** found west and north of the Allegheny Mountains. There are over 250 types of crayfish found in North America, and 29 different species in Louisiana alone. Turn over a rock in a slow-running pond or stream and there should be a crayfish for the grabbing. Regulations vary from place to place and should be checked before setting out. Also known as **crawfish, crawdad, creekcrab, yabbie,** and **freshwater lobster,** crayfish vary in size from one to 16 inches; however, only those species that reach at least three and one-half inches are considered edible.

Crayfish can be bought at fish markets in the South and West, but may be difficult to find in the East. They are sold either live or cooked in the shell and frozen. Freshly caught crayfish (those not purchased at the market) may be somewhat muddy or gritty. To help them rid themselves of grit, soak them in a large tub of water (to which has been added about 1 cup of coarse salt) for 10 to 20 minutes. Stir the crayfish around to keep them moving and then wait for the grit to settle to the bottom of the tub before removing the crayfish. Live crayfish can be kept on ice for 24 hours and any that do not move should not be eaten. The average crayfish is five inches long; about a dozen of these will yield one-half pound of meat from the claws and tail.

AVOCADO WITH CRAYFISH

⅓ cup sour cream
⅓ cup mayonnaise
3 tablespoons lemon juice
¼ teaspoon paprika
Salt and freshly ground pepper, to taste

¾ pound cooked, cleaned crayfish meat
2 or 3 ripe avocados

1. Combine sour cream and mayonnaise. Stir in lemon juice, paprika, salt, and pepper. Fold in the crayfish, stirring as little as possible so as not to break up the lumps.
2. Cut the avocados in half lengthwise. Discard pits. Fill the avocado halves with the mixture and serve.

Yield: 4 to 6 servings

CRAYFISH MANICOTTI

6 manicotti shells
¾ pound spinach
4 tablespoons butter
½ cup chopped onion
1 clove garlic, minced
3 tablespoons flour
2¼ cups milk

1 cup shredded Gruyère cheese
¼ cup grated Parmesan cheese
¼ teaspoon salt
1 pound cooked, cleaned crayfish meat, coarsely chopped
Freshly grated nutmeg (optional)

1. Cook manicotti in boiling salted water and drain.
2. Preheat oven to 350° F.
3. Wash spinach and steam briefly. Drain and chop coarsely.
4. In a saucepan, heat 2 tablespoons of the butter and sauté onion and garlic until just soft. Blend in flour, cooking briefly, and add milk. Cook and stir until thickened and bubbly.
5. Add Gruyère gradually and stir until melted.
6. Melt remaining 2 tablespoons of butter and in a bowl combine it with ½ cup of the sauce, the spinach, Parmesan cheese, and salt. Fold in crayfish. Stuff manicotti with crayfish mixture.
7. Pour half remaining sauce in a shallow 1½-quart baking dish. Place manicotti on sauce in pan. Pour remaining sauce over manicotti. Grate a little nutmeg over manicotti (if desired).
8. Cover and bake in a 350° F. oven for 30 to 35 minutes.

Yield: 6 servings

"Curry of Lobster. The meat of a lobster weighing between two and three pounds, one very small onion, three tablespoonfuls of butter, two of flour, a scant one of curry powder, a speck of cayenne, salt, a scant pint of water or stock. Let the butter get hot; and then add the onion, cut fine, and fry brown. When the onion is cooked add the flour and curry powder, and stir all together for two minutes. Add stock; cook two minutes, and strain. Add the meat of lobster, cut into dice, and simmer five minutes. Serve with a border of boiled rice around the dish."

—Miss Parloa's New Cook Book, 1880

Shrimp

The most popular American shellfish, shrimp are both freshwater and saltwater creatures that can be found in most of the world's waters. While there are hundreds of species of shrimp, all have ten legs and long, narrow bodies. Alive, they are a variety of colors—gray, brown, pink, yellow—but when cooked all shrimp are tones of reddish-pink on the outside and white on the inside. The most dramatic difference between species is in size. Shrimp range from the tiny **Alaskan pinks** (it takes nearly 180 to make a pound) to the gigantic *Macrobrachium*, which can be as long as 30 inches from claw to tail. Except for size, species of edible shrimp can barely be distinguished by the layman and often differ from one location to the other. For example, **pink shrimp** (*Penaeus duorarum*) and **brown shrimp** (*Penaeus aztecus*) are sometimes the same color, but some pink shrimp are lemon-yellow, while others are indeed pink. At least twelve different species of edible shrimps can be found in North American waters, and many more are sold in markets throughout the country. **Prawns**—a term used in the North American marketplace to refer to large shrimp—are actually separate (though related) beasts, with narrower bodies and longer legs.

For his now famous series of photographs documenting child labor, Lewis W. Hine caught these shrimp pickers at work at Biloxi, Mississippi, in 1911.

Regardless of size, only the tail portion of a shrimp is eaten. Except for **rock shrimp** (*Sicyonia brevirostris*), a large species with a firm meat similar to lobsterettes (which see), most shrimp have the same taste and texture.

When buying fresh (or "green") shrimp, one should look for those that are firm and do not smell. Frozen shrimp are also excellent. Because of their many sizes, shrimp can vary from three to a pound to up to 180 per pound. Shell-on shrimp are a better buy because the initial cost per pound is lower and the raw, peeled, and deveined shrimp may shrink as much as 25 percent when cooked.

BASIC SHRIMP

1. Wash the shrimp. (Shell and devein them before or after cooking.) Place shrimp in enough salted water (1 tablespoon salt for every quart of water) to cover.

Note: A court bouillon (Chapter 6) can be used instead. Also, pickling spices, beer, vinegar, or lemon juice can be added to the salted water.

2. Just as water reaches the boil, lower heat. Simmer small shrimp for 5 minutes or less. Larger shrimp can simmer for 8 minutes. Shrimp must never be boiled, since boiling or prolonged cooking will make them tough.
3. Drain shrimp and serve hot or cold.

SHRIMP RÉMOULADE

2 cups mayonnaise
2 tablespoons tarragon mustard
1 teaspoon anchovy paste
2 tablespoons minced gherkins
2 tablespoons minced capers
2 tablespoons minced fresh tarragon
2 tablespoons minced fresh chervil
2 tablespoons minced fresh parsley
Salt and freshly ground pepper, to taste
4 pounds shrimp, cooked, shelled, and deveined

1. Combine mayonnaise, mustard, anchovy paste, gherkins, capers, tarragon, chervil, and parsley. Season with salt and pepper.
2. Stir shrimp into mayonnaise sauce. Chill.
Yield: 12 servings

"Shrimp Salad. One quart of celery cut in small bits, two cans of shrimps, washed and picked to pieces, one dozen olives minced, one-fourth pound of grated cheese, one pint of mayonnaise, one head of lettuce in small pieces. Line salad bowl with lettuce leaves and mix ingredients. Garnish with parsley and whole olives. Set in a cool place until ready to serve."
—Good Housekeeping Family Cookbook, 1909

SHRIMP CUSTARD SOUP

1 small chicken leg, boned	4 eggs
4 tablespoons soy sauce	1 cup unseasoned chicken stock
3 large shrimp, shelled and	1 cup fish stock (Chapter 6)
deveined	1 teaspoon salt
6 mushrooms, sliced	Pinch of monosodium glutamate
2 tablespoons peas	(optional)

1. Preheat oven to 450° F.
2. Cut chicken into bite-sized pieces and let stand in 3 tablespoons of soy sauce about 5 minutes. Coarsely chop shrimp.
3. Into 6 small bowls, place equal amounts of shrimp, chicken, mushroom slices, and peas.
4. Beat the eggs and add chicken stock, fish stock, remaining tablespoon of soy sauce, salt, and monosodium glutamate (if desired). Mix well. Fill bowls with egg mixture and cover with aluminum foil.
5. Place bowls in a baking pan at least 2″ deep, half fill the pan with water and place in a 450° F. oven. Reduce heat immediately to 350° F. and cook for 30 minutes.

Yield: 6 servings

"We ate in pavilions on the sand. . . . Prawns fresh from the sea sprinkled with lime juice. They were pink and sweet and there were four bites to a prawn. Of those we ate many. Then we ate paella with fresh sea food, clams in their shells, mussels, crayfish, and small eels. Then we ate even smaller eels alone cooked in oil and as tiny as bean sprouts and curled in all directions and so tender they disappeared in the mouth without chewing."
—For Whom the Bell Tolls,
  Ernest Hemingway

PRAWN PILAU

3 tablespoons butter	1½ teaspoons salt
1 medium onion, sliced	1 tablespoon lemon juice
1½ teaspoons curry powder	1 tablespoon yoghurt
1 teaspoon turmeric	1½ pounds jumbo shrimp,
½ teaspoon chili powder	shelled and deveined
2 to 3 tablespoons chopped fresh	1 cup rice
parsley	2 cups boiling water

1. In a frying pan, heat half the butter. Add onion and sauté until brown. Add curry, turmeric, chili powder, parsley, and 1 teaspoon of the salt. Cook 3 minutes.
2. Add lemon juice and yoghurt. Increase heat a little and add shrimp, sautéing them for about 5 minutes on each side. Remove shrimp and keep them warm.
3. In a heavy saucepan, heat the remainder of the butter. Add remaining ½ teaspoon salt and rice. Stir well and cook 3 minutes over low heat.
4. Add spice-onion mixture and liquid from frying pan, and mix well. Add boiling water and bring back to the boil. Cover closely and cook over low heat for 20 to 30 minutes, or until liquid has been absorbed.
5. Serve rice garnished with shrimp.

Yield: 4 servings

SHRIMP ITALIANO

¼ cup olive oil
2 dozen large shrimp, shelled
  and deveined
2 shallots, finely chopped
2 cloves garlic, halved
½ cup dry white wine

6 tomatoes, peeled, seeded, and
  chopped
1 tablespoon tomato puree
Salt and freshly ground pepper,
  to taste
Dash of cayenne

1. In a frying pan, heat olive oil. Add shrimp and sauté for about 4 minutes. Add shallots and garlic and cook 1 minute longer.
2. Add wine, tomatoes, puree, salt, pepper, and cayenne. Cook over very low heat for 10 minutes.
3. Remove garlic, correct seasoning. Serve with rice.

Yield: 6 servings

POTTED SHRIMP

¼ cup lemon juice
6 tablespoons butter
Dash of nutmeg

2 cups cooked, coarsely chopped
  shrimp

1. In a small saucepan, heat lemon juice over low heat, stirring constantly until liquid is reduced by half. Add butter and continue stirring until melted. Sprinkle in nutmeg and remove from heat.
2. Pack the shrimp tightly into a 2-cup mold. Pour lemon butter over shrimp and place folded aluminum foil directly on top of mixture. Press down with a heavy weight. Refrigerate, keeping weight in place, for 8 hours, or overnight.
3. Spread on warm, buttered toast to serve.

Yield: 8 first-course servings, 16 hors-d'oeuvre servings

Prawns

SHRIMP PÂTÉ

1½ pounds shrimp, cooked,
  shelled, and deveined
8 tablespoons butter
Juice of 1 small onion (10 drops)
1 tablespoon dry sherry

Dash of mace
½ teaspoon dry mustard
Salt and freshly ground pepper,
  to taste

1. Grind shrimp very briefly in a blender or food processor.
2. Combine ground shrimp, butter, onion juice, sherry, mace, mustard, salt, and pepper.
3. Spoon shrimp mixture into a mold or shape into any design desired. Refrigerate, and serve on crackers or dark bread.

Yield: 2 cups

Crabs

There are over 4,000 species of crabs, most of which differ from region to region. They vary in size, color, and shape, but all edible varieties have a delicious flavor. In general, crabs are sold "green" (alive), cooked in the shell, frozen in the shell, or the meat alone frozen or canned. As a rule, 25 percent of the crab in the shell is edible; so four pounds will yield one pound of meat. Fresh crab should be cooked within 12 hours of being caught, and only live crabs should be used. It is generally best to cook crabmeat only once, so precooked crab should either be used in cold dishes or added to hot dishes at the last moment and cooked for as short a time as possible. Many recipes call for lump meat (the all white body meat) instead of claw meat, which is darker and in smaller shreds. The distinction, however, is one of appearance and not flavor.

BLUE CRAB: Native to the Western Atlantic, blue crabs (*Callinectes sapidus*) are the most popular of the edible species. They are found as far north as Nova Scotia and as far south as Brazil. These blue-hued crabs generally weigh from one-quarter to one pound and yield delicious white meat from the body and brownish meat from the claws. Like all crustaceans, crabs molt their shells. Before the new shell has hardened, they are known as **soft-shelled crabs.** While a number of species can be eaten at this point, almost all soft-shelled crabs marketed are blue crabs. They must be taken from the water both before the new shell hardens and before they are eaten by their older kin. Soft-shelled crabs generally weigh from two to five ounces and can be eaten "shell" and all.

DUNGENESS CRAB: The most popular of the Pacific Coast varieties, sometimes called **rock crabs,** on the West Coast, Dungeness crabs (*Cancer magister*) weigh from 12 ounces to four pounds and can be found from Alaska to Baja California. In the water they are pinkish-green to yellow, but when cooked their shells turn bright red.

KING CRAB: Called **Japanese crab, Russian crab,** and **Alaskan crab,** these gourmet delicacies inhabit the icy waters of the Northern Pacific. Average king crabs (*Paralithodes camtschaticus*) weigh about 10 pounds, but crabs as large as 20 pounds are not unknown. Although the body meat is very tasty, it is the legs of kings that are prized.

STONE CRAB: Heavy-shelled stone crabs (*Menippe mercenaria*) live in deep burrows in sandy shoals from North Carolina southward, but are most abundant around southern Florida. They measure five inches in width and have black-tipped claws,

"Deviled Crabs. *To the meat of one dozen hard crabs add pepper, salt, dry mustard and Worcestershire sauce to taste. Heat two cups of fresh milk, add two tablespoons of butter, six broken crackers and some chopped parsley. Stir and cook a few minutes. Remove from fire and mix with the picked crab meat. Fill each shell, cover with cracker crumbs with a bit of butter on top. Bake in oven until brown."*
—Good Housekeeping Family Cookbook, *1909*

which bear the meat for which they are known. Because the claws can be regenerated, fishermen trap stone crabs, twist off their claws, and toss them back into the water. In about 18 months these "retreads" will have sprouted new claws, which can once again be fished. Stone crab claws must be cooked as soon as they are caught and, because of the thickness of the shell, are usually served cracked.

SPIDER CRAB: Spider crabs include a number of species that range from those too tiny to be eaten to the largest of all crustaceans, the 11-foot-wide **Japanese spider crab.** As their name indicates, they are round-bodied, long-legged, hairy creatures that are sold under more appetizing commercial names: **snow crabs, queen crabs,** and **tanner crabs.**

RED CRAB: Deepwater crabs similar in taste to king crabs, red crabs (*Geryon quinquedens*) have bright red shells before cooking. Because they weigh only one to two pounds, their legs and claws are not as large as the king, although their pinkish meat is just as delicious.

JONAH CRAB: Jonah crabs (*Cancer borealis*) are usually found in open water from Nova Scotia to South Carolina, but in spring they can readily be caught from piers and bridges and are often found in lobster pots. They are especially plentiful along the south shore of Long Island. They are also called **mud crabs** or **rock crabs.** True **rock crabs** (*Cancer irroratus*) are found in the same waters.

BOILED CRABS

3 quarts water
5 tablespoons vinegar
⅓ cup butter
1 teaspoon lemon juice
1 tablespoon Worcestershire
   sauce

Salt and freshly ground pepper,
   to taste
2 2-pound crabs

1. Place water and ¼ cup of the vinegar in a large stainless-steel or enamel pot. Bring to a rapid boil.
2. Meanwhile, heat butter in a saucepan and stir over low heat until it turns dark brown. Add lemon juice, remaining tablespoon of vinegar, Worcestershire sauce, salt, and pepper.
3. Drop crabs into boiling water and cook for 10 minutes after water returns to a boil.
4. Cool crabs under running water, but do not soak them. Serve with butter sauce.

Yield: 2 servings

"TO MAKE HOT CRAB. Pick the meat out of a crab, clear the shell from the head, then put in the former, with a very small bit of nutmeg, salt, pepper, a bit of butter, crumbs of bread, and three spoonfuls of vinegar, into the shell again, and set it before the fire. You may brown it with a salamander. Dry toast should be served to eat it upon."
—A New System of Domestic
   Cookery, *1807*

CHESAPEAKE STEAMED CRABS

3 dozen blue crabs (about 4″ wide, ½ pound each)	1 tablespoon dry mustard
1½ cups coarse salt	1 teaspoon mustard seed
3 tablespoons cracked black pepper	1 teaspoon celery seed
2 teaspoons cayenne	1 teaspoon paprika
	2 cups water
	2 cups vinegar

1. Kill the crabs quickly by plunging them head first into rapidly boiling water.
2. Combine salt, pepper, cayenne, mustard, mustard seed, celery seed, and paprika.
3. Place water and vinegar in a large stainless-steel or enamel pot. Into pot, place a steaming rack that will hold the crabs above the liquid.
4. Place 6 of the crabs on the rack. Sprinkle the crabs with about 4 tablespoons of the crab spice. Place another 6 crabs on the rack and sprinkle with crab spice. Repeat this step until all crabs and crab spice are in the pot.
5. Bring to a boil over high heat, cover tightly. Lower heat and let crabs steam for 20 minutes.

Yield: 8 to 10 servings

"You are very fortunate to be assigned to duty at Fortress Monroe [on Chesapeake Bay]; it is just the season for soft-shelled crabs, and hog fish have just come in, and they are the most delicious pan fish you ever ate."

—General Winfield Scott, to General Benjamin Butler, *1861*

CRAB MOUSSE

6 ounces cream cheese	1 envelope unflavored gelatin
½ cup mayonnaise	1 tablespoon lemon juice
1 pound cooked crabmeat	1 tablespoon wine vinegar
Salt and freshly ground pepper, to taste	½ medium cucumber, sliced

1. Blend cream cheese and mayonnaise. Stir in crabmeat and season with salt and pepper. Set aside.
2. Place 5 tablespoons of cold water in a small saucepan and sprinkle gelatin into the liquid. Cook over low heat, stirring, until gelatin dissolves. Remove gelatin from heat and add lemon juice and vinegar.
3. Measure out 2 tablespoons of gelatin mixture and dilute with 2 more tablespoons water and reserve.
4. Stir remaining gelatin mixture into crabmeat. Blend well. Pour mixture into ¾-quart soufflé dish. Chill until set firm.
5. Soften the reserved gelatin mixture over low heat (if necessary), and spoon over surface of mousse. Arrange cucumber slices in the aspic and chill to set.

Yield: 4 servings

CRAB SOUFFLÉ

¾ cup fine bread crumbs
4 tablespoons butter
2 shallots, finely chopped
1 teaspoon curry powder
1 teaspoon paprika
1 tablespoon flour
½ cup milk
¾ pound cooked crabmeat

2 tablespoons heavy cream
2 tablespoons dry sherry
Dash of Tabasco sauce
Salt and freshly ground pepper,
   to taste
3 egg yolks
4 egg whites
½ cup grated Parmesan cheese

A California crab fisherman lowers his San Francisco Bay Cat, the area's original crab fishing boat, into the water.

1. Preheat oven to 375° F.
2. Butter inside of 1½-quart soufflé dish and dust with ½ cup of the bread crumbs.
3. In a frying pan, heat 2 tablespoons of the butter. Add shallots and sauté until they just begin to soften. Add curry powder and paprika and cook for 2 minutes.
4. Make a white sauce: in a saucepan, melt remaining 2 tablespoons of butter, add flour, mixing with a wire whisk, and cook over low heat for 1 minute. Stirring constantly, gradually add milk and cook over medium heat until slightly thickened and smooth. Remove from heat and cool slightly.
5. Combine crabmeat, cream, and sherry. Beat cooled white sauce into the crabmeat mixture. Add Tabasco sauce, salt, pepper, and egg yolks.
6. Whip egg whites and fold into mixture. Turn into prepared soufflé dish.
7. Combine remaining bread crumbs with cheese and sprinkle over top of soufflé.
8. Bake in a 375° F. oven for 20 to 30 minutes. Serve at once with dill, mushroom, or Mornay sauce (Chapter 6).

Yield: 4 servings

CRISS-CROSS CRAB

5 ounces crabmeat
1 medium cucumber, peeled,
  seeded, and diced
2 tablespoons chopped fresh dill
¼ cup finely chopped celery
  and leaves
¼ cup thinly sliced mushrooms

Dash of nutmeg
Dash of salt
3 tablespoons heavy cream
1 tablespoon dry sherry
  (optional)
1-crust pie dough
1 teaspoon butter

1. Make crabmeat filling: combine crabmeat, cucumber, dill, celery, mushrooms, nutmeg, salt, cream, and sherry (if desired).
2. Roll pie dough into rectangle about 12″ by 14″. Place on ungreased cookie sheet.
3. Preheat oven to 425° F.
4. Spread crab mixture lengthwise, down center of dough, covering an area about 4″ wide and 11″ long, leaving a border of dough on all sides. Dot top of stuffing with butter.
5. On the long sides of the rectangle, cut the dough into 6 strips of equal width, about 2¼″ each, at right angles to the stuffing, and stopping 1″ short of the stuffing. (The strips stay attached to the dough under the stuffing.) Starting at one end, bring the first two strips (one from each side) and cross them over on the top of the stuffing, at a slight angle, and overlapping in center. Continue to make this criss-cross pattern with the remaining strips. Tuck the short ends of dough under the criss-cross strips and pinch overlapping sections together to seal.
6. Bake in a 425° F. oven for 20 to 25 minutes, until top is browned. Serve with dill or caper sauce (Chapter 6).

Yield: 4 to 6 servings

Dungeness Crab

CRAB CROQUETTES

1 pound cooked crabmeat
2 eggs
1 teaspoon salt
1 teaspoon freshly ground
  pepper
1 tablespoon chopped fresh
  parsley or chives

1 teaspoon Worcestershire sauce
1 tablespoon sour cream
Flour, for dredging
Fine bread crumbs, for dredging
2 tablespoons butter

1. Shred crabmeat. Beat 1 of the eggs and add it to crabmeat along with salt, pepper, parsley (or chives), Worcestershire sauce, and sour cream, mixing all together lightly.
2. Form mixture into small egg shapes. Beat the remaining egg. Dredge croquettes in flour, dip in beaten egg and then roll in bread crumbs.

3. In a frying pan, heat butter and when frothy, brown croquettes well on all sides. Serve at once with tartar sauce (Chapter 6).

Yield: 4 servings

CRAB SOUP

2 cups milk	2 cups heavy cream
¼ teaspoon mace	Salt and freshly ground pepper,
2 strips lemon peel	to taste
1 pound crabmeat, shredded	¼ cup cracker crumbs
½ cup (1 stick) butter	2 tablespoons dry sherry

1. In the top of a double boiler, combine milk, mace, and lemon peel, and simmer for 3 minutes.
2. Add crabmeat, butter, and cream and cook for 10 minutes.
3. Season with salt and pepper and add cracker crumbs to thicken. Turn off heat and let stand a few minutes to develop flavor.
4. Add sherry just before serving.

Yield: 6 servings

Variation: If crabs used are she-crabs, save the roe and add it to the soup in Step 2.

DEEP-FRIED SOFT-SHELLED CRABS

8 soft-shelled crabs	1 egg, beaten
Salt and freshly ground pepper,	Fine bread crumbs, for dredging
to taste	Oil, for deep-frying

1. Prepare fresh crabs for cooking (Chapter 7).
2. Wipe crabs with paper toweling. Season with salt and pepper and dip in egg and then in bread crumbs.
3. In a heavy kettle, heat oil to 375° F. Drop crabs in and fry 3 to 4 minutes. Drain on paper toweling.
4. Season with cayenne and lemon juice.

Yield: 4 servings

"CRAB APPETIZER. Mix half a pint of sweet cream with the shredded meat from six boiled crabs, and when warmed through add three tablespoons of butter, salt, cayenne pepper to taste and two tablespoons of grated Italian cheese and the beaten yolk of one egg. Heat thoroughly, and place on squares of buttered toast. Place them in a pan and run into the oven for a few minutes, then serve each on a white lettuce leaf."
—Good Housekeeping Family Cookbook, 1909

Oysters

Oysters (*Ostrea*) are so popular with other, predacious forms of marine life that in order to satisfy man's appetite for them, oyster farming has been developed. Oyster cultivation was originated by the Romans more than 2,000 years ago, flourished under the Japanese, and is now used world-wide. Of the 10 species sold commercially in world markets, only a few are found in North America. By far the most popular are the three- to four-inch **Eastern oysters** (*Crassostrea virginica*), which have many names, depending on their home waters: **Blue Point, Cape Cod, Chincoteague, Kent Island, Cotuit,** and on and on. These are the best oysters for eating raw on the half shell. Native to waters from Maine to the Gulf of Mexico, Eastern oysters have been introduced to northern California, along with **Pacific** or **Japanese oysters** (*Crassostrea gigas*), a larger species that are rarely eaten raw. The two-inch **Olympia oysters** (*Ostrea lurida*) are a native Pacific variety. The **European oyster** (*Ostrea edulis*), transplanted to both coasts from Europe, may soon be readily available on the half-shell market.

Among the bits of folklore that have grown up around oysters is the belief that they make men more virile, which is doubtful, and the notion that they cannot be eaten in months whose names do not include the letter R, which is false. Months without an R roughly represent the oyster's spawning season (approximately May through October) during which it is perfect-ly *safe* to eat oysters—although the quality is generally consid-ered much lower than in the cooler months. Like clams and mussels, oysters should only be taken from unpolluted waters.

Two oyster farmers tend their beds in Olympia, Washington.

Oysters are sold fresh in the shell or shucked. Eat only those with a tightly shut shell. Shucked meats can be purchased frozen, smoked, and canned. At the market they are generally graded by size, ranging from about 160 to the gallon for extra large, to over 500 for the very small variety.

OYSTER CASSEROLE

1 quart shucked oysters (save oyster liquor)
6 tablespoons butter
1 clove garlic, crushed
6 slices white bread, trimmed
6 eggs
½ cup heavy cream
½ cup chicken bouillon
¼ teaspoon dry mustard
1 teaspoon paprika
½ pound Gruyère cheese, grated
1½ cups dry white wine

1. Preheat oven to 350° F.
2. In a saucepan, poach oysters in their own liquor until the edges just curl, about 2 minutes.
3. Cream butter and garlic together and spread on bread. Arrange bread slices in a shallow baking dish, buttered side down, and lay oysters and pan juices on top.
4. Beat eggs until foamy, then beat in cream. Add remaining ingredients. Pour this mixture over oysters and bread.
5. Bake in a 350° F. oven for 30 minutes, or until puffed and brown.

Yield: 6 servings

CREAMED OYSTERS

4 tablespoons butter
½ cup chopped onion
½ cup chopped celery
1 tablespoon flour
1 cup medium cream
1 teaspoon prepared mustard
1 teaspoon anchovy paste
½ teaspoon salt
⅛ teaspoon freshly ground pepper
Dash of cayenne
1½ cups shucked oysters (save oyster liquor)
2 tablespoons dry sherry

1. In a frying pan, heat butter. Add onion and celery and sauté until they just begin to soften.
2. With a wire whisk, stir in the flour and cook about 1 minute. Add cream, mustard, anchovy paste, salt, pepper, and cayenne, and blend gently.
3. Add oysters and their liquor and cook until edges just begin to curl. Heat sauce thoroughly, but do not boil.
4. Stir in sherry, warm briefly and serve on toast or English muffins. Garnish with chopped parsley.

Yield: 4 servings

"Southern Oyster Scallop. One layer of crumbled crackers with large lumps of butter and cream poured on quite moist, one layer of oysters, salt, pepper & pour on oyster juice to moisten well & do each layer the crackers followed by oysters until the pan you use may be full, being careful to make it rich with butter & cream & some juice always & the oysters well salted & peppered. It is much wiser to use 2 mediumly small pans for oyster scallop so one may be kept very hot in oven which the other is served. Use these as entrée dishes in baking dish & serve on meat plates with your meat & potatoes (& croquettes)—always have very hot or this dish loses its charm—3 pints will serve 12 people."

—old family recipe, collection of the author

OYSTER PIE

Crust:
2 cups flour
1 teaspoon baking powder
Dash of salt
2 tablespoons shortening
Milk

Filling:
3 dozen oysters, shucked (save
  oyster liquor)

4 hard-boiled eggs, sliced
4 tablespoons butter
Salt and freshly ground pepper,
  to taste
½ cup oyster liquor
½ cup milk
Flour

1. Make the crust: combine flour, baking powder, and salt. Cut in shortening and mix until mixture forms crumbs. Add enough milk so dough will hold together. Chill for 15 minutes.
2. Preheat oven to 375° F.
3. Divide pastry in half and roll out bottom crust. Return remaining dough to refrigerator. Line deep pan with crust and place half of the oysters on bottom.
4. Cover the oyster layer with half of the sliced egg. Dot with half the butter. Season with salt and pepper. Then, add in the following order, the rest of the oysters, eggs, and butter. Season again.
5. Pour oyster liquor and milk over top layer and sift a dusting of flour over liquid.
6. Roll out the top crust, cover the pie, crimp the edges and slash the center of the crust to permit steam to escape.
7. Bake in a 375° F. oven for 30 to 40 minutes, or until pastry is browned.

Yield: 6 to 8 servings

Among the foodstuffs required to satisfy Diamond Jim Brady's prodigious appetite were oysters, which he polished off at the rate of several dozen at a sitting. Restaurateur George Rector described the special arrangements his restaurant made to accommodate Diamond Jim: "We used to have our oysters shipped up to us from Baltimore daily, and every second or third shipment would include a barrel of Lynnhavens with the words 'For Mr. Brady' painted on the side of it. Even down in Maryland, the sea food dealers knew about Diamond Jim and saved all the giant oysters for him."

OYSTER STEW

2 cups milk
1 pint shucked oysters (save
  oyster liquor)
½ small onion, grated
1 stalk celery, grated
2 tablespoons butter

Salt and freshly ground pepper,
  to taste
1 tablespoon chopped fresh
  parsley
1 cup medium cream

1. Scald milk.
2. Heat oysters in their own liquor until edges begin to curl. Add onion, celery, butter, salt, pepper, parsley, and scalded milk. Add cream and heat through.
3. Serve at once.

Yield: 4 servings

OYSTER TURNOVERS

2-crust pie dough
2 dozen oysters, shucked and
  drained

½ cup spiced tomato sauce
  (Chapter 6) or ketchup

1. Preheat oven to 425° F.
2. Roll pastry about ⅛″ thick and cut into 2″ circles.
3. In center of each circle place 1 oyster and a little of the spiced tomato sauce (or ketchup). Fold pastry over and seal edges. Prick pastry with a fork to allow steam to escape.
4. Place on a cookie sheet and bake in a 425° F. oven for 15 minutes, or until pastry turns light brown.

Yield: 2 dozen

Clams

Clams are bivalve mollusks that burrow beneath the sand and mud in shallow waters close to the shoreline. Most clams can easily be had by treading or digging them out with one's toes or by using a special clam rake. But be sure to check local regulations before digging. The condition of the water from which the clams are taken must also be checked to ensure that they are not toxic.

Freshly dug clams are filled with mud and sand and must be cleaned before eating. Let the clams stand in a bucket of sea water for 15 or 20 minutes. Repeat the process with fresh saltwater two or three times to be sure the clams are clean. (Some fishermen suggest letting the clams soak for one hour in a solution of cornmeal and saltwater.) Clams need salt to stay alive, so if sea water is not available, use one-third cup of salt (preferably sea salt) to a gallon of fresh water. The shells can be scrubbed with a stiff brush.

Clams can be purchased at the market either fresh in the shell, shucked, or canned. As a rule, three dozen clams in the shell, one quart of shucked clams, or two seven-ounce cans will serve six people. When selecting fresh clams, choose only those that are tightly shut. When buying softshell clams, whose protruding siphons prevent the shells from closing, choose only those that have some constriction of the siphon when it is touched.

Hardshell clams or **quahaugs** (*Mercenaria mercenaria*), found only on the Atlantic Coast, are usually eaten raw on the half shell. Graded by size, quahaugs are sold as **little necks**—the smallest variety—and **cherrystones.** Quahaugs over three inches in diameter are commonly called **chowder clams. Softshell clams** (*Mya arenaria*), also found on the Atlantic Coast, are excellent for steaming. Less popular of the Eastern varieties are

"TO PICKLE OYSTERS. Take a quart of oysters, and wash them in their own liquor very well, till all the grittiness is out. Put them in a sauce pan or stew pan and strain the liquor over them. Set them on the fire, and scum them; then put in three or four blades of mace, a spoonful of whole pepper-corns, when you think they are boiled enough, throw in a glass of white wine. Let them have a thorough scald; then take them up, and when they are cold, put them in a pot and pour the liquor over them, and keep them for use. Take them out with a spoon."
—The Compleat Housewife,
1730

the large **skimmers** or **surf clams** (*Spisula solidissima*), found from Nova Scotia to South Carolina; these grow as large as eight inches and are the clams used in commercial clam chowders.

Razor clams are indigenous to both coasts. The Atlantic variety looks more like a straight-edged razor than does the more squat Pacific type. Both have sharp edges, a near-transparent shell, and cream-colored meat. **Butter clams** (*Saxidomus giganteus*) are a West Coast variety best eaten raw, while the **Pacific Coast littlenecks** (unlike the Eastern quahaugs of the same name), make fine steamers. This variety includes two species: **native littlenecks** (*Protothaca staminea*) and **Japanese littlenecks** (*Tapes philippinarium*), which were transplanted to the waters off California. Pacific Coast **geoducks** (*Panope generosa*), the largest American clams, grow to about five pounds. The large siphon protrudes from the shell and can be as long as three feet. Because their siphons spout gallons of water high in the air, geoducks can easily be spotted by clammers. **Horse clams** (*Tresus capax*), another Western variety, are similar to geoducks. The siphons of both clams can be ground and cooked.

Decked out in hip boots and derby, this clam digger uses a rake to pry steamers from tidal flats on Little Deer Island Maine.

QUAHAUG CHOWDER

¼ pound salt pork, cubed
3 medium onions, chopped
2 large potatoes, peeled and diced
4 cups chopped quahaug meat

2 cups quahaug liquor*
4 cups milk
2 cups medium cream
Freshly ground pepper, to taste

1. In a large saucepan, sauté the salt pork over low heat. If necessary, add a bit of water to prevent browning. Add onions and sauté until they soften.
2. Add potatoes and water to cover and cook until they are tender. Add quahaug meat and liquor and cook 5 minutes. Add milk and simmer 5 minutes longer. Do not boil. Do not overcook, or quahaugs will toughen.
3. When ready to serve, add cream. Heat through but do not boil. Season with pepper.
4. Serve in bowls with large pat of butter on top, accompanied by oyster crackers or pilot biscuits.

Yield: 6 servings

*Fresh from the shucked clams or bottled.

"But when that smoking chowder came in. . . . Oh! sweet friends, hearken to me. It was made of small juicy clams, scarcely bigger than hazel nuts, mixed with pounded ship biscuits, and salted pork cut up into little flakes! the whole enriched with butter, and plentifully seasoned with pepper and salt. Our appetites being sharpened by the frosty voyage, and in particular, Queegueg seeing his favorite fishing food before him, and the chowder being surpassingly excellent, we despatched it with great expedition. . . ."

—Moby Dick, Herman Melville

CLAMS À LA MARINARA

5 tablespoons olive oil	Salt and freshly ground pepper,
1 medium onion, finely chopped	to taste
2 tomatoes, chopped	6 dozen cherrystone clams
½ cup dry white wine	

1. In a frying pan, heat oil, add onion and sauté until it just begins to soften. Add tomatoes and continue cooking until the liquid thickens slightly.
2. Add wine, salt, pepper, and clams. Cook until all shells have opened. Garnish with chopped parsley and serve.

Yield: 4 servings

CLAM PASTA

1 pound pasta (egg noodles, spaghetti, or shells)	1½ cups razor or softshell clam meat (save the liquor)
3 tablespoons butter	1 cup medium cream
1 small onion, finely chopped	Salt and freshly ground pepper,
2 cloves garlic, minced	to taste
⅔ cup chopped fresh parsley	

1. Cook pasta according to package directions.
2. Meanwhile, in a frying pan, heat butter and sauté onion and garlic until just soft, about 5 minutes.
3. Add parsley, clams, and their liquor, and cook, stirring constantly, until clams turn slightly opaque. Do not overcook.
4. Add cream, salt, and pepper. Heat through but do not boil.
5. Serve clam sauce over pasta.

Yield: 4 servings

STUFFED CLAMS

1 dozen cherrystone clams	2 tablespoons butter, melted
4 tablespoons olive oil	Salt and freshly ground pepper,
1 medium onion, chopped	to taste
2 cloves garlic, minced	¼ teaspoon oregano
1 tablespoon chopped fresh parsley or chives	¼ cup grated Parmesan cheese
½ cup fine bread crumbs	Lemon juice

1. Preheat oven to 400° F.
2. Shuck clams, chop and set aside. Reserve half the shells, wash well, and set aside.
3. In a frying pan, heat olive oil. Add onion, garlic, and parsley (or chives), and sauté until just soft. Off the heat, add clams and toss lightly.

A clam chowder from Manhattan's famous Fulton Fish Market: "Fry one-half pound of fat salt pork until the fat is extracted. Skim out the scraps and put in an onion chopped fine and fry it a light yellow. Turn the contents of the frying pan into a pot. Add a cupful of the strained liquor of the clams and the same quantity of water, which should have been heated together to the boiling point. Put in one quart of tomatoes stewed, the hard portions chopped. Put one-half dozen whole allspice and the same number of whole cloves into a piece of cheese cloth, tie securely, and drop into the soup. Cook four hours. Half an hour before serving add the hard part of the clams, which should have been chopped very fine, and ten minutes before the soup is to be put into the tureen add the soft part of the clams. Season with a dash of red pepper and a teaspoonful of Worcestershire sauce. This recipe is for fifty clams."
—Grand Union Cook Book, 1902

4. Combine bread crumbs, butter, salt, pepper, and oregano.
5. Grease each clam shell. Divide clam mixture evenly among shells. Top each shell with crumb mixture. Sprinkle with Parmesan and a squeeze of lemon juice.
6. Place on baking pan and bake in a 400° F. oven for 10 minutes, or until crumbs are browned.
Yield: 6 servings

WHITE CLAM SAUCE

¼ cup olive oil
2 garlic cloves, minced
1 cup clam juice*
Salt and freshly ground pepper, to taste
Pinch of oregano

2 tablespoons chopped fresh parsley
24 littlenecks (the smaller the better)
4 tablespoons butter

1. In a large frying pan, heat oil, add garlic, and sizzle gently.
2. Stir in clam juice, salt, pepper, oregano, parsley, and clams. Simmer uncovered until the littlenecks open.
3. Add butter and stir very gently so the littlenecks don't come out of their shells. Serve over linguine or spaghetti.
Yield: 6 servings

Variation: For red sauce, substitute 1 cup tomato sauce for the clam juice and omit the butter.

*Fresh from the shucked clams or bottled.

Mussels

Mussels (*Mytilidae*) have never been as popular with Americans as other shellfish, but they are delicious and plentiful. Of all the species found in North American waters, only the marine **blue mussel** (*Mytilus edulis*) is considered edible. Colonies of mussels are readily found attached to rocks, pilings and seawalls along the Atlantic and Pacific coasts. The mussels attach themselves to the rocks by means of strong, coarse threads (called beard), but can be pried loose with a little effort. As with clams and oysters, mussels can be poisoned by their environment. From May through October, Pacific Coast mussels are known to be toxic, but even at other times water conditions should be checked with local authorities to be sure that the catch is safe to eat. Only harvest (or buy) those mussels that are tightly shut. Clean the mussels by scraping off any barnacles and scrubbing them with a stiff wire brush. Live mussels, covered with a damp cloth or seaweed, will keep for 24 hours. After cooking, discard any that have not opened.

"The inhabitants [of Cape Cod] measure their crops, not only by bushels of corn, but by barrels of clams. A thousand barrels of clam-bait are counted as equal in value to six or eight thousand bushels of Indian corn, and once they were procured without more labor or expense, and the supply was thought to be inexhaustible."
—Cape Cod, Henry David Thoreau

MUSSELS MARINIÈRE

3 pounds mussels
4 tablespoons butter
½ cup chopped scallions
1 teaspoon thyme
1 tablespoon chopped fresh
  parsley

Salt and freshly ground pepper,
  to taste
1 cup dry white wine
½ teaspoon lemon juice

1. Scrub mussels well.
2. In a large frying pan, heat 2 tablespoons of the butter. Add scallions and sauté until they just begin to soften. Add mussels, thyme, parsley, salt, pepper, and wine. Cook, closely covered, until shells open, about 5 to 10 minutes.
3. Push mussels to one side of the pan, add remaining 2 tablespoons of butter and lemon juice, and stir well. Serve mussels with broth.

Yield: 4 to 6 servings

Recording the bounty in the New World, William Strachey wrote, in 1612, "Oysters there be in whole banks and beds, and those of the best. I have seen some thirteen inches long. The savages use to boil oysters and mussels together and with the broth they make a good spoon meat, thickened with the flour of their wheat and its great thrift and husbandry with them to hang the oysters upon strings . . . and dried in the smoke, thereby to preserve them all the year."

KATE'S MUSSELS

Batter:
1⅓ cups flour
1 teaspoon salt
¼ teaspoon freshly ground
  pepper
1 tablespoon butter, melted
2 egg yolks, beaten
¾ cup flat beer

4 dozen mussels
4 tablespoons butter

2 cloves garlic, coarsely chopped
6 shallots or 2 scallions, chopped
½ teaspoon thyme
½ bay leaf
½ cup dry white wine
Lemon juice
Olive oil
Chopped fresh parsley
Oil, for deep-frying

1. In a bowl, combine flour, salt, pepper, melted butter, and egg yolks. Blend until smooth. Add slowly, stirring constantly, the beer. Cover the batter and refrigerate from 3 to 12 hours before using.
2. Scrub mussels well.
3. In a large frying pan, heat butter and sauté garlic and shallots (or scallions) until shallots soften.
4. In a small saucepan, simmer thyme, bay leaf, and wine for about 2 minutes. Add to garlic and shallots.
5. Place mussels in frying pan, cover tightly, and cook over medium-high heat for 6 to 8 minutes. Remove from the heat the minute the shells are open. Remove the mussels from the shells, discard shells and set mussels aside.
6. Make a marinade of 1 part lemon juice to 2 parts olive oil,

with 1 tablespoon chopped fresh parsley for every ½ cup of marinade (the amount of marinade needed will depend on how much it takes to barely cover the mussels). Steep the mussels in the marinade for 30 minutes.

7. In a heavy skillet, heat oil to 375° F. Dip mussels one at a time into batter and deep-fry until golden brown. Drain on paper toweling.

8. Serve with lemon wedges.

Yield: 8 servings

BILLI BI

1 pound mussels	2 tablespoons chopped fresh
3 tablespoons butter	parsley
1 medium onion, chopped	Salt and freshly ground pepper,
2 cloves garlic, chopped	to taste
1 cup dry white wine	1 cup heavy cream

1. Scrub mussels well.
2. In a frying pan, heat butter, add onion and garlic and sauté until onion just begins to soften.
3. Add mussels and wine. Cover closely and cook until shells open, about 5 to 10 minutes.
4. Remove mussels and set aside.
5. To the broth, add parsley and season with salt and pepper. Stir in cream and reheat very briefly. Serve in bowls garnished with mussels.

Yield: 4 servings

Scallops

Of the more than 400 species of scallops (*Pectinidae*) found in the world, five are native to the East Coast waters of the United States. Of these the **bay scallop** (*Argopecten irradians*) and the **sea scallop** (*Placopecten magellanicus*) are the most important. Bay scallops can be found in shallow waters from north of Cape Hatteras down to Florida and in the Gulf of Mexico. Their shells grow to three inches in diameter. The larger sea scallops live in deep waters from Labrador to New Jersey but abound off the coast of Maine. Their shells run to about five inches in diameter. Of lesser importance are the **calico, little northern,** and **thick scallops.**

Scallops are never sold in the shell. Because this bivalve mollusk cannot shut its shell tightly, it dries out and dies when taken from the water. Therefore, as soon as they are caught, the meat is removed and refrigerated. The meat of the scallop is actually the animal's large adductor muscle, which controls the

"TO FRY MUSCLES. Put them into a kettle, in which there is as much boiling water as will cover them. Being enough, take them up and beard them, then wash them in warm water, wipe them dry and flour them. Being fried crisp, dish them up with butter beaten with the juice of lemon and parsley throwed over them, fried crisp and green."

—The Family Dictionary, *1705*

opening and closing of the scallop shell. Although the rest of the scallop is edible, North Americans have never developed a taste for it. Scallops should always be cooked just before serving to ensure that they do not lose their fine, delicate flavor.

SAUTÉED SCALLOPS

1 pound bay or sea scallops
Flour seasoned with salt and
   freshly ground pepper, for
   dredging

3 tablespoons butter
1 tablespoon finely chopped
   fresh parsley
1 teaspoon lemon juice

1. Pat scallops dry with paper toweling. Put seasoned flour in a paper bag, add scallops and shake to coat evenly.
2. In a frying pan large enough to hold scallops in one layer, melt butter over moderate heat. Add scallops and sauté, shaking the pan often, or turning with a fork. Cook bay scallops about 5 minutes, larger sea scallops about 8 minutes.
3. When almost done, sprinkle with parsley and lemon juice. Serve with lemon wedges.

Yield: 4 servings

Variation: Add ¼ cup dry white wine or dry vermouth in place of lemon juice in Step 3.

Scallops

SCALLOPS IN THE SHELL

2 pounds bay scallops
1 cup sliced mushrooms
1 onion, finely chopped
1¼ cups dry white wine
4 tablespoons butter
½ cup flour
½ cup dry sherry

Milk
Salt and freshly ground pepper,
   to taste
⅔ cup heavy cream
Grated Gruyère or Parmesan
   cheese

1. In a saucepan, combine scallops, mushrooms, onion, and wine. Cover and poach for about 5 minutes. Strain, reserving the poaching liquid. Set scallop mixture aside.
2. In another saucepan, melt the butter. Add flour and cook for a few minutes without browning. Add reserved poaching liquid and sherry, and stir. If mixture gets too thick, thin with a bit of milk or cream.
3. Off the heat, add scallop mixture. Season with salt and pepper and lightly stir in cream. Reheat gently.
4. Divide evenly among 6 to 8 scallop shells. Sprinkle with grated cheese and brown under the broiler.

Yield: 6 to 8 servings

· SCALLOP STEW

5 tablespoons butter	2 cups light cream
¼ cup finely chopped celery and leaves	Salt and freshly ground pepper, to taste
½ pound sea scallops, quartered	Butter
¼ teaspoon Worcestershire sauce	Cayenne

1. In a frying pan, heat butter, add celery and leaves, and sauté until they just begin to soften. Add scallops and cook over low heat for about 2 minutes, stirring occasionally.
2. Add Worcestershire sauce and cream and bring to a simmer. Season with salt and pepper. Serve topped with a pat of butter and a dash of cayenne.

Yield: 2 to 4 servings

Conch

Indigenous to the Florida Keys and the Caribbean, the conch (*Strombidae*) boasts a beautiful shell and a large, edible foot. Not all conchs are edible, however; some conchs can cause nausea. Most popular of the edible conchs are **pink** or **queen conchs** (*Strombus gigas*). Other less well known, but also edible, species include **Verrill's conch, hawkwing conch,** and **milk** or **ivory conch.** Because conch meat is muscular, it does require tenderizing; and, unlike most shellfish, it should be well cooked. Conch is delicious as **scungilli,** chowder, in salads, or fried. From Florida north, fresh conch in markets or restaurants may actually be **channeled whelk** or **knobbed whelk.**

"The women once a day, as the tide gave way, resorted to the mussels and clambankes, which are a fish as big as horse-mussels, where they daily gathered their families food. . . . Quoth [one woman] 'and yet methinks our children are as cheerful, fat and lusty with feeding upon these mussels, clambanks and other fish, as they were in England with their fill of bread.' "
—Saviour in New England, 1654

CONCH SALAD

1 pound conch meat, thinly sliced	½ teaspoon oregano
2 to 3 stalks celery, chopped	¼ teaspoon basil
½ cup chopped fresh parsley	2 cloves garlic, crushed
2 medium tomatoes, coarsely chopped	Salt and freshly ground pepper, to taste
½ cup olive oil	½ cup bean sprouts
2 tablespoons white wine vinegar	

1. In a bowl, toss conch, celery, parsley, and tomatoes.
2. Combine olive oil, vinegar, oregano, basil, garlic, salt, and pepper, and pour over conch. Cover and refrigerate for 8 hours. Just before serving, toss with bean sprouts.

Yield: 6 servings

Abalone

A univalve mollusk, abalones are as prized for their beautiful, iridescent, ear-shaped shells, as for their flavorful meat. Only their large footlike organs (common to all gastropods) are edible. Practically all native abalone can be found along the California coast, but because of its scarcity, state laws prohibit the canning of abalone or the shipping of fresh or frozen meat. Abalone available outside California comes from Mexico or Japan and can be purchased frozen, canned, or dried. Fresh abalone is rubbery and should be pounded and tenderized before cooking. It is essential not to overcook the meat or it will become extremely tough. Abalone is also good raw in salads or as *sushi*.

ABALONE SESAME STEAKS

¼ cup sesame seeds
1 pound abalone, cut into 4 steaks
2 eggs
2 tablespoons milk
1 cup fine bread crumbs

⅛ teaspoon cayenne
Flour seasoned with salt and freshly ground pepper, for dredging
½ cup (1 stick) butter
2 teaspoons lemon juice

1. In a heavy frying pan, toast sesame seeds over medium heat until evenly browned. Shake pan often to prevent burning.
2. With a heavy mallet or veal pounder, pound abalone steaks until they are half their original thickness.
3. In a large, shallow bowl, beat eggs with milk. In another shallow bowl, combine toasted sesame seeds, bread crumbs, and cayenne.
4. Pat abalone dry. Dredge first in seasoned flour, then beaten eggs, then sesame-crumb mixture.
5. In a large frying pan, heat butter and lemon juice until frothy. Immediately add steaks and sauté over medium heat about 2 minutes on each side, or until browned. Do not overcook, or abalone will toughen. Serve with lemon wedges.

Yield: 4 servings

Squid

Squid is a lean-fleshed, highly proteinaceous, and greatly under-utilized (in North America) source of food. A remarkable 80 percent of the squid's tentacled, bullet-shaped body is edible. Squid range in size from a modest six inches to an enormous 60 feet (**giant squid**). Varieties common to North American waters are the **Atlantic squid** (*Loligo pealei*) and the **Pacific squid** (*Loligo opalescens*). Squid flesh is delicately flavored and naturally tender, but will get rubbery if overcooked. It is sold

---

"FISH STOCK. Place a saucepan over the fire with a good sized piece of sweet butter, and a sliced onion; put into that some sliced tomatoes, then add as many different kinds of small fish as you can get—oysters, clams, smelts, prawns, crabs, shrimps, and all kinds of pan-fish; cook all together, until the onions are well browned; then add a bunch of sweet herbs, salt and pepper, and sufficient water to make the required amount of stock. After this has cooked for half an hour pound it with a wooden pestle, then strain and cook again until it jellies."

—White House Cook Book, 1894

---

commercially in many forms: fresh, frozen, salted, pickled, dried, and canned. Small squid are usually cooked whole and stuffed; larger squid are cut into rings. The ink that the squid uses to hide from its prey is often eaten with the squid.

SQUID FRITTERS

1 pound squid, cleaned	**2 eggs, separated**
1 cup flour	**⅔ cup milk**
¼ teaspoon nutmeg	**Oil, for deep-frying**
⅛ teaspoon cayenne	
Salt and freshly ground pepper,	
to taste	

1. Cut squid into 3″-by-1″ strips.
2. Combine flour, nutmeg, cayenne, salt, and pepper. Lightly beat egg yolks with milk and add to flour, mixing well.
3. Beat egg whites until stiff and fold into batter.
4. In a deep, heavy kettle, heat oil to 375° F. Dip squid strips in batter and fry in oil until golden brown. Drain on paper toweling.

Yield: 4 servings

Octopus

Octopus

Although rarely eaten by Americans, the eight-armed, round-bodied octopus features prominently in many Oriental and Mediterranean dishes. Octopus is sold fresh, frozen, smoked, and canned and has a fine flavored, firm flesh. The commercial catch of octopus in North America is almost entirely of **Pacific octopus** (*Octopus dofleini*), although there is an **Atlantic octopus** (*Octopus vulgaris*) as well. As with squid, the octopus has an ink sac whose "ink" can be used in octopus recipes.

OCTOPUS IN WINE

1¾-pound octopus, cleaned	**1 bay leaf**
4 tablespoons olive oil	**¼ cup dry white wine**
2 large onions, sliced	
Salt and freshly ground pepper,	
to taste	

1. Cut the octopus into bite-sized chunks.
2. In a frying pan, heat olive oil. Add octopus and cook for about 10 minutes, turning regularly.
3. Add onions, salt, pepper, bay leaf, and wine. Cover and simmer gently until octopus is tender, about 15 minutes.

Yield: 4 servings

6: Stocks, Sauces & Side Dishes

FISH HERBS

The following herbs are those that best complement the flavors of fish; they can be used in sauces, herbed butters, or in poaching liquids: **dill, parsley, chives, shallots, scallions, chervil, basil, savory, thyme, tarragon, marjoram,** and **rosemary.** If using whole, fresh herbs, crumple or crush them slightly before adding them to bring out their flavors.

Stockpot

FISH STOCK I

Use fish stock to make sauces, soups, and aspics. Fish stock can be used immediately, or stored for later use by freezing or refrigerating. If stored in the refrigerator, the stock must be brought to a boil every 3 days to prevent spoilage.

2 pounds fish heads, bones, and trimmings
5 cups water
3 cups dry white wine
2 medium onions, chopped
3 to 4 sprigs fresh parsley
¼ teaspoon marjoram
¼ teaspoon thyme
6 peppercorns
Pinch of salt

1. Place all ingredients in a large stockpot and simmer gently, uncovered, for 30 to 45 minutes, until reduced by half.
2. Strain through cheesecloth or a fine sieve.

Yield: 4 cups

Note: Add shellfish shells, or clam or oyster liquor to enhance flavor.

FISH STOCK II

3 tablespoons vegetable oil
⅓ cup chopped onions
⅓ cup sliced carrots
⅓ cup sliced celery
4 cups white wine
4 cups water
2 pounds fish heads, bones, and trimmings
Pinch of fennel seeds
4 sprigs fresh parsley
1 bay leaf
Salt and freshly ground pepper, to taste

1. In a large stockpot, heat oil and cook onions, carrots, and celery gently until soft.
2. Add wine, water, and fish. Bring to a boil. Skim off foam.
3. Add fennel, parsley, and bay leaf and simmer, uncovered, for 30 to 45 minutes, until reduced by half.
4. Strain through cheesecloth and season with salt and pepper.

Yield: 4 cups

◀*An Illinois cook stands over her new, 1911-model gas range.*

COURT BOUILLON

Court bouillons are seasoned liquids used for poaching. The amount of liquid required will depend on the size of the fish to be poached, but the proportion of ingredients should remain the same. The recipe listed here will accommodate at least 6 pounds of fish.

5 quarts water
4 cups dry white wine
¾ cup white wine vinegar
2 carrots, roughly sliced
1 large onion, roughly sliced

4 sprigs fresh parsley
1 sprig fresh thyme
1 bay leaf
6 peppercorns
2 tablespoons salt

1. In a large pan or fish poacher, bring water to a boil. Add the remaining ingredients.
2. When the liquid returns to the boil, add fish, reduce heat to a simmer and cook according to the recipe.

Note: A court bouillon can be saved and used again, but will not keep longer than 2 or 3 days refrigerated. It can also be made into a fish stock by boiling it to reduce it by half.

"Red Vegetable Salad. One pint of cold boiled potatoes, one pint of cold boiled beets, one pint of uncooked red cabbage, six tablespoonfuls of oil, eight of red vinegar . . . two teaspoonfuls of salt . . . half a teaspoonful of pepper. Cut the potatoes in thin slices and the beets fine, and slice the cabbage as thin as possible. Mix all the ingredients. Let stand in a cold place one hour; then serve. . . ."
—Miss Parloa's New Cook Book, 1880

BROILING BUTTERS

Basic butter mixture:
4 tablespoons butter
2 tablespoons lemon juice
Dash of cayenne

To be combined with:
½ clove garlic, crushed
¼ teaspoon curry powder
¼ teaspoon chili powder
¼ teaspoon paprika
¼ teaspoon crushed celery seed

¼ teaspoon marjoram
¼ teaspoon thyme
2 teaspoons anchovy paste
¼ cup toasted slivered almonds
¼ cup toasted hazelnuts
¼ cup ground peanuts
¼ cup dry white wine (eliminate lemon juice)
¼ cup orange juice (eliminate lemon juice)

1. In a saucepan, melt butter, add lemon juice, cayenne, and one of suggested additions.
Yield: ¼ cup

MUSTARD BUTTER

½ cup (1 stick) butter
1½ teaspoons salt
2 teaspoons lemon juice

1 teaspoon prepared mustard
Dash of freshly ground pepper

1. In a small saucepan, melt butter and add remaining ingredients.
Yield: ½ cup

WHITE SAUCE

2 tablespoons butter
2 tablespoons flour
1½ cups milk

Dash of nutmeg (optional)
Salt and freshly ground pepper,
   to taste

1. In a saucepan, melt butter, add flour, mixing with a wire whisk, and cook over low heat for 1 minute.
2. Stirring constantly, gradually add milk and cook over medium heat until slightly thickened and smooth. Season with nutmeg (if desired), salt, and pepper.

Yield: 1½ cups

THICK WHITE SAUCE

3 tablespoons butter
3 tablespoons flour
1 cup milk

Dash of nutmeg (optional)
Salt and freshly ground pepper,
   to taste

1. Follow instructions for WHITE SAUCE.

Yield: 1 cup

PARSLEY SAUCE

1½ cups white sauce
1 tablespoon lemon juice

3 tablespoons chopped fresh
   parsley

1. Make white sauce. Just before serving, stir in lemon juice and parsley.

Yield: 1½ cups

CELERY-FLAVORED WHITE SAUCE

1½ cups white sauce

½ cup minced celery and leaves

1. Make white sauce and add celery. Stir to heat, then serve.

Yield: 1½ cups

MUSHROOM SAUCE

1 tablespoon butter
1 cup chopped mushrooms

1½ cups white sauce

1. In a saucepan, heat butter and sauté mushrooms until they just soften. Remove mushrooms and set aside.
2. In the same pan, make the white sauce. Then return the mushrooms to the sauce and stir to warm.

Yield: 2 cups

"Sauce Matelote
Peel about twenty button onions, then put a teaspoonful of powdered sugar in a stew-pan, place it over a sharp fire, and when melted and getting brown, add a piece of butter the size of two walnuts, and your onions, pass them over the fire until rather brown; then add a glass of sherry, let it boil, then add a pint of brown sauce and ten spoonfuls of consomme, simmer at the corner of the fire until the onions are quite tender, skim it well; then add twenty small quenelles, ten heads of mushrooms, and a teaspoonful of essence of anchoves, one of catsup, one of Harvey sauce, and a little cayenne. . . ."
—Frank Forester's Fish and Fishing of the United States and British Provinces of North America, 1864

MORNAY SAUCE

2 tablespoons butter
2 tablespoons flour
¼ teaspoon salt
Dash of freshly ground pepper
1 cup milk

½ cup fish stock (page 185)
¼ cup grated Gruyère cheese
¼ cup grated Parmesan cheese
1 egg yolk, lightly beaten

1. In a saucepan, melt butter, add flour, mixing with a wire whisk, and cook over low heat for 1 minute.
2. Stir in salt and pepper, then add milk and fish stock. Cook, stirring constantly, until mixture thickens and bubbles. Add cheese and stir until melted. Remove from heat.
3. Pour small amount of hot mixture into egg yolk, stirring constantly. Return warmed egg yolk to sauce and, stirring constantly, continue cooking until mixture thickens.

Yield: 1½ cups

VELOUTÉ SAUCE

3 tablespoons butter
2 tablespoons flour
Salt and freshly ground pepper,
    to taste

¾ cup milk
1½ cups fish stock (page 185)

1. In a saucepan, melt butter, add flour, mixing with a wire whisk, and cook over low heat for 1 minute.
2. Season with salt and pepper, then add milk and fish stock all at once. Cook, stirring constantly, until mixture thickens and bubbles. Remove from heat.

Yield: 1½ cups

EGG SAUCE

4 tablespoons butter
2 tablespoons flour
¾ teaspoon dry mustard
1¼ cups milk
½ teaspoon salt

Dash of freshly ground pepper
2 hard-boiled eggs, chopped
1 tablespoon chopped fresh
    parsley

1. In a saucepan, melt butter, add flour and mustard, mixing with a wire whisk, and cook over low heat for 1 minute. Stirring constantly, gradually add milk and cook over medium heat until slightly thickened and smooth.
2. Add salt and pepper. Add eggs and parsley and heat through.

Yield: 1½ cups

"Sauce for Salmon Loaf. Heat one pint of milk and thicken with one tablespoon of corn-starch and two tablespoons of butter, rubbed together. Add the liquor from one can of salmon, one tablespoon each of tomato ketchup and Worcestershire with a pinch of cayenne. Pour over a well beaten egg, beat well and serve."
—Good Housekeeping Family Cookbook, 1909

EGG AND SHRIMP SAUCE

4 tablespoons butter
2 tablespoons flour
1¼ cups milk
½ teaspoon salt
Dash of freshly ground pepper

2 hard-boiled eggs, chopped
1 cup cooked, chopped shrimp
1 tablespoon chopped fresh
  parsley

1. In a saucepan, melt butter, add flour, mixing with a wire whisk, and cook over low heat for 1 minute. Stirring constantly, gradually add milk and cook over medium heat until slightly thickened and smooth.
2. Add salt and pepper. Add eggs, shrimp, and parsley and heat through.

Yield: 2 cups

SHRIMP SAUCE

2 tablespoons butter
2 tablespoons flour
1 cup fish stock* (p. 185)

2 tablespoons lemon juice
Salt and cayenne, to taste
1 cup cooked, chopped shrimp

1. In a saucepan, melt butter, add flour, mixing with a wire whisk, and cook over low heat for 1 minute. Stirring constantly, gradually add fish stock and cook until thickened and smooth.
2. Add lemon juice, salt, and cayenne and mix. Add shrimp and warm through.

Yield: 2 cups

Variation: Add 2 egg yolks and ½ cup medium cream to make a richer sauce. Warm in a double boiler to make thick, like custard.

*If fish stock is unavailable, use ½ cup water in which shrimp were cooked and ½ cup medium cream.

GREEN SAUCE I

4 egg yolks
1 tablespoon tarragon vinegar
Salt and freshly ground pepper,
  to taste

1½ cups olive oil
2 tablespoons heavy cream
½ cup cooked, pureed spinach

1. In a bowl small enough to be placed in a pan of water, mix egg yolks, vinegar, salt, and pepper. Set the bowl in a pan of warm water and heat over medium heat.
2. Stirring constantly, add oil, cream, and spinach.
3. As soon as mixture becomes thick and smooth, serve hot.

Yield: 2¼ cups

"TO MAKE SHRIMP SAUCE. Wash half a pint of shrimps very clean. Mince and put them in a stew pan, with a spoonful of anchovy liquor and a pound of thick melted butter; boil it up for five minutes and squeeze in half a lemon. Toss it up and put it in a sauce boat."

—The Virginia Housewife,
1825

GREEN SAUCE II

1 cup chopped fresh spinach
½ cup chopped watercress
2 scallions, chopped
4 tablespoons chopped fresh
  parsley
1 teaspoon chopped fresh
  tarragon

1 cup sour cream
2 cups mayonnaise (p. 191)
Dash of Tabasco sauce
Salt and freshly ground pepper,
  to taste

1. In a blender or food processor, blend spinach, watercress, scallions, parsley, and tarragon. Add sour cream, then mayonnaise, blending until just mixed. Add Tabasco sauce and season with salt and pepper and blend very briefly.
Yield: 3 cups

DILL SAUCE I

2 eggs
2 tablespoons olive or vegetable
  oil
Salt and freshly ground pepper,
  to taste

½ cup heavy cream
½ teaspoon Worcestershire
  sauce
2 tablespoons chopped fresh dill

1. Beat eggs until light.
2. Beating constantly, add remaining ingredients.
Yield: 1 cup

"Mousseline Sauce. Beat a tablespoon of butter to a cream; add the yolks of three eggs, one at a time, then add three tablespoons of lemon juice, half a teaspoon of salt and a dash of cayenne. Cook over hot water until the sauce thickens, then add another tablespoon of butter and half a cup of sweet cream. When the sauce is hot, serve. It should be quite thick and frothy."
—Good Housekeeping Family
      Cookbook, *1909*

DILL SAUCE II

2 cups mayonnaise (p. 191)
3 tablespoons chopped fresh dill
1 tablespoon chopped fresh
  chives

1 tablespoon Dijon mustard
1 tablespoon lemon juice
½ cup heavy cream

1. Combine all ingredients, except cream, and chill.
2. Just before serving, whip cream and fold into mayonnaise mixture.
Yield: 3 cups

CUCUMBER SAUCE

1 large cucumber
¼ cup heavy cream
1 tablespoon lime juice
10 watercress leaves

½ cup sour cream
Salt, to taste
Tabasco sauce, to taste
1 teaspoon grated lime rind

1. Peel and seed cucumber and cut into small pieces.
2. Drop pieces into blender or food processor with cream, lime

juice, and watercress leaves. Blend until the cucumber is pureed and the mixture is pale green.
3. Stir the puree into the sour cream.
4. Season with salt and Tabasco sauce. Stir in lime rind.
Yield: 2 cups

MAYONNAISE

Be sure that all ingredients are at room temperature.

4 egg yolks
2 teaspoons Dijon mustard or ½
teaspoon dry mustard
Pinch of salt

1 tablespoon lemon juice or
vinegar
1¼ cups olive oil

1. Beat egg yolks until lemon-colored. Beat in mustard, salt, and lemon juice (or vinegar).
2. Beating constantly, add olive oil drop by drop (this is very important) until the mixture begins to thicken. Then add the rest of the olive oil in a thin, continuous stream, beating all the time. As the oil is added, the sauce will continue to thicken. Should it become too thick, add a few more drops of lemon juice (or vinegar) and mix.

Note: If the sauce curdles, drop an egg yolk into a new bowl, and stirring constantly, add the mayonnaise a little at a time.
Yield: 2 cups

Variation: As a sauce for fish, flavor with fish herbs, freshly grated horseradish, lemon rind, or lobster coral.

"Red Mayonnaise Dressing. Lobster 'coral' is pounded to a powder, rubbed through a sieve, and mixed with mayonnaise dressing. This gives a dressing of a bright color. Or the juice from boiled beets can be used instead of 'coral'."
—Miss Parloa's New Cook Book, 1880

FOOD PROCESSOR MAYONNAISE

1 egg
½ teaspoon dry mustard or 1
tablespoon Dijon mustard
1 teaspoon salt

1 tablespoon lemon juice or
vinegar
⅓ cup vegetable oil
⅔ cup olive oil

1. Place plastic blade in work bowl. Put egg, mustard, and salt in bowl and process for 20 seconds.
2. Pour in lemon juice (or vinegar) and process.
3. Combine oils. With the processor turned on, pour oil very slowly through the feed tube until the mixture starts to thicken, then pour the remaining oil in a little faster. If too thick, add 1 tablespoon hot water. The longer the machine is run, the thicker the mayonnaise becomes.
Yield: 1¼ cups

HOLLANDAISE SAUCE

½ cup (1 stick) butter
2 egg yolks*
2 teaspoons lemon juice

¼ teaspoon salt
Pinch of cayenne

1. In a small saucepan, heat butter until it begins to bubble.
2. Meanwhile, in a blender or food processor, beat egg yolks very briefly. Then add remaining ingredients and turn blender or food processor on and immediately off.
3. Turn blender or food processor on again (blender on high speed) and pour in hot butter in a slow thin stream. When last drop is mixed, turn off.

Note: If sauce gets too thick, add 1 teaspoon of cold water.

4. Serve warm.

Yield: 1 cup

* For a thinner sauce, use 3 egg yolks.

WALNUT SAUCE

½ cup ground walnuts
1¼ tablespoons sugar
1 teaspoon salt
1 cup water
¼ cup vinegar

1 tablespoon chopped fresh coriander
1 tablespoon chopped fresh parsley

1. In a saucepan, combine walnuts, sugar, salt, and water, and simmer for 10 minutes.
2. Add vinegar, coriander, and parsley, and simmer for another 5 minutes.
3. Serve hot or cold.

Yield: 1 cup

MUSTARD SAUCE

¼ cup dry white wine
¼ cup fish stock (p. 185)
1 tablespoon chopped shallots
1 cup velouté (p. 188)

1 tablespoon Dijon mustard
1 tablespoon butter
1 teaspoon chopped fresh parsley

1. Combine wine, fish stock, and shallots. Reduce by ⅓ by quick boiling.
2. Add velouté and mustard and bring to a boil.
3. Add butter and parsley, stir to mix, and serve.

Yield: 1⅓ cups

"Beet Fritters a la Dickens. *Cut beets, after boiling, into slices an eighth of an inch thick; mince a few mushrooms with one-eighth their bulk in onions; press between two slices of beet and dip in a batter made by beating the yolk of an egg, adding a tablespoon of oil or melted butter, four of flour, and lastly the whipped white, with salt and pepper to taste; fry these fritters in very hot fat.*"

—Good Housekeeping Family Cookbook, *1909*

TARTAR SAUCE

1 cup mayonnaise (p. 191)
1 tablespoon minced sweet
  pickle
1 tablespoon minced fresh
  parsley

1 tablespoon minced capers
1 tablespoon minced onion

1. Mix all ingredients together thoroughly. Chill.
Yield: 1¼ cups

CAPER SAUCE

½ cup white wine vinegar
4 tablespoons lemon juice
1 scallion, minced
2 tablespoons chopped fresh
  parsley

½ teaspoon salt
½ teaspoon sugar
¼ teaspoon freshly ground
  pepper
3 tablespoons chopped capers

1. Combine all ingredients and let stand for at least 1 hour.
Yield: 1 cup

SOUR CREAM CAPER SAUCE

2 egg yolks
1 cup sour cream
1 tablespoon tarragon vinegar
⅛ teaspoon salt

⅛ teaspoon paprika
⅛ teaspoon Tabasco sauce
3 tablespoons chopped capers

1. Place egg yolks in top of a double boiler, over hot but not
   boiling water. Stir in cream, vinegar, salt, paprika, Tabasco
   sauce, and capers. Continue stirring until smooth and thick.
Yield: 1¼ cups

"TO MAKE A DISH OF RICE TO BE SERVED UP WITH THE CURRY IN A DISH BY ITSELF *Take half a pound of rice, wash it clean in salt and water. Then put it into two quarts of boiling water, and boil it briskly twenty minutes. Strain it through a colander and shake it into a dish, but do not touch it with your fingers nor with a spoon. Beef, veal, mutton, rabbits, fish, etc. may be curried and sent to the table with or without the dish of rice. Curry powder is used as a fine flavored seasoning for fish, fowl, steaks, chops, veal cutlets, hashes, minces, a-la-modes, turtle soup, and in all rich dishes, gravies, sauces, etc., etc."*
—The Virginia Housewife,
1825

HORSERADISH SAUCE

½ cup white wine vinegar
4 tablespoons lemon juice
1 scallion, minced
2 tablespoons chopped fresh
  parsley
½ teaspoon salt

½ teaspoon sugar
¼ teaspoon freshly ground
  pepper
1½ tablespoons grated fresh
  horseradish

1. Combine all ingredients and let stand for at least 1 hour.
Yield: 1 cup

TOMATO SAUCE

2 tablespoons butter	Dash of sugar
1 onion, sliced	Dash of ginger
2 tablespoons flour	1 bay leaf
1½ cups chopped tomatoes	1 tablespoon pine nuts
Salt and freshly ground pepper, to taste	

1. In a frying pan, heat butter, add onion and sauté until golden. Remove onion and set aside. Add flour, blend well and brown slightly.
2. Add tomatoes, sautéed onion, salt, pepper, sugar, ginger, and bay leaf. Heat to boiling point. Reduce heat and simmer 20 minutes. Just before serving add pine nuts.

Yield: 1 cup

SPICED TOMATO SAUCE

16 large tomatoes	2 cups sugar
4 large sweet red peppers, chopped	2 cups cider vinegar
1 small hot green pepper, minced	1 tablespoon salt
	1 tablespoon celery seeds
2 large onions, chopped	1 tablespoon dry mustard
2 cups chopped celery	Dash of Tabasco sauce
	Dash of cayenne

1. Core tomatoes and cut into chunks.
2. Place tomatoes and all remaining ingredients in a large kettle and bring slowly to a boil, stirring often. Lower heat and simmer 2 to 3 hours, or until mixture is as thick as desired.
3. Pour mixture into hot, sterilized jars. Seal. Process 15 minutes in a water bath.

Yield: 8 cups

SEAFOOD SALAD DRESSING

2 tablespoons sugar	1½ tablespoons minced onion
1 teaspoon dry mustard	2 sprigs fresh dill
1 teaspoon salt	1 cup vegetable oil
½ cup cider vinegar	

1. Blend all ingredients in a blender or food processor.

Yield: 1½ cups

Variations: Any of the following may be added to the basic dressing: fresh tarragon, poppy seeds, or celery seeds.

"TO MAKE AN EXCELLENT CATSUP WHICH WILL KEEP GOOD MORE THAN TWENTY YEARS *Take two gallons of stale strong beer, or ale, the stronger and staler the better. One pound of anchovies, cleansed from the intestines and washed. Half an ounce each of cloves and mace, one quarter do. of pepper, six large roots of ginger; one pound of eschalots and two quarts or more of flap mushrooms well rubbed and picked.*

Boil these ingredients over a slow fire for one hour. Then strain the liquor through a flannel bag, and let stand till quite cold when it must be bottled and stopped very close with cork and bladder, or leather. One spoonful of this catsup to a pint of melted butter, gives an admirable taste and color, as a fish sauce, and is by many preferred to Indian soy."

—The Universal Receipt Book, 1814

COLE SLAW

⅔ cup mayonnaise (p. 191)
2½ tablespoons vinegar
1 tablespoon grated onion
1 teaspoon caraway seeds
1 teaspoon sugar
½ teaspoon salt

¼ teaspoon freshly ground
  pepper
5 cups shredded cabbage
1 medium green pepper, finely
  chopped
2 large carrots, shredded

1. Combine mayonnaise, vinegar, onion, caraway seeds, sugar, salt, and pepper.
2. Toss cabbage, green pepper, and carrots with the dressing. Garnish with a dash of paprika.

Yield: 8 servings

Variation: Substitute lemon juice for vinegar, and chopped fresh dill for caraway seeds.

POTATO SALAD

4 cups cooked, diced potatoes
1 cup diced celery
½ cup chopped dill pickle
2 tablespoons chopped pimiento

2 tablespoons minced onion
½ cup mayonnaise (p. 191)
Salt and freshly ground pepper,
  to taste

1. Combine potatoes, celery, pickle, pimiento, and onion. Add mayonnaise and toss. Season with salt and pepper and toss again.
2. Garnish with sliced hard-boiled eggs and green pepper slices.

Yield: 6 servings

SWEDISH CUCUMBER SALAD

2 large cucumbers
½ medium onion, thinly sliced
⅓ cup vinegar
⅓ cup water

⅓ cup sugar
½ teaspoon salt
Dash of freshly ground pepper
1 tablespoon chopped fresh dill

1. Peel cucumbers and cut into thin slices. Place cucumber and onion in a serving bowl.
2. Combine vinegar, water, sugar, salt, pepper, and dill, and shake well. Pour over cucumbers and onion and toss lightly to coat evenly.
3. Cover bowl and refrigerate for several hours, until cucumber is wilted. Serve garnished with chopped fresh dill or parsley.

Yield: 6 servings

"To pickle Cucumbers. Let your cucumbers be small, fresh gathered, and free from spots; then make a pickle of salt and water, strong enough to bear an egg; boil the pickle and skim it well, and then pour it upon your cucumbers, and stive them down for twenty four hours; then strain them out into a cullender, and dry them . . . and take the best white wine vinegar, with cloves, sliced mace, nutmeg, white pepper corns, long pepper, and races of ginger . . . boil them up together, and then clap the cucumbers in, with a few vine leaves, and a little salt. . . ."

—American Cookery, by Amelia Simmons, 1796

MARINATED BEET SALAD

2 cups grated beets   ¼ cup red wine vinegar

1. Place grated beets in a bowl and add vinegar. Mix and let stand in the refrigerator at least 1 hour before serving.
Yield: 8 servings

STEWED TOMATOES

4 medium tomatoes, peeled and   1 tablespoon sugar
  quartered   Salt and freshly ground pepper,
¼ cup crumbled salted crackers   to taste
1 tablespoon butter

1. In a saucepan, combine all ingredients and cook until tomatoes have softened.
Yield: 4 servings

GRILLED TOMATOES

4 large tomatoes   1 tablespoon minced onion
2 tablespoons butter, melted   2 tablespoons grated Parmesan
Salt and freshly ground pepper,   cheese
  to taste

1. Preheat oven to 450° F.
2. Cut tomatoes in half and place in a shallow, buttered baking dish. Brush tops of tomatoes with melted butter and season with salt and pepper. Sprinkle with onion and cheese.
3. Bake in a 450° F. oven for 10 minutes. Place tomatoes under broiler and broil until tops turn light brown.
Yield: 4 to 8 servings

PUFFED SPINACH

1 cup dried bread crumbs   1¼ cups chicken broth
⅓ cup grated Parmesan cheese   4 eggs, separated
¼ cup sliced scallions   1 cup cooked, chopped spinach
½ teaspoon oregano   1½ cups chopped tomatoes
½ teaspoon salt
¼ teaspoon freshly ground
  pepper

1. Preheat oven to 350° F.
2. In a bowl, combine dry bread crumbs, cheese, scallions, oregano, salt, and pepper.

"Rice Borders. . . . Put one cupful of rice on to boil in three cupfuls of cold water. When it has been boiling half an hour, add two tablespoonfuls of butter and one heaping teaspoonful of salt. Set back where it will just simmer, and cook one hour longer. Mash very fine with a spoon, add two well-beaten eggs, and stir for three minutes. Butter a plain border mould, and fill with the rice. Place in the heater for ten minutes. Turn upon a hot dish. . . ."
—Miss Parloa's New Cook Book, 1880

3. In a saucepan, bring chicken broth to a boil. Remove from heat and blend in egg yolks, one at a time, blending well after each addition. Blend in spinach and tomatoes and pour over bread-crumb mixture. Stir to blend.

4. Beat egg whites until stiff but not dry. Fold ⅓ of the egg whites into spinach-tomato mixture to lighten it, then fold in remaining whites.

5. Spoon mixture into a well-buttered loaf pan or 4 individual casserole dishes, and bake in a 350° F. oven for 55 to 60 minutes for loaf pan and 30 to 35 minutes for individual casseroles.

Yield: 4 servings

POTATO PUFFS

3 medium potatoes	½ teaspoon salt
¼ cup milk	1 tablespoon chopped fresh
1 tablespoon butter	parsley
1 egg, beaten	1 tablespoon chopped fresh
½ cup flour	chives or dill
1 teaspoon baking powder	Oil, for deep-frying

1. Peel and cut potatoes, and boil in salted water until soft. Mash, adding milk, butter, and egg.

2. Combine flour, baking powder, and salt and add to potatoes, mixing well. Add parsley and chives (or dill) and mix well.

3. In a deep, heavy kettle, heat oil to 375° F.

4. Form potato puffs with a spoon and drop into hot oil. Fry until golden brown and drain on paper toweling.

Yield: 4 servings

POTATO GUGELIS

1 tablespoon butter	½ cup oatmeal
1 medium onion, finely chopped	2 eggs, beaten
4 medium potatoes	1 teaspoon salt
1 cup milk	1 tablespoon caraway seeds

1. Preheat oven to 350° F.

2. In a frying pan, heat butter and sauté onion until soft. Set aside.

3. Peel potatoes and grate into a large bowl.

4. Bring milk to the boil and pour immediately over potatoes to prevent discoloring. Add onion, oatmeal, eggs, salt, and caraway seeds and mix well.

5. Pour into a buttered 1½-quart casserole and bake in a 350° F. oven for 35 minutes.

Yield: 6 servings

"TO STEW MUSHROOMS. *The large buttons are best, and the small flaps while the fur is still red. Rub the large buttons with salt and a bit of flannel; cut out the fur and take off the skin from the others. Sprinkle them with salt, and put into a stew pan with some pepper-corns. Simmer slowly till done; then put a small bit of butter and flour, and two spoonfuls of cream. Give then one boil and serve with sippets of bread."*

—The American Domestic Cookery, 1822

7: Preparation Techniques

Many of the instructions in this chapter make reference to the parts of a fish's body: for example, dorsal, pectoral, and pelvic fins; or the vent hole, or lateral line; or gill openings and covers. In order to clear up any possible confusion, use the following diagram of a typical round fish as a guide. The actual placement and size of fins will, of course, differ from fish to fish.

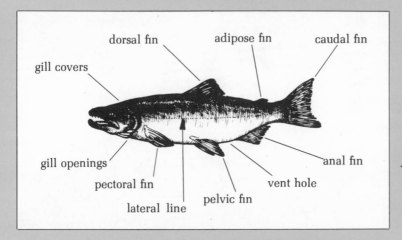

HOW TO FREEZE FISH: Only freeze fish that are fresh and cleaned. Dip leaner species for 20 seconds in a salt solution (½ cup to 8 cups of water) in order to firm the flesh. Freeze small fish on a cookie sheet, then wrap tightly in freezer paper or plastic wrap and seal in a freezer bag. For larger, whole fish, freeze on a cookie sheet, then dip frozen fish in ice-cold water and return to the freezer. Repeat several times to create a glaze, then wrap tightly in freezer paper or plastic wrap and seal in a freezer bag. Label and date package.

Fish may also be frozen in a block of ice to prevent drying or freezer burn. To do this, place fish in a strong plastic bag, empty milk carton, or ice cube tray, cover with water and freeze.

For best results, store fatty species (e.g., salmon, mackerel, lake trout) for a maximum of 3 months. Store lean species (e.g., cod, haddock, ocean perch, pike, smelt) for a maximum of 6 months. Keep fish frozen at 0° F. (−18° C.) or lower.

When thawing fish, keep it cold until it is to be cooked. Wash off ice from glazed fish with cold water. Melt an ice block with running tepid water, then place freed fish in cold water until just thawed, or cover and set in the refrigerator to thaw. Cook as soon as possible after thawing. Do not refreeze, as flavor will be lost and flesh texture will be mushy.

Smoked and salt-cured fish can be carefully wrapped and frozen in the same ways as for fresh fish.

HOW TO SMOKE FISH: Virtually all species of fish (and many varieties of shellfish) can be smoked. Fresh fish are best,

◄A Northwest Coast Indian woman prepares to dress a large salmon. Traditionally, Indians preserved salmon by splitting, smoking, and pounding them, later reconstituting the dried fish in boiling water.

The simplest hot smokehouse is a tepeelike arrangement of sticks covered with canvas. Eastern Woodland Indians, from whom the design is borrowed, traditionally used birch bark. A fire is started in a bucket or kettle and placed under the fish hung head down from the top of the tepee.

but frozen and thawed fish can also be used. Fish can be smoked in either a small, portable, commercially-available smokehouse, following the manufacturer's directions, or in one of several types of homemade smokehouses (see drawings).

Fish are smoked whole, with their heads on if small; in chunks; or as fillets, butterflied or halved. With the exception of those with odd or unpleasant tasting skin, all fish should be smoked with the skin on. Before smoking, fish are cured with salt, either in solution (as a brine) or dry. Fish must be properly cleaned before curing. After curing, fish are smoked in one of two ways: hot smoking (85° F. up to 150° F.) or cold smoking (85° F. maximum). A variation of flavor and flesh texture can be obtained depending on the smoking method used and the amount of salt used in the curing process. Smoking fish is in some ways like the art of wine making: the taster's thrills lie in the subtle variations.

The amount of salt used to cure fish not only affects its taste, but also determines the length of preservation. In the dry-salting method—generally used for larger fish, such as salmon—the fish is gutted and butterflied, or cut into two fillets, salted, left for several hours to cure, rinsed, wind-dried, and smoked. The following recipe gives the proportions for a dry-salt cure. The amount of salt and spices needed will depend on the size of the fish, but should be applied to a depth of at least 1/16″. Be sure to use kosher salt, not table salt, which has preservatives in it. Also, the fish can be dry-cured with salt alone, no spices.

SALT CURE

4 cups coarse salt	2 tablespoons freshly ground pepper
2 cups brown sugar	2 tablespoons crushed bay leaves

1. Take freshly caught fish, remove guts and gills, head and tail, but do not skin or scale. Then split along side of backbone until fish is lying in two halves. Remove exposed backbone and rib cage. 2. Place two halves on table, meat side up. Sprinkle generously with salt cure: 1/16″ to 1/8″. (Use more pepper for highly seasoned fish.) 3. Place fish in dry, cool, shaded area for several hours, until a glaze forms on the surface of the fish. Fish should be somewhat dehydrated.

The brining method is used for smaller fish, generally those under 6 pounds. Fish are first brined (gutted whole, or in fillets), then rinsed, wind-dried, and smoked.

FISH BRINE

2 gallons water	2 cloves garlic, crushed
4 cups coarse salt	2 tablespoons minced onion
1 cup brown sugar	4 sprigs fresh dill (optional)
½ cup lemon juice	

1. Mix the brining solution in an earthenware crock or a large glass, enameled, or plastic container. (Neither wood nor metal

pans should be used; in particular, avoid aluminum.) 2. Add salt gradually, stirring constantly to dissolve. When the solution has enough salt, an egg will float in it. (Measured with a salinometer, the solution should be 80% salt—although some brining solutions can have a lower concentration.) Brine should be kept at 60° F. 3. The time allowed for brining depends on the weight and the saltiness desired. As a general rule, fish under ¼ pound should be brined for 30 minutes; fish ¼ to ½ pound, for 45 minutes; fish ½ to 1 pound, for 1 hour. For each additional pound, add 1 hour. 4. Drain excess fluid off fish, rinse, and dry in a cool, shaded area until a glaze forms on surface of fish, about 2 to 3 hours.

Once the fish has been salt-cured, it can be either hot or cold smoked. In hot smoking, the fish is actually cooked and smoked at the same time. The initial heat level is 85° and is then increased to 150° F. (higher in commercial smokehouses). The cured, wind-dried fish is hot smoked for 8 to 10 hours, and will keep for several weeks, if refrigerated. Un-cured fish can also be hot smoked, but they will take longer to smoke, won't have as much flavor, and will not stay good for as long (5 days or so, refrigerated).

In cold smoking, the fish must be salt cured and wind dried. Cold smoking dries the fish out with warm smoke at temperatures not exceeding 85° F. This process may take several days. The fire should not produce too much smoke during the first 12 hours, but after that a dense smoke should be maintained. Cold-smoked fish will have a smokier flavor and will keep much longer without refrigeration.

In both hot and cold smoking, wood used to produce the smoke should be hardwoods, not resinous, piney woods. Hickory, oak, maple, beech, alder, pecan, or quaking aspen are all excellent. Slightly green wood will burn more slowly and produce better results. Be sure to remove any bark, moss, or lichen, which may impart odd flavors to the fish. Dried corn cobs can also be used, but must be carefully watched as they tend to catch fire and cook the fish too quickly.

To start a homemade smokehouse fire, a fire of charcoal briquets is burned until they're reduced to coals, more charcoal is added and then topped with the hardwood. Once the fire is ready, fish are placed in the smokehouse. If the smokehouse has racks, lay fish with meat side up, skin side toward the fire. If it has hooks, hang the fish head side down. With small fish smoked whole, place metal hooks under gill covers and hang on rods. Check fire and smoke volume every 2 to 3 hours.

One of the simplest ways of making a cold-smoker is to take a barrel or metal drum, remove both ends, and cover the top with canvas. Drill holes near the top and run a stick or rod through them. From this rod hang S-hooks to which the fish are attached. A smoke pit is dug under the barrel, and a fire pit is dug several feet away, slightly lower down, with a metal cover. A section of drainage pipe or stove piping carries the smoke from the fire to the smokehouse.

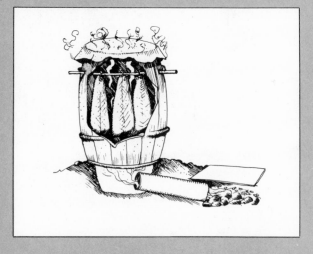

HOW TO SCALE: Dampen fish and lay flat. With one hand, grip fish firmly by the tail. Holding a blunt knife or scaler in the other hand, at a 45° angle, begin working instrument from tail to head, using short, firm strokes. Turn fish over and repeat. Then rinse off loose scales.

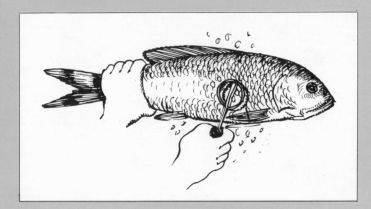

HOW TO GUT, LEAVING ON HEAD AND TAIL: Insert knife in vent hole and slice along belly to head. Remove viscera and run thumbnail firmly along spine to remove blood and membrane (*drawing*). Cut gills where they are attached to base of fish's skull and between lower jaws. Then pull out gills with thumb and forefinger, and cut away side pectoral fins as well. With a short semicircular movement, cut away the pelvic fins, if desired. Run water into the cavity to clean fish. Dry with paper toweling.

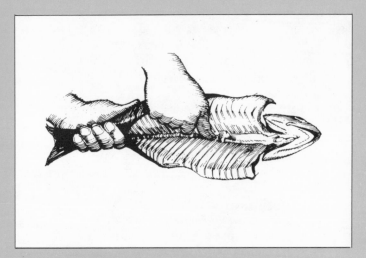

HOW TO GUT A FISH WITHOUT CUTTING IT: A fairly small fish can be gutted without cutting it. Insert index finger into the gill opening, hook the gill and pull. The gill will come out with the gut attached.

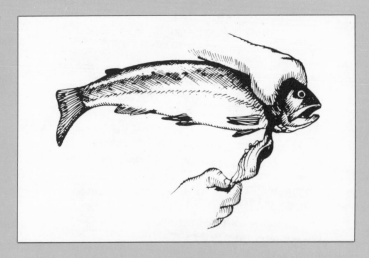

HOW TO GUT, REMOVING HEAD AND TAIL: Place fish bellyside down and with one hand, hold fish firmly in the center of the back. Using as sharp a knife as possible, cut off head, making a semicircular slice just behind gills from the back to the throat. Roll fish onto its side, hold onto tail and insert knife in vent hole and slice belly to head (*drawing*). With knife tip or fingertips, push out all viscera. Run thumbnail hard against fish spine toward head, thus pushing out blood and membrane. Cut off tail that has served as handle. Run water into the cavity to clean fish. Dry with paper toweling.

To cut away dorsal fin, hold fish in upright position and make two sharp

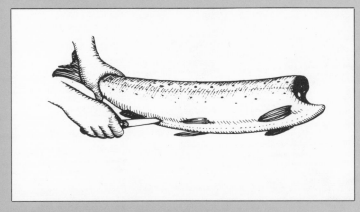

cuts as close as possible to left and right of dorsal fin. Lift fin and projecting bones free of fish. On smaller fish, the two pelvic fins and single anal fin can remain in place; they are more easily removed after cooking.

HOW TO FILLET: If the fish has scales and is not to be skinned, remove scales before filleting. To fillet, use a knife that has both a sharp edge and point. The best filleting knives are made of strong, thin, flexible steel. The blade should be about 8″ long and narrow. Run the filleting knife along the center of the fish's back (starting at the tail), cutting through skin and flesh to the backbone (*top drawing*). At the back of the head, make a cut across the fish to the belly. Then, holding the knife flat against the fish, cut along one side from head to tail, easing the knife over the rib bones (*bottom drawing*). Remove the fillet. Turn the fish over and repeat on other side. Save bones and head for fish stock.

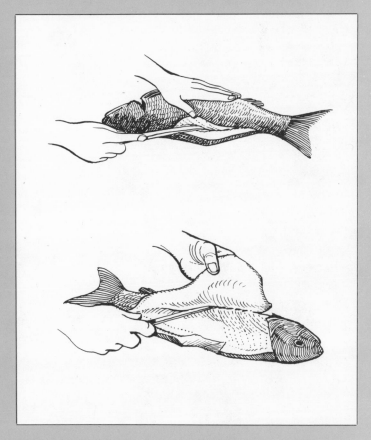

HOW TO SKIN A FILLET: Place the fillet skin side down. Holding the tail firmly with one hand, cut the skin from the flesh with quick, short strokes. Angle the knife blade toward the skin so that no flesh is wasted.

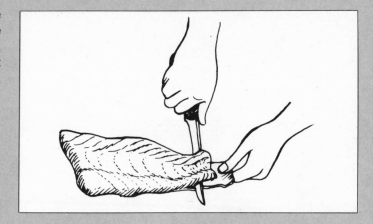

HOW TO BUTTERFLY: Holding fish flat with one hand, cut along the center of the back just above the backbone. Slide knife along the ribs, following the shape of the rib cage without cutting any bones (*drawing*). Turn fish over and repeat on the other side of the backbone, detaching the other fillet from the rib cage in the same manner. Cut down through fish, but do not cut through the stomach skin. Sever the backbone at the throat and tail. Carefully lift skeleton and pull out viscera with it. Cut off head and tail. With the bones removed, the double fillet can be opened like the pages of a book.

HOW TO SERVE COOKED FISH: Pull away any fins that were left on during the cooking. Cut along the center of the back from tail to head, running a knife through the skin and meat to the depth of the backbone. Peel off the top skin. Cut along the center of the fish from head to tail along the lateral line. Divide the top fillet into serving portions by slipping a wide knife from the center of the back over the rib bones to the middle.

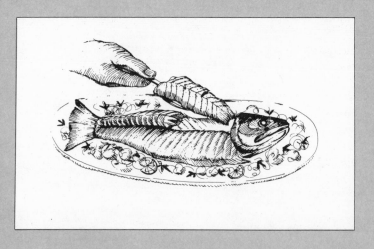

HOW TO REMOVE BONES FROM COOKED FISH: If some of the fins have been left on (as with smaller fish) pull away the dorsal fin, anal fin, and pelvic fins. Run a knife to the depth of the backbone up the center of the back from tail to head. Slit across upper tail and from the tail to the stomach opening. Then with the aid of a knife and fork, lift the entire upper fillet away from the skeleton, raising first the rear, then the middle and the front, being careful to peel meat slowly from the rib bones. Lay aside this fillet and holding the tail, lift up the spine from tail to head, pulling away the entire skeleton in one complete section. To reconstruct the boned fish, replace top fillet over bottom one.

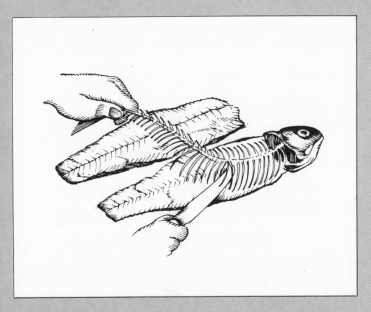

HOW TO CUT STEAKS: Lay the gutted fish on its belly and remove head by making a crescent cut behind the gills. According to thickness desired, cut downward through fish from back to belly. Steaks are only cut from round fish and some very large flatfish. To skin steaks, insert a small, sharp knife between skin and meat. Continue cutting around entire steak until all skin is removed.

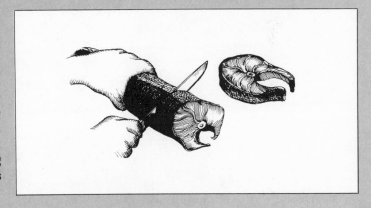

HOW TO MAKE BONELESS ME-DALLIONS: After removing outer skin of steak, cut out central bone and the three sets of long, thin bones attached to it. There will be two comma-shaped pieces per steak. Invert one comma so that it will fit snugly into the right-side-up comma. Press the commas together to form a compact circle and pin the comma tails in place with toothpicks.

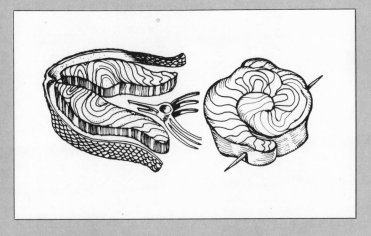

HOW TO SKIN A FLATFISH:

Place the flatfish, head removed, bellyside (white side) down and cut the skin where the body joins the tail. With fingernail or knife point, raise a skin flap large enough to allow a firm grip (*top drawing*). Cover tail with a paper towel and use one hand to pin it to the work surface. With the other hand, pull skin flap vigorously toward the head (*bottom drawing*). If fish is to be cooked whole, remove only dark back skin; the white belly skin will hold the fish together during cooking. If not cooked whole, turn fish over and repeat the process to remove belly skin.

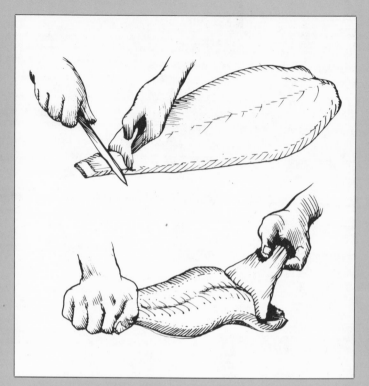

HOW TO FILLET A FLATFISH:

Lay the skinned fish bellyside (white side) down with its eyes facing up. Insert a knife just behind the head, cut down to the backbone and slice along the center of fish from head to tail. Beginning at the head, hold one fillet with one hand and, holding the knife horizontally, cut outward from the center backbone along the ribs. Cutting with short strokes along the length of the fish, lift up the fillet (*drawing*). Cut the fillet off the fish. Cut away the second top fillet in the same manner. Under one of the two top fillets, just behind the eyes, will be the viscera, to be discarded. There may also be a sac of roe or milt to be saved for cooking. After cutting two top fillets, turn the fish over and repeat the process for the two fillets on the belly side.

HOW TO SKIN A CATFISH: Wearing a thick glove for protection against the fish's stinging fins, hold fish firmly by the head. (The catfish can also be held in place by nailing its head to a board.) Use a sharp knife to make an incision just in back of the head (*top drawing*), then cut down to just behind the pectoral fins. Roll the fish over and continue to cut across the other side of the fish, finally coming full circle to meet the original incision. Because a catfish's skin is too tough to remove with a knife, grasp the cut edge of the skin with pliers (*bottom drawing*) and pull vigorously toward the tail. The skin will come off in strips.

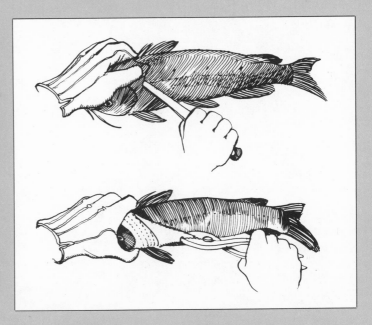

HOW TO STUFF A ROUND FISH: Spoon any prepared stuffing into the cleaned body cavity of a round fish, beginning at the tail and working forward. Using a large darning needle and heavy thread, sew up the fish with a few diagonal or criss-crossed stitches. Or insert metal skewers through the top layer of flesh into the bottom layer and secure by criss-crossing a thin string (*drawing*).

HOW TO STUFF A FLATFISH:
Scale fish, leave on head and tail, and remove dark skin from top. Lay fish bellyside (white side) down with its eyes facing up. Insert a knife just behind the head, cut down to the backbone and slice along the center of the fish from head to tail. Beginning at the head, hold one fillet with one hand and holding the knife horizontally, cut outward from the center backbone along the ribs. Cutting with short strokes along the length of the fish, lift fillet away from the rib bones (see drawing for how to fillet a flatfish). Leave the fillet attached at head and tail. Repeat for the fillet on the other side. Remove the viscera from behind the eyes. If desired, the backbone can be removed before cooking. To do this, cut the backbone at the head and tail ends, pry it up with the tip of a knife and pull it out. This will create an empty envelope into which the prepared stuffing can be placed.

HOW TO POACH: Fish can be poached whole, in large fillets, or as steaks. Fish are poached by completely covering them with a barely simmering poaching liquid: a court bouillon of lean, flavored stock (Chapter 6) or a water-wine mixture. An oval saucepan big enough to hold the fish and necessary liquid can be used, but a long fish poacher fitted with an inner removable rack (*drawing*) is better. When cooking a whole fish, wrap it in cheesecloth or muslin to prevent the possibility of the fish falling apart. This may not always be necessary when using a fish poacher with a removable rack, but will make the operation somewhat less risky. To poach, bring the poaching liquid to a boil in the closed poacher, then lower the fish into the already hot liquid. When the poaching liquid returns to

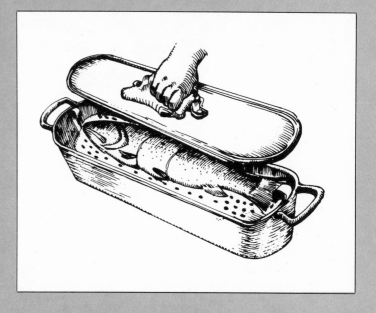

the boil, reduce heat to simmer. When done, gently tip the rack and slide the fish onto a serving platter.

HOW TO PREPARE A FISH EN PAPILLOTE: To cook en papillote, the fish is enclosed in an oiled or buttered wrapping to contain the fish's juices. Aluminum foil now commonly takes the place of the traditional kitchen parchment paper, but once natural materials such as palm, grape, and cabbage leaves were used. Place fish and any seasonings or sauce makings in the center of a piece of buttered foil. Seal the fish in a "bag" by lifting up two sides of the foil, crimping them together, and rolling them down onto the fish. Next, crimp and roll up the ends, completely sealing the packet. The fish is served in the foil.

HOW TO GRILL: In an outdoor grill or fireplace, start a wood or charcoal fire and burn until there are hot coals (the briquets are ready when their surface is covered with a gray ash). Make the bed of coals slightly wider than the fish to be cooked. Place fish in a well-greased, hinged wire grill. A simple, flat, hamburger-type grill with legs (*top drawing*) works well for fillets and small fish; whole large fish can be grilled in specially designed fish-shaped grills with legs (*bottom drawing*). To give fish distinctive grill marks, heat grill before placing well-basted fish in it. Fish should be cooked approximately 4″ from the coals for 10 minutes for every inch of the fish's thickness (see Canadian fish cooking rule, Chapter 1). While grilling, the fish should be liberally basted with butter or sauce, and turned at least once. Fish can also be marinated ahead of time and then basted with the marinade, or cooked wrapped in heavy foil carefully

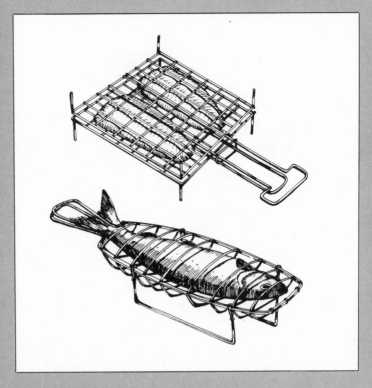

sealed to keep in moisture—although this will bake/steam the fish instead of grilling.

HOW TO COOK INDIAN STYLE: Prepare a whole fish butterfly style, removing head and tail. Do *not* remove skin. Take two sharpened sticks and thread them through the butterflied fish (*drawing*). Plant the sticks at an angle over a campfire. Use heavy rocks at their base to keep sticks from falling over.

HOW TO PLANK COOK: Prepare a whole fish butterfly style, removing head and tail. Do *not* remove the skin. Rinse clean and salt lightly, then place skin side down on a hardwood (*not* resinous) board and nail flat. Use stainless-steel, *not* iron nails. Prop board at an angle beside a campfire (*drawing*), with the thicker end of the fish (head end) on the bottom, near the fire. The cooked fish may be eaten directly from the plank. To plank cook in an oven, first generously oil a hardwood plank and place in a cold oven. Set the temperature to 400° F. and allow the plank to heat up gradually. When the oven temperature reaches 400° F., re-oil the plank, place fish on it and bake for 10 minutes for every inch of the fish's thickness (see Canadian fish

cooking rule, Chapter 1). Serve fish on plank.

HOW TO SKIN AN EEL: Grasp the fresh-killed eel's body with a dry cloth. With a sharp knife, cut into the skin behind the gills and cut a complete circle around the eel's body. Holding the head with the cloth to avoid slipping, grasp the cut edge of the skin with pliers (*drawing*) and pull off skin whole. With a knife, cut off eel's head about three inches behind gills and pull, thus removing all viscera.

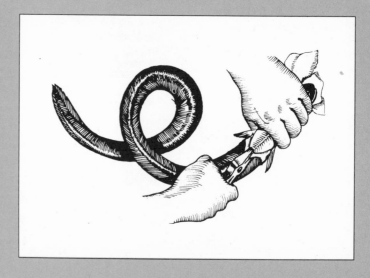

HOW TO CLEAN AN UNCOOKED LOBSTER: A thin, sharp knife point pierced between the eyes of the lobster will kill it instantly. Lay it on its back and with a sharp knife cut firmly down the middle of the belly (but not through the top shell), split-ting it from head to tail. Press the two halves outward and apart and remove viscera from head and along middle of the body and tail. The lobster can now be broiled or baked in its shell. Spiny lobster can be treated in the same manner.

HOW TO REMOVE MEAT FROM A COOKED LOBSTER: Lay lobster on its back and with a sharp knife slit down the middle of the belly, cutting it from head to tail. Turn over and let drain briefly. Break tail off the body and crack off the endmost flippers by bending them back. Push the tail meat out of the shell, pressing from the narrow end with a fork or fingers, and cut out and discard the intestinal vein. Break off the two front claws and crack with a lobster or nut cracker. Discard the stomach sac or "lady" behind the head. Save the liver (tomalley) and roe (coral) for sauces. The spiny lobster can be treated in the same manner as the American lobster.

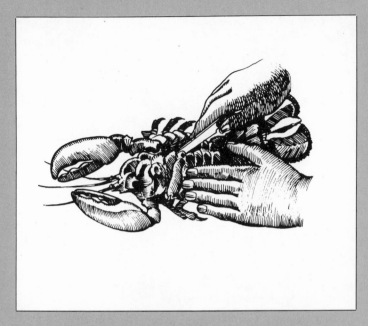

HOW TO REMOVE MEAT FROM A CRAYFISH: Separate head from tail. Remove shell from tail and remove intestinal vein from backside of tail meat. With a small knife remove the orange fat (crayfish butter) from behind the head and save it for use in recipes that call for it.

HOW TO CLEAN SHRIMP: This method of cleaning can be used before or after shrimp are cooked. Separate tail from head. Holding the shrimp tail bellyside up, use thumbs of both hands to pry shell apart and away from body. Peel off the shell, removing the legs in the same motion. (Save shells for adding to a fish stock.) Using the tip of a sharp paring knife, make a very shallow slit down the middle of the back. This will reveal the intestinal tract, which can now be pulled out. Deveining, as this is called, is mostly a matter of aesthetics and can be skipped.

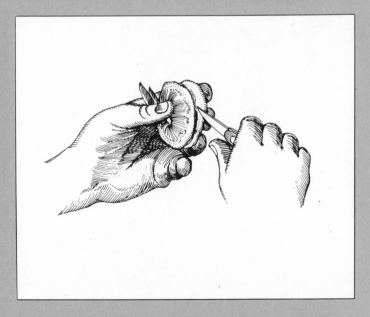

HOW TO CLEAN AN UNCOOKED CRAB:

For smaller hardshell crabs (such as blue crabs), hold crab in the cup of one hand with fingers firmly placed between the two large front claws and against the body to avoid getting bitten. Pry off the top shell and the apron. With a knife, cut away the eyes and mouth, and remove viscera and gills. For small softshell crabs, simply cut out eyes, lungs, and apron to prepare for cooking.

HOW TO REMOVE MEAT FROM A COOKED CRAB:

Starting with the smaller legs, pull them off singly, leaving body sections on the legs. Pull off two front claws. Remove the crab's back shell, which will pull off easily (*drawing*). Scrape out inedible viscera and gills, or wash out under running water. Snap off the apron. Pick out body meat and the creamy parts (crab butter) from the inside of the shell. Crack legs and claws with a crab/lobster or nut cracker.

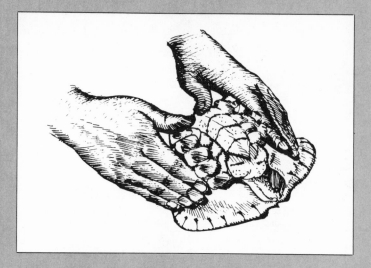

HOW TO SHUCK AN OYSTER:

Scrub each shell clean under cold running water before opening. (Do *not* leave oysters standing in water.) Hold each oyster with the deep half of the shell down and the hinge toward the palm of the hand. Carefully insert the point of a sharp, stiff-bladed oyster knife between the shells, near the hinge. With a hard, steady twisting motion, run the knife blade around the oyster until it cuts the muscle, which is located off center, near the hinge. When the muscle is cut (*drawing*), the shell will open. Be sure to save the oyster liquid, which will drain off, for cooking.

HOW TO SHUCK A SCALLOP:

Scallops are most often sold shucked, for once taken from water they dry out and die. To open very freshly harvested scallops, scrub the shells, then place them on top of a warm stove. When the top shell rises slightly, use a knife to carefully cut the muscle where it is attached to the top shell. Then cut the muscle away from the bottom shell. Discard the membrane and guts around the muscle—although the whole scallop is edible, North Americans only eat the muscle.

213

HOW TO SHUCK A CLAM: Hold clam in one hand with hinge toward the palm of the hand. Grip firmly. Insert the blade of a clam knife between the top and bottom shells. Slide blade toward the hinge (*drawing*) until the muscle is severed. Clam can then be freed from both halves of its shell. Be sure to save the clam liquor for cooking.

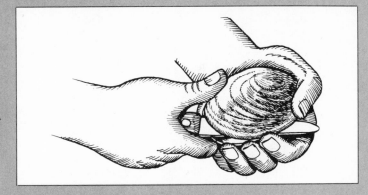

HOW TO CLEAN A SOFTSHELL CLAM: If steaming softshell clams, the most common cooking method, the shells will open as they cook. If using softshell clam meat for other purposes, run a knife between the two halves of the shell, cut the meat away from the top shell and then the bottom. Cut the clam meat from around the stomach area to eat raw or cook lightly. Cut off the long neck, or siphon, removing the dark, sandy tip and outer skin, and cut up this slightly tougher meat for chowders or creamed dishes.

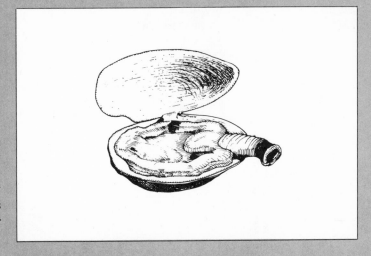

HOW TO CLEAN A MUSSEL: The mussel's beard (silklike threads used by the mussel to attach itself to rocks and pilings) should be left in place until just before cooking. Then scrub mussels well to trim the beard and any grit and grass on the shells. Wash in several changes of water. Mussels will split open when cooked. Discard any that do not open.

HOW TO CLEAN A SQUID: Pull head and tentacles away from body. Cut tentacles off head (*drawing*) and reserve. Discard head. Remove the ink sac and the thin, transparent pen from the body cavity. Reserve ink sac if called for in recipe. Rinse body well and pat dry. If only white meat is desired, pull off dark, outside skin by holding squid in one hand and using fingers of the other hand to peel off. The body can be left whole or cut into rings.

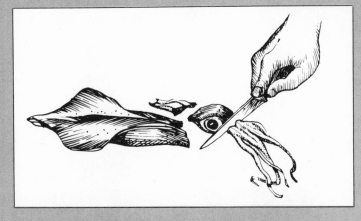

WEIGHTS AND MEASURES

KITCHEN METRICS

1 liter (L.)	=	10 deciliters (dL.)
1 deciliter (dL.)	=	10 centiliters (cL.)
1 centiliter (cL.)	=	10 milliliters (mL.)
1 kilogram (kg.)	=	1000 grams (g.)
1 gram (g.)	=	1000 milligrams (mg.)
1 meter (m.)	=	100 centimeters (cm.)

METRIC CONVERSION FACTORS

WHEN YOU KNOW	MULTIPLY BY	TO FIND
Weight		
ounces (oz.)	28	grams (g.)
pounds (lb.)	450	grams (g.)
pounds (lb.)	0.45	kilograms (kg.)
Volume		
teaspoons (tsp.)	5	milliliters (mL.)
tablespoons (Tbsp.)	1.5	centiliters (cL.)
fluid ounces (fl. oz.)	3	centiliters (cL.)
cups (c.)	2.4	centiliters (cL.)
cups (c.)	0.24	liters (L.)
pints (pt.)	4.7	centiliters (cL.)
pints (pt.)	0.47	liters (L.)
quarts (qt.)	9.5	centiliters (cL.)
quarts (qt.)	0.95	liters (L.)
gallons (gal.)	3.8	liters (L.)
Length		
inches (in.)	2.54	centimeters (cm.)
feet (ft.)	30	centimeters (cm.)
feet (ft.)	0.3	meters (m.)
Temperature		
Fahrenheit (° F.)	5/9 (after subtracting 32)	Celsius (° C.)

KITCHEN MEASUREMENTS

3 teaspoons	=	1 tablespoon
2 tablespoons	=	1 fluid ounce
4 tablespoons	=	2 fluid ounces or ¼ cup
8 tablespoons	=	4 fluid ounces or ½ cup
16 tablespoons	=	8 fluid ounces or 1 cup
1 cup	=	8 fluid ounces or ½ pint
2 cups	=	16 fluid ounces or 1 pint
4 cups	=	2 pints or 1 quart
1 pint	=	16 fluid ounces
1 quart	=	32 fluid ounces or 2 pints

INGREDIENTS

Almonds, 1 pound unshelled	=	1½ cups nut meats
Bread, 1 pound, crumbled	=	9 cups
Bread crumbs, dried, 1 pound	=	3½ cups
Butter, 1 pound	=	2 cups/32 tablespoons/4 sticks
Butter, 1 stick	=	¼ pound/½ cup/8 tablespoons
Cheese, 1 pound	=	5 cups grated/2⅔ cups cubed
Crabmeat, 1 pound cooked	=	2 cups
Eggs, 4 to 6	=	1 cup
Fish, 1 pound cooked	=	2 cups
Flour, all-purpose, 1 pound	=	4 cups, sifted
Flour, whole-wheat, 1 pound	=	3½ cups
Gelatin, 1 envelope	=	1 tablespoon
Lobster meat, 1 pound cooked	=	2 cups
Noodles, 1 pound uncooked	=	7 cups cooked
Onions, 1 medium	=	½ cup chopped
Potatoes, 1 pound	=	2½ cups sliced or diced/2 cups mashed
Rice, ½ pound	=	1 cup
Rice, 1 cup uncooked	=	3 cups cooked
Shrimp meat, 1 pound cooked	=	2 cups
Spaghetti, 1 pound uncooked	=	7 cups cooked
Sugar, granulated, ½ pound	=	1 cup
Sugar, brown, ½ pound	=	1½ cups
Tomatoes, 1 pound	=	1 2-pound can, drained
Walnuts, 1 pound unshelled	=	2 cups nut meats

RECIPE CROSS INDEX

Although the recipes in this book have been designed for particular fish, many of them are suitable for more than one fish type; use this Recipe Cross Index for suggested substitutions. The numbers refer to pages on which recipes appear.

Credits (page num 218 shown)

Credits

Front Cover—Library of Congress, photograph by Otto M. Jones. Back Cover—James Houston. Half Title—Library of Congress, photograph by Otto M. Jones. Title—The Whaling Museum, New Bedford, Massachusetts. 6—Photography Collection/University of Washington Library. 9—Glenbow-Alberta Institute. 10—The American Museum of Natural History. 12—Library of Congress/photograph by Otto M. Jones. 14—International Museum of Photography at George Eastman House/photograph by Nathan Lazarnick. 16—Southern Oregon Historical Society. 18, 19—Colorado Historical Society. 23—Arizona Historical Society. 26—Photograph by William Lyman Underwood, courtesy Helen Baker. 27—Glenbow-Alberta Institute. 29—Library of Congress, photograph by Seneca Ray Stoddard. 30—The American Museum of Natural History. 35—Photography Collection/University of Washington Library. 38—Public Archives Canada, PA 21080. 42—Photography Collection/University of Washington Library, photograph by Asahel Curtis. 46—Asahel Curtis Collection/Washington State Historical Society. 51—Library of Congress. 52—Photography Collection/University of Washington Library. 55—Library of Congress, photograph by Ben Gifford. 56—Public Archives Canada, PA 40997. 58, 59—Photography Collection/University of Washington Library, photograph by Asahel Curtis. 60—Library of Congress. 65—State Historical Society of Wisconsin. 68—State Historical Society of Wisconsin, photograph by Charles Van Schaick. 71—Rio Grande Collection/Colorado Historical Society, photograph by William Henry Jackson. 76—Collection of Hobart L. Morris, Fayette, Missouri. 78—State Historical Society of Wisconsin, photograph by A. A. Bish. 81—Archives of Ontario. 82—Public Archives Canada, C-19836. 88—National Archives, photograph by D. C. Herrin. 90—Library of Congress, photograph by Otto M. Jones. 93—Library of Congress. 94—Library of Congress. 96, 97—State Historical Society of Wisconsin. 98—Library of Congress. 101—California Historical Society Library, photograph by P. V. Reyes. 105—The Whaling Museum, New Bedford, Massachusetts, photograph by Albert Cook Church. 112—Library of Congress. 116—Fish and Wildlife/National Archives. 120—The Whaling Museum, New Bedford, Massachusetts, photograph by Thomas E. M. White. 124—Fish and Wildlife/National Archives. 131—State Historical Society of Wisconsin. 134—British Columbia Provincial Museum, Victoria, British Columbia, photograph by Richard Maynard. 139—The Whaling Museum, New Bedford, Massachusetts. 144—Geological Survey of Canada, Ottawa. 149—California Historical Society Library. 151—Photograph by William Lyman Underwood, courtesy Helen Baker. 152—State Historical Society of Wisconsin, photograph by Charles Van Schaick. 156, 157—The Whaling Museum, New Bedford, Massachusetts, photograph by Thomas E. M. White. 160—International Museum of Photography at George Eastman House, photograph by Lewis W. Hine. 167—National Maritime Museum, San Francisco. 170—Washington State Historical Society, photograph by Asahel Curtis. 174, 175—Fish and Wildlife/National Archives. 184—Chicago Historical Society.

Acknowledgments

The author wishes to express her gratitude to the following individuals:

General: Dr. Clement A. Griscom, Division of Marine Resources, University of Rhode Island, Narragansett, Rhode Island; Messrs. Don, Tony, and Frank Degenarro, Quality Fish Market, New Haven, Connecticut; Becky More, Benefit Street Cooking School, Providence, Rhode Island; Yvonne Brockman; Bella Martin; Ruth Martin; Nancy Patterson; Judy Poston; Mary Plowden-Wardlaw; Barbara Saxon; Lephe Smith. **Historical:** Ida Lipson; Elizabeth Watson; Carolyn Zelaney. **Trout & Salmon:** Mary Harvie; Valerie Osborne; Pitsiolala; Kathleen Sherbrooke; Clara Weber. **Freshwater:** Denise Robert. **Saltwater:** Betty Anne Caldara; Rebecca Dawson; Mimi Dyer; Nancy Fabbri; Jean Ferguson; Gabriel Ferreux; Ellie Harvey; Francis Knight; Borge Lambert; Barbara Parker; Nancy Richartz; Benita Sanders; Mary Thompson. **Shellfish:** Ann Parker; Christine Zadora-Gerlof. **Stocks, Sauces & Side Dishes:** Lester Lewis; Lillian Poston. **Photographs:** Helen Baker; Nancy Claflin; Emily Hoxie; Betsy Johnson; Anne Lunt; Amanda Martin; Gladys Segar; Ken McPherson, Archives of Ontario, Toronto, Ontario; Laverne Mau Dicker, California Historical Society; Dan Savard, British Columbia Provincial Museum, Victoria, British Columbia; Judith Golden, Colorado Historical Society, Denver, Colorado; Georgeen Barrass, Glenbow-Alberta Institute, Calgary, Alberta; Helen Burgess, Hudson's Bay Company Library, Winnipeg, Manitoba; Leroy Bellamy, Library of Congress, Washington, D.C.; Judith Ciampoli and Susan Riggs, Missouri Historical Society, St. Louis, Missouri; National Maritime Museum, San Francisco, California; Christopher Kirby, National Museums of Canada, Ottawa, Ontario; John R. Bockstoce, Old Dartmouth Historical Society, New Bedford, Massachusetts; Kathy Flynn, Peabody Museum, Salem, Massachusetts; Barbara McLennan, Provincial Archives of British Columbia, Victoria, British Columbia; George Talbot, Christine Schelshorn, and Myrna Williamson, State Historical Society of Wisconsin; Bob Monroe and Dennis Anderson, University of Washington Library, Seattle, Washington; Jeanne Engerman, Washington State Historical Society, Tacoma, Washington.

INDEX
Entries in boldface refer to recipes.